76 Tips For Investing in an Uncertain Economy For Canadians For Dummies

Smoothing Out Financial Uncertainties

You may not be able to control the markets, but you're not at their mercy. Here are some ways you can protect yourself against life's financial uncertainties (along with a few notes on where you can find more information in this book):

- Plan for life's certainties and prepare for life's uncertainties (covered throughout the book).

- Invest in and protect your ability to earn money; it's likely your most valuable asset (Tips #3 and #4).

- Adequately insure yourself, your stuff, and your income stream (Tips #5 and #6).

- Maintain an emergency reserve fund (Tip #8).

- Minimize or eliminate debt (Tip #9), and focus on building a great credit score (Tip #10).

- Invest for your goals, time horizon, and risk tolerance (covered throughout).

- Diversify your portfolio across a broad mix of asset classes (covered throughout).

- Monitor and rebalance your portfolio to maintain your target asset allocation (Tip #39).

Your Risk Profile

Consider the following to determine your personal risk profile:

- **Risk capacity:** How much risk *should* you take, assuming a worst-case scenario? Take into account your age, family situation, income, and your other assets and resources. Keeping these factors in mind, how much risk should you take to achieve your goals?

- **Risk tolerance:** How much risk *can* you take? Consider your ability to stick with your investment plan without losing sleep or getting stressed out. Don't take on any more risk than you can comfortably tolerate.

- **Risk required:** How much risk *must* you take? You're exposed to certain risks whether you like it or not. However, you can minimize or avoid many financial risks. Doing so usually means accepting a lower return on your investments. To meet your personal goals and objectives in the time frame you'd like, you need to take some risks, but take no more risk than you must to achieve your goals.

For Dummies: Bestselling Book Series for Beginners

BESTSELLING
BOOK SERIES

76 Tips For Investing in an Uncertain Economy For Canadians For Dummies®

Calculating Interest

Years Until Goal	3% Average Inflation: Multiply Cost by	4% Average Inflation: Multiply Cost by
5	1.16	1.22
10	1.34	1.48
15	1.56	1.80
20	1.81	2.19
25	2.09	2.67
30	2.43	3.24

Web Resources to Help Find or Check Out a Financial Advisor

The following Web sites can help you in your search for a financial advisor:

✔ **Investment Industry Regulatory Organization of Canada (IIROC):** Click on "investors" at www.iiroc.ca and go to the section called "Member/Firm Registrant Info" to get the low-down on the registration and disciplinary history of member firms. Don't stop there, though. Your provincial securities commission may have information that isn't available on the IIROC site. Doing due diligence is worth your while!

✔ **Financial Planners Standards Council:** Visit www.fpsccanada.org to locate a Certified Financial Planner (CFP) in your area. The CFP designation is the most widely recognized educational credential for financial advisors and planners. A professional designation indicates that an advisor has completed certain educational and examination requirements. However, professional designations don't guarantee that you'll get competent or objective advice that best meets your needs. Quality personal financial planning education is critical, but it's only part of the criteria to consider when choosing a financial advisor.

✔ **Institute of Advanced Financial Planners (IAFP):** Visit the IAFP's Web site at www.iafp.ca. The institute offers the Registered Financial Planner (RFP) designation, which is considered the gold standard for financial planning in Canada. Like CFPs, RFPs adhere to educational and ethical standards. But they must also have a minimum five years of specific planning experience.

For Dummies: Bestselling Book Series for Beginners

76 Tips For Investing in an Uncertain Economy For Canadians

FOR DUMMIES®

76 Tips For Investing in an Uncertain Economy For Canadians

FOR DUMMIES®

by Sheryl Garrett

Garrett Planning Network

Camilla Cornell

John Wiley & Sons Canada, Ltd.

76 Tips For Investing in an Uncertain Economy For Canadians For Dummies®

Published by
John Wiley & Sons Canada, Ltd.
6045 Freemont Blvd.
Mississauga, ON L5R 4J3
www.wiley.com

For general information on John Wiley & Sons Canada, Ltd., including all books published by Wiley Publishing Inc., please call our warehouse, Tel. 1-800-567-4797. For reseller information, including discounts and premium sales, please call our sales department, Tel. 416-646-7992. For press review copies, author interviews, or other publicity information, please contact our publicity department, Tel. 416-646-4582, Fax 416-236-4448.

Library and Archives Canada Cataloguing in Publication Data

Garrett, Sheryl
    76 tips for investing in an uncertain economy for Canadians for dummies / Sheryl Garrett, Garrett Planning Network, Camilla Cornell.

Issued also in electronic format.
ISBN 978-0-470-16099-2

    1. Investments. 2. Investments—Canada. I. Cornell, Camilla II. Garrett Planning Network III. Title. IV. Title: Seventy-six tips for investing in an uncertain economy for Canadians for dummies.
HG179.G38 2009   332.6
C2009-900545-X

Printed in the United States

1 2 3 4 5 RRD 13 12 11 10 09

About the Authors

Sheryl Garrett, CFP, founder of The Garrett Planning Network, Inc., has made it her mission to "help make competent, objective financial advice accessible to all people." Sheryl's fresh approach as a financial advisor working with clients on an hourly, as-needed, fee-only basis has evolved into an international network of like-minded financial advisors, the Garrett Planning Network. This book is a collaborative effort brought to you by more than 70 professional financial advisors who are members of the Garrett Planning Network (www.garrettplanningnetwork.com).

As a vocal advocate for financial education, Sheryl has frequently been interviewed on CNNfn, Bloomberg, ABC World News Now, and Fox-TV; NPR's *All Things Considered* and *Marketplace;* and in *Business Week, Newsweek, Time, Forbes, Kiplinger Personal Finance, Money, Smart Money, MarketWatch, U.S. News & World Report, Glamour, Parade, Better Homes and Gardens,* the *New York Times, USA Today,* and the *Wall Street Journal.* For four years straight, Sheryl was recognized by *Investment Advisor* magazine as "One of the Top 25 Most Influential People in Financial Planning." The National Association of Personal Financial Advisors (NAPFA) honored Garrett with the prestigious *Robert J. Underwood Distinguished Service Award* for her contributions to the development of the financial planning profession.

Camilla Cornell is a Toronto-based freelance writer and three-time National Magazine Awards recipient. She has been writing about personal finance for 20 years for a wide range of Canadian newspapers and magazines, including *National Post, MoneySense, Today's Parent, Profit,* and *Canadian Family.* Camilla's first book, *How to Pay Less for Just About Anything* (Reader's Digest) came out in 2005 and launched her as a spokesperson for Uniroyal Canada's More Mileage for Your Money campaign offering money-saving tips for Canadian families. Her most recent book, *Flipping Houses For Canadians For Dummies,* appeared in 2008.

Dedication

Sheryl: On behalf of the members of the Garrett Planning Network, I dedicate this book to you, the reader. Our goal is to help answer your questions and empower you to make smarter financial decisions so that your most cherished life goals become reality.

Camilla: To all the many people I know (and those I don't) who are struggling to hold onto their dreams, goals, and retirement plans in the face of the market's ups and downs. I hope this will provide a road map so you can calm down and endure — if not enjoy — the ride. And to my husband and kids, who put up with my tight deadlines and the slap-dash meals I produce in order to meet them. See ya at dinner!

Authors' Acknowledgements

Sheryl: The passion and devotion of my colleagues in the Garrett Planning Network made this book possible. We all share the mission to help make competent, objective financial advice accessible to *all* people. This book is an extension of that mission.

Thank you to Jeff Alderfer, David Anderson, Diane Blackwelder, Kevin Brosious, Barbara Camaglia, Kay Conheady, Peggy and Chad Creveling, Helga Cuthbert, Debbra Dillon, Paul Dolce, Jake Engle, Christine Falvello, Cynthia Freedman, Eileen Freiburger, Robert Friedland, Deidra Fulton, Gwen Gepfert, Garry Good, Angela Grillo, Kathy Hankard, Katherine Holden, Will Humphrey, Ben Jennings, Kim Jones, Jean Keener, Derek Kennedy, Michael Knight, Cheryl Krueger, Derek Lenington, Charles Levin, Jennifer Luzzatto, Roland Mariano, Warren McIntyre, Herb Montgomery, Thomas Nowak, Robert Oliver, Kevin O'Reilly, Michael Oswalt, Abigail Pons, Dylan Ross, Brooke Salvini, Martha Schilling, Corry Sheffler, Brian R. Smith, Bruce Sneed, Janice Swenor, James Taylor, Denisa Tova, Gigi Turbow Marx, Neil Vannoy, John Vyge, Liane Warcup, and Richard Weimert. Without your insight and contributions, this book would not have been possible.

My collaborative and support team, including Shawnda Hubbard, Jamie Breeden, Thomas Arconti, John Belluardo, Rick DeChaineau, William Keffer, Buz Livingston, David McPherson, Kevin Sale, Louise Schroeder, and Michael Terry, were indispensible. Thank you all for your endless energy and steadfast devotion to this project.

I'd be remiss not to acknowledge the army of folks involved in this project at Wiley Publishing. Thank you for taking on this challenge and for having faith that we could deliver.

Camilla: Thanks to all the financial planners and experts who have freely shared their knowledge and opinions with me over the years. Among them, Janet Freedman, Lynn Biscott, Adrian Mastracci, Patricia Lovett-Reid, Joanne Anderson, Fran Goldberg, and Sucheta Rajagopal.

Publisher's Acknowledgements

We're proud of this book; please send us your comments through our Dummies online registration form located at www.dummies.com/register/.

Some of the people who helped bring this book to market include the following:

Acquisitions, Editorial, and Media Development

Acquisitions Editor, US Edition: Mike Baker

Senior Project Editors, US Edition: Tim Gallan, Christina Guthrie

Editor: Robert Hickey

Project Manager: Elizabeth McCurdy

Project Coordinator: Pauline Ricablanca

Copy Editor: Heather Ball

Technical Editors: Christopher Cottier, John Vyge, CFP

Editorial Assistant: Katie Wolsley

Cover photo: TK

Cartoons: Rich Tennant (www.the5thwave.com)

Composition Services

Vice-President Publishing Services: Karen Bryan

Project Coordinator: Lynsey Stanford

Layout and Graphics: Reuben W. Davis, Melissa K. Jester,

Proofreader: Laura L. Bowman

Indexer: Claudia Bourbeau

John Wiley & Sons Canada, Ltd.

 Bill Zerter, Chief Operating Officer

 Jennifer Smith, Vice-President and Publisher, Professional and Trade Division

Publishing and Editorial for Consumer Dummies

 Diane Graves Steele, Vice President and Publisher, Consumer Dummies

 Kristin Ferguson-Wagstaffe, Product Development Director, Consumer Dummies

 Ensley Eikenburg, Associate Publisher, Travel

 Kelly Regan, Editorial Director, Travel

Publishing for Technology Dummies

 Andy Cummings, Vice-President and Publisher, Dummies Technology/General User

Composition Services

 Gerry Fahey, Vice-President of Production Services

 Debbie Stailey, Director of Composition Services

Contents at a Glance

Table of Contents

Introduction

*T*he only certainty in investing — and probably in life — is *uncertainty.* That can make investing seem like an adventure; however, it's more like a transcontinental expedition than a day trip to an amusement park. You can't anticipate the turbulent waters or the snowstorms you may encounter along the way, but you'll reach your destination if you plan ahead and prepare for all possibilities.

If you feel uneasy about the current economic environment or your ability to protect yourself and your nest egg, you're not alone. You live in truly interesting and uncertain times. Treat this book as your survival guide — it can help you limit your risks, plan for the long term and the short term, and invest in ways that let you sleep comfortably at night, no matter what the markets throw your way.

About This Book

Over 70 professional financial advisors collaborated to bring you *76 Tips For Investing in an Uncertain Economy For Canadians For Dummies.* (To be honest, if you add 'em all up, there are more than 76 tips, but we figured you wouldn't mind getting a few extra.) The book contains seven parts, each focusing on an investing theme — accumulating wealth, preparing for retirement, and so on. Focus on the tips or parts that address your specific needs at this time. Then refer back to this book whenever you have questions or need some guidance in your personal financial life.

Conventions Used in This Book

While writing this book, we used a few conventions to make your life just a bit easier. Here's what you can expect:

- ✔ We use *italics* when we define a word or phrase that's important to understanding a topic. And when we get especially excited, we may throw in some italics for extra emphasis.

- ✔ When you see text in **bold,** you can expect it to be either a step in a numbered list or a key word in a bulleted list.

- ✔ All Web addresses appear in `monofont`.

- ✔ When this book was printed, some Web addresses may have needed to break across two lines of text. If that happened, know that we haven't put in any extra characters (such as hyphens) to indicate the break. So when using one of these Web addresses, just type in exactly what you see in this book and ignore the line break.

✔ Grey shaded boxes, otherwise known as *sidebars,* contain interesting but nonessential information. Feel free to skip 'em if you're short on time.

Foolish Assumptions

To provide the tools and advice you need, we made some of the following assumptions:

✔ You recognize the need to become more informed about the financial markets and your personal finances. You don't want to become a victim of self-serving sales pitches, and you need answers now.

✔ You have some interest in taking a more active and productive role in managing your personal financial life, or you at least want to make sure you don't do anything really stupid or get ripped off.

✔ You have access to the Internet, whether at home, work, or your local library.

How This Book Is Organized

76 Tips For Investing in an Uncertain Economy For Canadians For Dummies is organized into seven distinct parts, each covering a major area involving your financial life. Here's a summary of what you can find in each part.

Part I: Laying a Solid Foundation

Before you start pulling money out of current investments or pouring money into new ones, you should make sure you have the right mindset toward your finances, investments, and the market at large. This part gives you a historical perspective of market cycles, helps you assess your finances and goals, and reviews some financial tips to help you get a good foundation in investing.

Part II: Using Investment Vehicles and Accounts throughout the Economic Cycle

The investment marketplace offers lots of options — as well as futures, commodities, stocks, bonds, mutual funds, exchange-traded funds, cash accounts, retirement accounts, and more! This part gives you an overview of your choices and explains when certain types of vehicles or accounts may be right for you.

Part III: Demystifying Risk: Accumulating and Protecting Wealth

You may think the only risk involved with investing is losing value when the market goes down. However, other risks — emotional reactions, inflation, job loss, and so on — are major financial risks you have to consider in your planning. In this part, you explore types of risk, gauge your risk tolerance, and discover how to design a portfolio that enables you to limit risk while still getting the returns you need to meet your goals.

Part IV: Investing for Accumulators

This part helps you save and accumulate money for your emergency fund, major purchases, and goals such as university education and retirement. It also outlines various investment vehicles and tips tailored to how much investment experience you have.

Part V: Heading into Retirement

Your retirement savings may have to support you for 30 years or more, so this is one investment area you need to get right. In this part, you discover how to prepare for surprises such as having to assist aging parents or adult children. You examine employer retirement plans, Canada/Quebec Pension Plan and Old Age Security, and other potential sources of retirement income. You also look at asset allocation and gauge whether you're on track to have enough money during retirement.

Part VI: Living on Your Investment Earnings and Drawing Down Your Assets

This part takes you into retirement, helping you maximize pension and/or Canada/Quebec Pension Plan and Old Age Security benefits and reduce your taxes as you decide which retirement accounts to use first. It also helps you develop a strategy for tapping into your assets and continuing to invest them so they offer you a steady stream of income while minimizing the risk of running out of money during your golden years.

Part VII: The Part of Tens

The Part of Tens is a classic *For Dummies* part consisting of top-ten lists. In this part, you find ten tips for building a solid financial foundation and ten ways to minimize risk.

Icons Used in This Book

As you flip through this book, you see a few different icons that draw your attention to specific issues or examples. Check them out:

If you're looking for a timesaving tool or insider suggestion that you can use immediately, the text next to the Tip icon has what you want.

If you don't read anything else, pay attention to the info next to this icon, which points out information that we just had to stress because it's *that* important to your financial well-being.

This icon alerts you to common pitfalls and dangers that you have to look out for when managing your personal finances.

This icon marks ideas you should pay special attention to when the economy looks shaky or you're really struggling.

Where to Go from Here

This book is organized so you can go directly to the part or tips that matter to you right now. Worried about debt and your credit score? Flip to Tips #9 and #10. Need information on diversifying your stock portfolio? Tips #39 through #42 can help you out.

If you're just beginning to get your financial house in order, we suggest you start with Part I and possibly work through to Part IV. If you're getting closer to retirement, you may want to peruse Parts I and II and skip to Part V. If you're already in retirement, Part VI is specifically for you.

Part I

Laying a Solid Foundation

The 5th Wave — By Rich Tennant

In this part...

Before you make any investment decision, you can benefit from balancing current events with some historical perspective. Life is full of uncertainties, so in this part, you get a thorough review of some personal financial planning tips to help you minimize or avoid plenty of the financial uncertainties you face.

Keep Your Feet on the Ground

By Derek Lenington, CFP, and Dylan Ross, CFP

*Y*ou can be forgiven for chewing your nails in these uncertain times. But, successful investors are grounded. They're logical and disciplined, and they don't let emotions drive investment decisions. Successful investors understand and embrace the idea that the economy is *always* uncertain; it may have seemed more certain in the past, but only with the benefit of hindsight.

The Canadian economy has cycled between good and bad times, and you can expect that trend to continue (see Tip #2 for more historical perspective). Unless you think the economy will always be either booming or slow forever, every bad period must be followed by a good period and every good stretch has to be followed by a bad one. The big unknown is how long each period will last.

People often focus on an unanswerable question: When are things going to turn around? When times are good, your investments do well and you hear rumours of bigger bonuses at work this year. The question of when it'll all change seems less crucial, but the answer remains uncertain. That question is more pressing during bad times, when investments tank or talk of a recession picks up. However, if you embrace the fact that the economy is *always* uncertain, the tips in this book can help you make better investing decisions.

You can't single-handedly turn around the economy. But this book is filled with information on the tactics, strategies, and steps you can take with your money. This particular section focuses on how *you* — the key player in your financial life — need to prepare for and approach your finances. The following guidelines help you ensure that your attitude, decisions, and behaviour truly support your desire to invest successfully during uncertain times.

Invest in Yourself

You are your biggest asset, thanks to your ability to earn money, and you need to protect and develop that asset. Think of yourself as Me, Inc. Focusing on Me, Inc., involves more than the occasional doctor's visit and an hour at the gym. You can sink into a rut, afraid to move, or you can challenge yourself to earn a new degree; seek out a more rewarding job; or master new technologies and apply them in your professional life.

You may also need to retool your physical plant, so to speak — losing weight, improving your focus and energy level with exercise, or budgeting for additions to your wardrobe so you look good.

No matter your age, show a real interest in being a part of fast-paced change, or risk being a dinosaur (remember — they're extinct). Not only do these steps better position you for the uncertainties of life that we discuss in Part I, but they also help you increase your value:

- ✔ **Make yourself indispensable at work.** See Tip #4 for suggestions about beefing up your networking efforts, sharpening your skills or adding new ones, and going back to school.

- ✔ **Exercise, eat well, and get enough sleep.** Strength and flexibility, proper nourishment, and a good night's sleep may increase your productivity and help to keep your mind sharp.

- ✔ **Be creditworthy.** For ideas on improving your credit and debt, see Tips #9 and #10.

- ✔ **Prioritize, prioritize, prioritize.** Making more money sounds great, but at what expense? Take some time to get your priorities in order and find the balance that works for you. Think about family, sleep, and mental and physical health.

- ✔ **Talk to someone.** If your finances are causing you mental and/or emotional stress — or distress — get help! A financial professional can help you take control of your finances and map out a plan to get things back on track. If financial concerns are only one of a number of issues causing you to feel overwhelmed, speaking with a counsellor or other mental health professional can help lighten that load, which will make everything on your plate more manageable.

Know Your Financial Situation

You can't make savvy financial decisions without first understanding your current personal financial situation. You need to assess your strengths and weaknesses as well as the current economic environment. This check-up can make you anxious — you may be doing fine in some areas and need improvement in others — and that's okay. But avoiding coming up with a plan to improve your financial situation is not okay. (Part I of this book can help you assess your financial health across a range of categories.)

If you need help with your self assessment or financial review, consider hiring a fee-only financial planner. Because fee-only planners don't sell products or get commission, their advice isn't constrained to certain products and should be in your best interest. Unfortunately, most advisors in Canada are commission based, so you may not have a choice in the matter. At least opt for a Registered Financial Planner (www.iafp.ca) or a Certified Financial Planner Professional (www.fpsccanada.org). Both have minimum education requirements and ask members to adhere to a code of ethics. In addition, Registered Financial Planners need at least five years of planning experience to hold the designation.

Tips #7 through #13 can help you address potential weak links in your financial picture, and Parts II and III can give you tools and techniques to make change happen. If you haven't yet thought about retirement in a concrete way, Parts V and VI offer tips to reduce the risk of outspending your resources.

Keep Your Emotions in Check

Completely ignoring emotions is a tall order for most folks. Fear and greed are powerful emotions that can influence your investment decisions for better or worse (usually for worse). Although worrying is okay at times, you have to work around some powerful emotions to be a successful investor. Keep these tips in mind:

- ✔ **Acknowledge your emotions.** Admit when you're feeling fearful or greedy. Only by acknowledging those feelings can you guard against their influence on your actions.

- ✔ **Don't wait for feelings of fear or greed to disappear before you act.** They may never totally vanish. This book can help you develop financial plans and strategies to guide decision making. When your emotions surge, refer to this book to stay on course.

- ✔ **Understand how emotions fit into the economic cycle.** You probably feel best about investing when markets have been going up, up, up. The higher the recent increase, the better you may feel about putting your money in. But only people who already had their money in the market, *before* it started going up, got those big, attractive gains. They had their money in the market when it didn't feel so great.

- ✔ **Remember, everyone's in the same boat.** If the economy is slowing down or contracting, it also impacts your neighbours, co-workers, other consumers, and producers. You're not being left behind while everyone else is passing you by.

✔ **Avoid people who try to exploit your feelings.** Turn off the financial channels. Their programming is intended to play to your emotions to keep you tuned in. If you must watch, remember that the news is sensationalized at times.

✔ **Don't dwell on things beyond your control.** Instead, focus on what you *can* control. (See the next section.)

Control What You Can

Events that can affect your personal financial situation fall into one of two categories: events that you can control and events that you can't. Recognizing things that are beyond your sphere of influence is important. You have no control over the following: inflation, tax increases, stock market returns, interest rates, and what others are doing. You can control these factors:

✔ How much you spend

✔ How much you know about personal finance and investing

✔ Where you put your hard-earned money (see Part II for detail)

✔ How much risk you take (see Part III)

✔ How you react to what you can't control

Put Your Goals in Writing

You may have heard the old saying "If it isn't being measured, it probably won't change; and if it does change, you probably won't notice." This holds true for financial goals, too. Part IV is all about setting and achieving goals, from buying a home to raising children and preparing for retirement. Setting realistic targets is important, but devising a system for tracking your progress is equally important. You'll enjoy checking off goals as you reach them.

You may be tempted to give yourself a bit too much leeway in meeting your targets, so find yourself an accountability partner to work with: a spouse, partner, or friend. Partners don't need to know every intimate detail, but they do need to know the following:

✔ Your goal

✔ The info you'll be reporting

✔ How often to expect updates

Offer to do the same in return — keep it fun and get started.

Realize That This Has Happened Before (And Will Happen Again)

By Debbra Dillon, CFP

Uncertain economic times come and go — you have about as much control over them as you do over the weather. Although you can't know exactly when a major economic event will occur, if you're prepared, you stand a good chance of weathering the storm.

When you're preparing for uncertain economic times, understanding what's happened in the past can help. History provides clues to help you avoid making common mistakes during challenging times. So what kinds of events create uncertain economic times, and what clues do they hold for you today? This tip takes a look at three types of events that can unexpectedly affect your financial security.

Weathering Major Economic Events

Most major economic events, such as stock market crashes, happen when a normal economic cycle goes off balance. Imagine looking forward to a big dinner, and when dinner arrives, you eat until you feel you'll burst. Afterward, you regret the overindulgence and swear you won't do it again. But soon, you forget feeling stuffed and start planning for another indulgent meal. Economic cycles work this way, too: You see periods of rapid growth often inspired by exciting technological advances. Occasionally, investors overindulge and a bubble develops. Unfortunately, when the bubble bursts, people suffer until things even out again.

Stock market bubbles and crashes

One of the most famous bubbles of the last century occurred in the so-called Roaring Twenties, which came to a startling end with the stock market crash of 1929. The overindulgence of credit and spending combined with wild speculation in the stock market, plummeting exports, and drought in the Prairie provinces led to the Great Depression. At its peak, an estimated 30 percent of Canadians were unemployed. Will we experience another depression like the Great Depression? Who knows, but you can prepare yourself just in case. Here's how to position yourself well:

✔ **Steer clear of consumer debt.** In the Great Depression, those in debt got hammered when they had to pay up.

✔ **Pay your mortgage off as soon as possible.** Minimizing your mortgage debt is a smart thing to do. Having too much debt — of any kind — puts you in jeopardy if you lose your income, run out of savings, and can't borrow more money.

✔ **Save for emergencies.** Those with cash set aside (ideally covering three to six months of expenses) can roll with the punches.

✔ **Take advantage of future investment opportunities.** Some people took advantage of lucrative investment opportunities, buying stock and real estate at a discount, for example. Believe it or not, some people actually prospered during the Great Depression.

✔ **Develop a broad skill set.** Jobs were extremely hard to come by during the Depression. Those with many skills had an easier time finding work.

Although depressions are rare, stock market bubbles and ensuing crashes are not. In fact, Canada has experienced four *bear markets* (times in which the stock market lost more than 20 percent of its value) since 1980. But take heart; over that same period, the market gained overall, in spite of the crashes.

Bubbles are surprisingly similar to each other. Take the dot-com bubble of the 1990s. As in the 1920s, investors were convinced that they could get rich quickly with the stock market. Internet and technology stock prices soared to dizzying heights until the bubble burst in March 2000 and the party was over. The dot-com bust didn't lead to a depression, but it did a lot of damage to people's investments. Here's how to avoid getting hurt when a stock market bubble bursts:

✔ **Maintain a diversified portfolio.** Investors who were seriously hurt in the tech wreck had most of their cash in dot-com and technology stocks. If you have a diversified portfolio and remain invested for the long term, don't panic when a bubble bursts. Stay the course and let the market work things out.

✔ **Avoid the next hot investment.** Resist the urge to get caught up in the irrational exuberance of new technology.

Real estate bubbles and crashes

Bubbles aren't limited to just the stock market. The meltdown in the U.S. housing market has left many Canadians wondering if we're next. The good news: More conservative lending practices in Canada mean Canadians were not as hard hit. Nonetheless, the Canadian Real Estate Association is predicting a 2.1 percent drop in housing prices for 2009, with areas like British Columbia expecting a 7.8 percent decline. To protect yourself from a crash, do the following:

✔ **Don't rely on your mortgage lender or real estate agent to tell you how much house you can afford.** Work out your budget and make sure you can handle the mortgage payments and housing expenses.

✔ **Put at least 10 percent (preferably 25 percent to avoid the Canada Mortgage and Housing Corporation insurance fee) down on the home.** Pass on 5 percent down payment financing. If you can't afford a good-sized down payment, you likely can't afford the home.

✔ **If you don't plan on being in a house for at least five years, don't buy one.** Rent instead. In most cases, breaking even on a home purchase takes at least five years due to the costs involved in buying and selling a home.

✔ **Must sell now? Make sure the deal is ironclad before buying another property.** Don't get stuck carrying two houses.

✔ **Avoid using home equity lines of credit for consumer purchases.** Save them exclusively for emergencies only.

✔ **Don't rely on a home equity line of credit as your sole source of emergency funds.** Keep an emergency fund in cash reserve accounts, like high-interest savings accounts or money market funds. If, however, you deplete these accounts in a prolonged emergency, you can then turn to your home equity line of credit.

If you don't pay back a home equity line of credit, you could lose your home.

Rapidly rising commodity prices

Speculative bubbles aren't the only cause of economic events. The OPEC Oil Embargo in 1973 quadrupled gas prices around the world. The Canadian economy slipped into a recession, leading to a nasty decade of *stagflation* (high unemployment and double-digit inflation). Take these steps to prepare for periods of rapidly rising commodity prices:

✔ Cut back on your energy use. Ride your bike or drive a fuel-efficient car. Invest in energy-efficient home appliances.

✔ Maintain an emergency fund to cover unexpected price increases.

✔ Buy staples in bulk.

Standing Strong During Political Events

Political events are often unanticipated and shocking. Assassinations, terrorist attacks, and political instability can tempt you to panic. Historically, these types of events have caused only short-term economic uncertainty. Take the September 11, 2001, terrorist attacks on the World Trade Center and the Pentagon that shocked the U.S. and Canada. The S&P/TSX Composite Index lost more than 10 percent in a week. Fortunately, it recovered the lost ground within 47 days. Here's how to stay safe during an unexpected political event:

✔ **Don't panic.** Knee-jerk reactions can come back to haunt you.

✔ **Maintain a diversified portfolio.** This is the single best way to weather economic uncertainty.

Witnessing Global Conflicts

You may think that wars have a negative impact on the economy, but actually, for the most part, the opposite is true. World War II was the most costly war in terms of government expenditures and human lives. Gearing up for and supporting the war actually produced a booming economy.

On the other hand, the Vietnam War and the War on Terror south of the border have had relatively negative effects on the U.S. economy. The Vietnam War lasted for 16 years, and the average return for the S&P 500 during that time was a dismal 3.91 percent. Here's how to survive long periods of low market returns:

✔ Don't depend on high investment returns when planning for your retirement or other financial goals.

✔ Keep investing periodically throughout these periods.

✔ Include fixed-income investments, such as government bonds and guaranteed investment certificates, in your portfolio.

Plan for Life's Uncertainties

● ●

By Denisa Tova, CLU, ChFC, CFDP, CFP

● ●

It's a bright, beautiful morning, and you walk outside, feeling on top of the world. You set your coffee cup on top of the car, and you realize that the cup is slanted. Either the horizon has changed or something's wrong with your car. You look down, and suddenly you're not having such a great day. You have a flat tire.

Or it's a bright, beautiful morning, and your telephone rings. Your real estate agent tells you the property on the lake that you've wanted for years has just been put on the market. Now you're really feeling on top of the world. But a thought crosses your mind: Do you have enough money set aside? It's such short notice!

Life can throw you curve balls in the form of financial frustrations or opportunities. But life doesn't always time those surprises at the peak of the financial markets. In this tip, discover how to make sure your savings are ready — even if the market isn't.

Keep an Eye on Social Trends

For years, the market may grow with gusto and vigour and then suddenly go south. Likewise, many of your lifelong goals — such as going to university or college, getting married, buying a house, having children, helping pay for your children's education and weddings, and at long last enjoying your retirement — may suddenly turn out to be more expensive than you thought. Other factors can increase the uncertainty of reaching your goals, too. Consider the following:

- ✔ University tuition fees are growing at nearly three times the current inflation rate.

- ✔ Companies are cutting back on or entirely cutting out their traditional defined benefit pension plans. Only about 26 percent of Canadians are covered under such plans.

- ✔ New retirees may need 70 to 80 percent or more of their current income to maintain their standard of living.

- ✔ A 2007 report by Fidelity Canada says that retirees are on track to replace only 50 percent of their pre-retirement income.

✔ Canada Pension Plan (CPP) hasn't been immune to the market mayhem and recently reported a loss of $10 billion in the value of its assets. If the red ink continues, CPP might have to consider raising contributions or reducing benefits.

✔ Unexpected events around the world can send inflation soaring at the same time the economy is slowing down or in a recession.

Good financial planning involves setting goals, developing a plan to get from where you are to where you'd like to be, and then monitoring what's happening and making adjustments when needed. Monitor things like the national economy, your local economy, your job and your employer, your family situation, and your personal life. Your plan should include ways to deal with the unexpected. Stay aware at all times of how each thing you monitor affects your planning; doing so enables you to adjust your plan and keep heading in the right direction.

Motivate Yourself to Save and Develop a Plan

If you haven't planned ahead like you need to, it's never too late. You don't have to become a recluse or take up meditation to relieve your troubled mind. Nor should you just work as long as you can and hope for the best or buy a weekly lottery ticket.

Do yourself a big favour and start planning today. Planning allows you to protect your future, live comfortably, and know your options.

Practically speaking, you may need to motivate yourself to save money. Think of it this way: If you lost $20 down a drain in the road, would you recover? Would your life continue? Would you starve, or would you just have to buy less ice cream and fewer DVDs? How about $100? That'd be a harder hit, but you should still be able to withstand the blow.

If you've never thought about the uncertainties that can sabotage your financial goals or the unexpected opportunities that might pop up, start thinking about them now. And start saving your money for future contingencies rather than spending it on stuff you can do without. The reality of life is that things like ice cream and DVDs are ways to throw your money down the drain. You know they're fun to have, but think about the overwhelming anxiety that can occur when something bad happens or when you're financially unprepared for a good opportunity. That anxiety far outweighs the benefits of seeing the latest movie or getting your chocolate fix.

If *saving* and *self-restraint* aren't normally part of your vocabulary, you can motivate yourself to start saving and keep saving with these five steps:

1. **Adjust your attitude.**

   When you save money, think of it as buying your future.

2. **Give thought to all the life events that may be possible and decide which ones you want to be a part of your life.**

   Those life events may be starting a business, buying a house or vacation home, travelling, or taking art classes.

3. **Create two funds and start to save money for your goals.**

   Make sure you have the following funds:

   - An emergency fund (see Tip #8 for details on a rainy-day fund)

   - A make-my-life-great fund (see Tip #11 for more on setting goals)

4. **Pay off high-interest debt.**

   Why? Because paying down debt gives you even more bang for your buck than investing, particularly in a volatile market. By paying down a credit card, you can eliminate the interest charged on that debt — in some cases 18 percent or more. You're making an after-tax return of 18 percent without speculating!

5. **Don't let anything intimidate you.**

   It doesn't matter how small the amounts you save seem at first. Remember that they grow over time.

 If all the details of planning seem overwhelming, seek professional help. You can find a Certified Financial Planner Professional in your area by searching at www.fpsccanada.org, or you can find a Registered Financial Planner at www.iafp.ca.

Finally, remember that putting money only into your chequing, savings, or money market account isn't enough. These accounts are fine to park cash that you may need within three to five years, but they're lousy choices to fund retirement needs 10, 20, or even 30 years in the future. To make all your financial sacrifices worth the trouble, you need to invest the money in one or more portfolios (depending on the length of time to each goal). This book discusses investment types and how to build a portfolio in Parts II, III, IV, and V.

Protect Your Ability to Earn Income

· ·

By Gwen Gepfert

· ·

In today's uncertain economy, job changes are sometimes forced on people when companies go out of business, lay off employees to cut costs, or just downsize due to competitive pressures. Take the following quiz to see whether you're prepared to face the next round of cuts:

- ✔ Have you conducted a recent (and honest!) assessment of your strengths and weaknesses at work?
- ✔ Have you recently reviewed your job description to make sure that you're meeting or (better) exceeding your job responsibilities?
- ✔ Do you hear about jobs that are available in other companies but aren't advertised?
- ✔ When your co-workers leave your company to take a new job, do they recommend you for any open positions in their new company?
- ✔ Have you found easy ways to gain further education or training in your chosen career?

If you didn't answer *yes* to all these questions, perhaps you're not as secure in your current job as you imagine or as well prepared to make a job change. Your career and financial goals are too important to leave in the hands of your employer. Don't let yourself be surprised or unprepared. Instead, concentrate on meeting the recommendations in this tip.

Make Yourself Indispensable

No one is 100 percent indispensable, but you should strive to become an employee that your company would have trouble replacing. Not only does this tip reduce the likelihood that you'll receive a layoff notification, it also puts you in the driver's seat in terms of potential promotions, raises, and other workforce benefits. Here are some ways to become *almost* irreplaceable:

✔ **Take initiative.** Take on new responsibilities outside of your current job description. Bring your manager solutions, not new problems. Jump in to help your company when staff vacancies occur.

✔ **Keep your skills up-to-date.** Stay current in your field of knowledge. Read industry magazines and reports, monitor pending legislation and technology advancements, and learn new software that can make you more efficient.

✔ **Develop an impeccable reputation for dependability.** Do your homework and be prepared for meetings and projects. Meet deadlines. Be punctual. Take responsibility for your actions and mistakes to highlight your professional integrity.

✔ **Be a considerate and positive team player.** Maintain a positive attitude and don't keep company with complainers or naysayers. Be *nice* to your co-workers and support them. Prove yourself to be trustworthy and someone for inexperienced members of your organization to look up to.

Building a good reputation takes a lot of hard work, but developing a bad one is fairly easy. Pay attention to how others perceive you and listen openly to performance feedback. Act promptly to fix any issues that have tarnished your reputation as a model employee.

Schmooze with the Best of Them

One crucial skill during uncertain economic times is your ability to network. Professional relationships can be a great source of referrals for potential job openings. Don't let shyness interfere with building a strong list of personal contacts. Follow these simple steps:

✔ **Talk to strangers.** Launch conversations with new people, and don't forget to exchange business cards. Join professional organizations and go to meetings to develop a wider range of contacts.

✔ **Compile your contacts.** You never know when you may need to ask someone to make an introduction for you into a company. Consider creating a database or special file of contacts. Be sure to keep in touch so you can stay abreast of changes in their career as well as contact information.

✔ **Never burn bridges.** You may be tempted to tell off your previous boss or co-workers on the way out the door. Don't. They can provide great leads to potential jobs as well as informal personal references.

✔ **Put your knowledge on display.** When you write articles for trade or industry periodicals, you get to see your name in print, *and* you increase your professional profile within your industry.

✔ **Remember that networking is a two-way street.** Professional relationships can be a great asset to you throughout your career, but don't drop the ball when someone asks you for help.

✔ **Say "Thank you."** A personalized thank-you note to a helpful contact goes a long way to show your appreciation. Remember, you may need that person's help again someday.

Many open jobs are filled by word of mouth. Most employers are more comfortable hiring applicants who are recommended by trusted employees or partners versus hiring qualified candidates who just walk in from the street. Some companies even pay a finder's fee to employees who recommend successful hires. Make sure your contacts are recommending you for these jobs!

Even if you're content in your job, always keep your eyes open for new and better opportunities. Many of the best career opportunities come when you're least expecting them. In case you want to respond to a sudden opportunity, make sure your resume is up to date and relevant. (*Resumes For Dummies,* 5th Edition, written by Joyce Lain Kennedy and published by Wiley, contains lots of helpful hints about preparing your resume.)

Broaden Your Skill Set

Today's most effective employees don't allow life's circumstances to get in the way of their full income potential. These people embrace the concept of lifelong learning and find this journey both rewarding and enjoyable. Make a conscious effort to develop your own plan for continuing to learn and grow in your job. These simple steps enable you to be better prepared for your next job opportunity:

✔ **Conduct a personal skill review.** Check your last company performance evaluation and make sure you're actively improving noted areas of weakness. Compare your skills to those required by the job you'd *like* to have — the Internet is a great resource for conducting both skill and salary research.

✔ **Develop a career path.** Create a roadmap that can take you from your current job to your dream job. Break it into a series of realistic baby steps. Document the skills you need to take you from today's job to tomorrow's.

✔ **Capitalize on your natural skills and interests.** When you do what you love, success is a natural byproduct. Build on your strengths by improving your skills in your current position.

✔ **Act now, while you're still employed.** Having the right skills and qualifications for any position you apply for is essential. Start developing those new skills or get the training while you're still employed.

✔ **Take advantage of easily accessible training tools.** There are many simple ways to gain additional training; you just need to look for them. They include the following:

- Reading business books and training manuals

- Watching training videos

- Attending industry seminars and conferences

- Researching industry topics on the Internet

- Learning from a mentor

- Attending adult education classes

- Downloading podcasts to your MP3 player and listening to them in your car or while you exercise

Go Back to School

Whether you're going back to school to gain a competitive edge in the job market, to obtain additional education to keep current, or to work toward your dream job, choose the right school:

1. **Select a widely recognized certification or degree.**

2. **Pick an accredited school.**

3. **Decide how you want to attend classes.**

4. **Check all possible sources for financial assistance.**

Ask your human resources office whether your company offers a tuition assistance program or whether you'll be reimbursed for all or a portion of your tuition. Your school's financial aid officer can check to see if you're eligible for any low-cost loans, assistance-ships, fellowships, scholarships, or grants. To research grants or scholarships online, visit www.scholarshipscanada.com or www.studentawards.com. Depending on your family income level, you may qualify for a grant or loan from Canada Student Loans (www.hrsdc.gc.ca/en/learning/canada_student_loan/index.shtml), but you must apply through your provincial or territorial student aid program.

#5

Assess Your Disability Insurance

By Neil Vannoy, MBA

Your chance of becoming disabled during your prime income-earning years is much higher than your chance of dying. And yet, about 30 percent of all Canadians dispense with disability insurance coverage. If you're one of them, ask yourself how long you could survive without a paycheque? According to Canadian Life and Health Insurance Association Inc., almost half of all mortgage foreclosures are due to disability.

 Disability insurance (DI) protects your ability to earn a living. Especially in uncertain economic times, don't underestimate the importance of insuring your paycheque.

The Nuts and Bolts of Disability Insurance

Here's a rundown of what you need to know about DI:

- ✔ **What's covered:** Most policies cover disabilities resulting from accidents, though some also cover disabilities caused by illness. Because younger people are more apt to be disabled by accidents and older people by illness, you need to know what kind of coverage your policy provides.

- ✔ **How much coverage:** Benefits are usually between 40 and 70 percent of your income. Why don't insurance companies cover a higher percentage of your income? Well, how much incentive would you have to recover and return to work if you could earn the same amount watching TV?

- ✔ **Qualifying for payments:** Before you can collect benefits from your DI policy, you have to satisfy the *elimination period,* or waiting period. This is the insurance company's way of making sure you're really disabled before they go to the expense of sending you money. The elimination period varies by policy.

✔ **How long payments last:** DI policies can have either a short- or long-term benefit period. *Short-term policies* usually pay benefits for three to six months, although some provide benefits for up to two years. The elimination period for short-term policies generally ranges from 1 to 14 days.

✔ The benefit period for *long-term policies* can range from a few years to the rest of your life. The most popular benefit period for long-term policies is *to age 65.* The elimination period for long-term policies ranges from 30 to 365 days.

Look Under the Hood of a DI Policy

Here are some details to pay attention to — you can find them in the policy itself or as *riders* (optional amendments added to the policy).

Defining disability

So who decides whether you're disabled? The insurance company, of course, so knowing how it defines disability is important:

✔ **Own occupation:** By this definition, you're disabled if you can't do your usual job, even if you could perform other work. So a pilot with an eye injury would qualify for benefits.

✔ **Any occupation:** You're considered disabled only if you can't work at any job that you're qualified for by education, training, and experience.

✔ **Total disability:** You're disabled only if you're unable to work at any job at all. Yikes! You may be able to flip burgers at a fast-food restaurant, but would you *want* to do that for a living? Try to get another definition of disability in your DI policy.

Tacking on riders

You may want to consider putting some of these additional provisions on your policy:

✔ **Cost of living adjustment (COLA):** This rider increases your benefit of the policy with inflation up to a maximum that you elect, generally from 3 to 8 percent. The benefit continues to increase every year that you remain disabled. This rider is extremely important, especially when you're younger.

✓ **Automatic increase:** This rider usually allows for a total bene-fit increase of 20 to 25 percent over the first three to five years of the policy. Your premiums go up with the benefit.

✓ **Future increase option (FIO):** If you qualify for only a small amount of disability coverage now but expect to be making big bucks later in your career, you can guarantee that you can increase your coverage later, regardless of your health, by selecting the FIO. This rider allows benefit increases — usually up to age 55 — by providing proof of higher income. You won't have to prove insurability!

✓ **Waiver of premium:** This rider waives premiums while you're disabled.

✓ **Residual benefit (partial disability):** This benefit allows you to return to work part-time while continuing to receive a portion of your benefits. Most policies require a minimum earnings loss (such as a 20 percent reduction) to qualify for residual benefits.

Choosing renewability provisions

All DI policies contain renewability provisions that explain how your coverage will continue. Most policies are one of the following:

✓ **Guaranteed renewable:** The insurance company will continue to renew the policy, but the premiums can be increased for an entire group of policyholders (for instance it may be increased by province or occupational class).

✓ **Non-cancellable and guaranteed renewable:** The insurance company can't cancel or raise the premiums.

✓ **Conditionally renewable:** Policies can be renewed at the insurer's discretion. Unless you believe your insurance company has a big heart and loves you, stay away from these policies!

Purchase Your Policies

Many employers offer group coverage without a medical exam if you sign up during the initial enrollment period. Some pre-existing conditions may be excluded from group coverage for up to two years. Group DI is generally less expensive than an individual policy because most employers pay a portion of the premium. Some plans have a *portability option* that allows you to convert your group coverage to an individual policy when you leave your job.

You can buy individual disability insurance directly from an insurance company or through an insurance broker. Unlike group insurance, you have to go through underwriting to get the policy. One of the greatest benefits of individual DI is that changes in your health, employment, or occupational class don't affect your coverage after the policy is issued. Even if you become uninsurable in the future or switch to a risky occupation, your individual policy remains in force as long as you keep paying the premiums.

The higher the chance you could become disabled and the larger the benefit, the higher the premium. To see all the factors that go into it, check out the following table.

Factor	*How It Affects the Premium*
Age	Premiums increase with age.
Gender	Women are at greater risk of disability than men, so their premiums are higher.
Occupation	Riskier occupations have higher premiums.
Elimination period	You pay a higher premium for a shorter elimination period.
Benefit amount	The more the potential benefit amount, the higher the premium.
Riders	Premiums increase if you add riders.
Definition of disability	Policies with more favourable definitions of disability (for instance, "own occupation") have higher premiums than policies with less favourable definitions.
Renewability provision	A non-cancellable and guaranteed renewable policy has a higher premium than a conditionally renewable policy.

Don't forget about taxes! If you pay the premiums for your policy, the benefits you receive are generally tax free. If your employer paid part or all of the premiums, part or all of the benefits may be taxable.

The government pays disability benefits as well. Some insurers subtract those benefits from their payments:

> ✔ Employment Insurance pays a sickness benefit of 55 percent of insured weekly earnings up to a maximum of $435 weekly. You can collect for 15 weeks at the most, following a two-week waiting period.

✔ Canada/Quebec Pension Plan pays a benefit providing you meet their very stringent definition of being disabled (see www.hrsdc.gc.ca/eng/isp/cpp/adjudframe/cppadjud.shtml for more information). You can begin collecting in the fourth month following the month you were disabled. The amount depends on the number of years you've been contributing and how much you've paid. The maximum benefit in 2008 was $1,077 per month.

Assess Your Life Insurance

By Neil Vannoy, MBA

One of the most uncertain times for a family is after the unexpected death of a loved one — especially someone the family depended on for financial support. Reviewing your life insurance policy can help ensure that you have the right amount of coverage to protect your loved ones if something happens to you . . . and that you're not overpaying for your safety net.

Calculate Needed Coverage

Two simple methods for estimating your life insurance needs are the income replacement approach and the needs approach.

Income replacement approach

The income replacement approach to estimating life insurance needs has you predict how much you'll earn from now until you retire. Here's the formula:

Life insurance needs = Annual income × Years until retirement

For example, suppose Gail is 35 years old and plans on retiring in 30 years at age 65. She currently earns $65,000 per year. Gail's life insurance needs are $1,950,000 (or $65,000 × 30).

Although the income replacement approach is great for a rough estimate, it doesn't account for a rising salary or for inflation.

Needs approach

The needs approach, which accounts for the short- and long-term needs of your beneficiaries, is more accurate than the income replacement approach. Most professionals use this method. To determine how much your family will require, imagine if you were to die. Would your husband or wife be left with debts, including a mortgage? Would your children need full-time child care or money for university? How much income would you have to replace? After you figure out your beneficiaries' needs, subtract your available financial resources, such as mortgage insurance or Registered Education Savings Plans (RESPs). Then apply the formula:

Life insurance needs = Money required for short- and long-term needs – Available financial resources

When using this approach, be as accurate as possible. Inflation will affect the future value of your beneficiaries' needs. Consider contacting a fee-only advisor for help using the needs approach.

Compare Current Life Insurance Coverage to Your Calculated Need

After you know how much life insurance coverage you need, compare that amount to your current coverage. If you're underinsured, you have two options:

- ✔ **Replace your current life insurance policy (or policies) with a single policy.** Most life insurance policies offer *breakpoints* (discounts) when you purchase large amounts of coverage. So having one large policy rather than several small ones is usually less expensive.

- ✔ **Buy an additional policy.** The cost of insurance increases as you age. So in some cases, purchasing an additional policy may be less expensive than replacing an old policy.

If you discover you have too much coverage, consider the following:

- ✔ **Think about your future needs.** If you foresee new kids, debts, or big raises on the horizon, or if your health has changed, you may want to hang on to what you have.

- ✔ **If you're certain you don't need all your life insurance, you can usually reduce or cancel a policy.** If you have a term policy, contact the agent about reducing the coverage or just stop paying the premium. If you do need part of the coverage, compare the cost of the reduced policy to your options on the market.

- ✔ **If you have a permanent policy — either whole life or universal life — ask your agent for the net surrender value.** The *net surrender value* is the amount of your *cash value* (the accumulated cash in your account) that you get to keep after surrender charges. If you're reducing coverage, a charge to your cash value may still apply, even though you're keeping the policy. You may find that you're better off keeping the policy, at least until the surrender charges no longer apply.

If you decide to replace an existing life insurance policy, never cancel your existing policy until you've obtained replacement insurance.

Pick the Right Type of Life Insurance for Your Situation

Two types of life insurance policies exist: term and permanent. Think *term* for a temporary need and *permanent* for needs that'll last for your lifetime.

Term life insurance

For most families, term insurance is the only option that makes sense. It's cheap and effective. You pay a set yearly premium for a specified period of time, from 1 to 20 years, or even to age 100, and the policy pays off only if you die. Consider matching the term of the policy to specific milestones, such as when children leave home, when university is paid for, or when you retire. You pay for the policy for the entire period. At the end of the term, the policy expires, just like auto or homeowner's insurance.

Term coverage costs less than permanent because it's temporary and very few policies actually result in claims (that is, most are cancelled or expire). The lower cost of term insurance makes it a great choice if you have a limited budget and need a lot of coverage.

Because term insurance expires, you may want a policy that allows you to renew the policy for an additional term or to switch to a permanent policy before the policy terminates:

- ✔ *Renewable term insurance* allows you to renew the policy at the end of the term without providing proof of insurability, although the premiums will increase because you'll be renewing at a higher age.

- ✔ *Non-renewable term insurance* is less expensive than renewable term insurance because it automatically expires at the end of the term.

✔ *Convertible term insurance* allows you to convert term insurance to a permanent policy before the end of the term. Premiums on the permanent policy are based on your age when you convert. This is a great way to secure low-cost coverage now and have the option to switch to a permanent insurance policy later.

✔ *Non-convertible term insurance* is less expensive than convertible term insurance because it doesn't give you the right to convert it to a permanent policy.

Permanent life insurance

Permanent life insurance doesn't expire after a specific term (providing that you continue to pay the premium), and both your payments and the benefits remains the same. Permanent policies include an investment portion, referred to as the *cash value*. But keep in mind that the cash value is essentially funded from the higher premiums you pay. So what you're *really* getting is term insurance coupled with a savings or investment account. The problem is that these savings and investment accounts operate like no others.

Consider your average whole life policy. Typically, you have to own that policy for a year or two before any cash value shows up in your account. At that point, the insurer pays you a very low rate of return. Adding insult to injury, you can only access the cash value in the form of a loan that you have to pay interest on. (Remember, this cash value comes from your own premium overpayments, so you're actually paying interest on your *own* money to the insurance company!) Finally, if you die, be warned that your beneficiary will receive only the *face value* (or death benefit) of the policy. The cash value will revert to the insurer, minus any loans you've taken against it.

Universal life policies also include an insurance policy, coupled with an investment account (often a money market fund). Unlike whole life, universal life policies allow you to raise or lower your contributions and withdraw from your accumulated cash value with no interest charges. Both the cash value and the death benefit go to your beneficiaries if you die. On the down side, administrative fees are usually high and investments are frequently restricted.

Variable universal life policies have all the features of universal life, except that you allocate the cash value yourself to a range of investments that might include stocks, cash, and bonds. Your account either grows or shrinks with time. Again, administrative fees are high. And although you have a greater range of investment choices, you're usually restricted to a certain family of securities.

The only real advantage that permanent life insurance policies offer is that earnings accumulate tax free. Unless you've exhausted your Registered Retirement Savings Plan (RRSP) (see Tip #30) contribution room, you probably shouldn't consider such a policy. Why? Because RRSP contributions give you an immediate tax deduction and shelter future earnings from tax. If you expect your heirs to face a hefty tax bill when you pass away, and you want to cover that bill, you might consider permanent life insurance. Just make sure you completely understand the policy's complexities.

You'd be wise to shop around for term insurance. Start your research at www.term4sale.com, a Web site run by Compulife, which produces life insurance comparison software. You'll get a listing of dozens of available policies and prices after providing some basic information (age, sex, health status, and so on).

Purchase Your Life Insurance

Calculate the amount of life insurance coverage you need, determine whether to increase your current coverage, and pick the best type of policy for your needs. Next, get the coverage. You can choose between an individual policy and a group policy.

Opt into a group policy

Most employers provide group life insurance without *underwriting* (a medical exam to show evidence of insurability). Group insurance is a taxable benefit, but it's a great option if you have health problems that would keep you from being approved for an individual policy.

Many group life insurance policies can be converted to individual policies without proof of good health when or if you leave your job, but a converted policy may be more expensive than an individual policy because you don't have to prove insurability.

Go it alone with an individual policy

You can purchase individual policies through an insurance broker or directly from a life insurance company. Unlike group insurance, you can select the insurance company, the policy, and the coverage amount.

One of the greatest benefits of individual policies is portability. You don't have to worry about losing coverage if you change jobs. And changes in your health don't affect your coverage after the policy is issued. Use an individual policy to supplement employer-provided life insurance and to ensure continued coverage regardless of changes in your employment or health.

Take Stock of Your Current Financial Picture

By Cheryl Krueger

Finding a good route to your destination is difficult if you don't know where you're starting. During uncertain economic times, one of the first steps to meeting your major financial goals is to find out where you are now. A net worth statement is a great tool to find out where you are financially. After you know that, you can compare it to where you want to be.

Prepare a Net Worth Statement

You may think of what you own and what you owe as the most important parts of your financial life, but the combination of the two is what truly matters. If you have $1 million in assets, that sounds like a lot. But what if you also owe $930,000 in mortgages, student loans, and credit card debt? The difference between your assets and your liabilities is your *net worth,* which is what gives you stability in times of financial uncertainty.

Think of your current net worth statement as the You Are Here sticker on your financial map. Your net worth statement summarizes what you own, what you owe, and what would be left if you paid off all debt. *Assets* include money, investments, the fair market value of your house and furniture, your car, other real estate, and anything else you own. *Liabilities* include mortgages, car loans, credit card debt, and any other amounts owing. Here's how to determine your net worth:

Net worth = Assets – Liabilities

To meet many of your financial goals, you need to increase your net worth, either by increasing the amount of assets you have or by reducing your liabilities. A regular review of your net worth statement tells you a lot about how you're progressing. For example, you'll be able to see the following:

✔ Whether you're increasing your assets through saving or decreasing your assets through spending

✔ Whether your invested assets are growing at the rate you expect

✔ How you're doing in your quest to eliminate your debt

✔ Whether you're drawing down your assets too quickly during retirement or you can afford to take that month-long European cruise after all

Preparing the net worth statement isn't difficult; it just takes a bit of time and access to your financial statements. If you use personal finance software like Quicken or Microsoft Money Essentials — Canada, much of your net worth statement is available to you already. Or check out the online net worth calculator at `http://money.mytelus.com/calc/calculators.asp`. Figure 1-1 shows a sample net worth statement.

Net Worth Statement

Date: _____

Assets	Balance	Liabilities	Balance
Cash		Credit card _____	_____
Checking Accounts	_____	Credit card _____	_____
Savings Accounts	_____	Credit card _____	_____
Money Market Accounts		Auto Loan(s)	_____
		Student Loan(s)	_____
Investments		Mortgage	_____
GICs	_____	Line of Credit	_____
Mutual funds	_____	Personal loans you owe	_____
Stocks, bonds, etc.	_____		
Employer savings plans	_____		
Value of employer pension(s)	_____		
RRSPs	_____		
		Total Liabilities	_____
Other assets			
Home	_____		
Personal Property	_____		
Auto	_____		
Life insurance cash value	_____		
Business interest	_____	**TFSA Total Net Worth**	_____
Total Assets	_____		

Figure 1-1: A sample net worth statement.

Use the Net Worth Statement to Reach Your Goals

Tracking your net worth over a period of time can help you weather the ups and downs of an uncertain economy. By looking at the big picture, you don't get as discouraged when an investment stumbles, as long as other investments are still gaining in value. Knowing that hitting a bump in the road doesn't mean you'll never reach your destination can help get you back on track to meet your long-term financial goals.

How does this work? Don't simply complete one net worth statement and call it a day. Here's how to look at your net worth:

1. **Commit to calculating your net worth periodically.**

   This can be quarterly, semiannually, or annually. More frequently than quarterly is overkill; less frequently than annually may put you way off course when you do review your position.

2. **Calculate your initial net worth.**

3. **Re-calculate your net worth at the next calculation period.**

4. **Compare the changes in assets, liabilities, and overall net worth.**

   Are you getting closer to your goals or farther away from them? Make a point of understanding the general direction of each category. Are your assets lower now because your investments are down with the market? Or are your investments down while the market is up? Are you spending more than you're earning and depleting your assets to cover your living expenses?

5. **Identify where you have control over improving your financial direction.**

6. **Plan actions to increase your net worth before the next review period.**

Tracking your net worth periodically through the ups and downs in the economic cycle can prevent you from losing sight of your financial progress.

Assess Your Current Location

So where are you on the financial roadmap? Knowing where you are and how you're progressing toward your goals of building assets or paying down debt helps you focus on your financial resources and obligations. Consider each of the following three levels and find out which one best describes your financial situation.

Level 1: Shaky

Are you always feeling off-balance in your financial life? You're at the Shaky level if one or more of these statements apply to you:

- ✔ Your employment or retirement income sources don't provide regular and sustainable income.

- ✔ You're unable to save any part of your income.

- ✔ You need to use credit to provide for regular living expenses (food, rent or house payment, and so on).

- ✔ You have significant debt payments.

- ✔ Your net worth is decreasing year to year.

If you're a Shaky individual, weathering any financial environment, let alone an uncertain one, is difficult. Shaky individuals need to either increase their income or decrease their expenses, fast. Sometimes, you may need to take extreme measures to bolster your financial stability, such as selling your home to reduce your housing costs; selling a nice but too-expensive car; getting a second job; or going back to work if you've taken time off. Pay particular attention to Tip #4 and Tip #9.

Level 2: Stable

Stable individuals feel comfortable about today but may not be prepared for future shakeups. If you're a Stable individual, many of these statements describe you:

- ✔ You have regular and sustainable income.

- ✔ You're able to break even or even save a little every month.

- ✔ You have auto and homeowner's (or renter's) insurance but no other significant insurance.

- ✔ You don't have large amounts of consumer debt.

- ✔ You don't know how much money you need for retirement.

- ✔ Your net worth is level or slowly increasing.

If you're a Stable individual, you may be setting yourself up for tough times if things get turbulent. You're not struggling from pay-cheque to paycheque, so you feel okay about your current location on the financial map. But a single devastating event can send you veering off course. It's time to move to the next level, where your net worth is increasing noticeably each year (or if you're retired, continuing to increase or stay at a level that'll meet your needs). For now, make sure you read the tips in Part I of this book.

Level 3: Secure

If you're a Secure individual, you not only live within your means today but also plan for the future. The following statements describe you:

- ✔ You have a cash account with enough money to cover at least three months worth of expenses in case of a financial emergency.

- ✔ You know your most significant financial risks and have a plan in place to deal with unexpected events like job loss.

- ✔ You save for major purchases, such as automobiles and university education, to reduce or eliminate borrowing for them.

- ✔ You have a growing retirement portfolio (or if retired, you have a plan to invest and spend down your portfolio). You know how much money you'll need for a comfortable retirement.

- ✔ Your net worth is increasing regularly toward your ultimate goals.

Secure individuals are in the best position to weather the ups and downs of an uncertain economy. But even Secure individuals have some areas where they could improve their planning for volatile times. If you're in the Secure category, make sure you read through Parts II and III, and read the tips from Parts IV through VI that most apply to you now.

#8

Save

By Kim Jones, CFP

Likely lurking somewhere in your past (or present) is a grandmother who badgered you about saving money. Perhaps she didn't nag. But at the very least she probably counselled, advised, suggested, instructed, and just plain told you to save.

For most children, the future is tomorrow morning. But for the savvy saver who listened to Gramma, the future is that rainy day when you need cash but your current income isn't high enough to cover the unexpected downpour.

You can be certain a rainy day will arrive; you just can't be certain when.

Just Save It

You can find as many ways to save as you can to spend your money. And no matter how much your paycheque increases, you'll probably have no trouble finding more things to buy with the extra money.

So what's a hard-working gal or guy to do? Follow these two rules:

- ✔ Rule #1: Just do it.
- ✔ Rule #2: Pay yourself first.

You can't spend what you don't have. That's why you set aside a portion of your paycheque each month and then spend what's left. If you find this concept painful, play a game with yourself. Tell yourself that you'll just try it for a month or two.

Some folks call this strategy, "Set it and forget it." First you set it, and then you forget it. Soon you'll be on your way to feeling smug about that tidy sum in the bank.

Decide Where to Put that Rainy-Day Nest Egg

Common advice from financial gurus is to sock away an emergency reserve of three to six months' worth of living expenses in easily accessible savings. That way you won't put yourself in a bind by having to ask Uncle Henry for a loan (yikes!) or by borrowing too much on credit cards when a budget crisis crops up. Even worse would be liquidating a long-term investment account such as your Registered Retirement Savings Plan (RRSP) (which would cost you not only income tax on the amount withdrawn, but also a 10 to 20percent penalty!).

Your emergency fund should be

- ✔ Readily available on short notice
- ✔ Relatively safe
- ✔ Earning interest or dividends

You could put your dollars in a piggy bank. But piggy banks don't pay interest (and they're so-o-o easy to raid!). Instead, stash your money in a Tax-Free Savings Account (see Tip #32 for more on this), bank money market account, or a money market mutual fund. Have your credit union or bank directly debit your pay-cheque or chequing account before you have a chance to spend the money. The bank will be delighted to do it, and you'll get excited seeing your rainy-day fund grow each payday. You'll also heave a sigh of relief (rather than cringe) the next time an unexpected expense comes up.

Make Room for More Savings

Want to know the most important, most brilliant financial tip that exists in the world today? *Spend less than you make.*

If you automate those rainy-day savings (also a good strategy for long-term savings such as your RRSP), you spend less than you make without having to think about it.

Suppose you want to amass a $7,500 nest egg (three months of expenses at $2,500 per month). At 3 percent interest, saving $200 per month will allow you to reach your $7,500 goal in three years if you pay no income tax on your 3 percent.

Perhaps you're still insisting that you can't budget for savings. Well, take a look at what you spend on things that aren't absolutely essential, that don't match your life goals, or that don't give your life pleasure. Keep track of your spending for several weeks. Carry a little log book in your pocket and write down everything you spend. After a few weeks, pull out the log book and your regular monthly bills. Look at where your money goes. (During this exercise, having a glass of wine or your mug of favourite tea by your side is helpful.)

Ponder these questions:

- ✔ Do you need a landline *and* a cellphone?

- ✔ Do you need to buy books or is the library a better choice?

- ✔ Are you an impulse shopper at the supermarket? Try planning a weekly menu and make a shopping list of ingredients. Stick to the list, and you'll cut out expensive impulse buys.

- ✔ Can you host a potluck instead of meeting at a restaurant?

- ✔ Can you (heaven forbid!) make your own coffee at home and invest in a travel mug?

- ✔ Could you live in a modest home?

- ✔ Could you buy a used car rather than the latest new model? Or better yet, join a car co-op like www.zipcar.com?

- ✔ Do you have subscriptions to magazines you never read or health club memberships you never use?

- ✔ Can you make your own wine or beer?

The idea is not to feel deprived, but rather to make conscious spending decisions. Looking closely at where your money goes can help you decide where to cut, so that you can free up enough savings for the emergency fund without feeling bereft.

Hey, you may find that the joy of watching your savings grow far exceeds the momentary pleasure of an impulse purchase!

If you need a little boost, try this: The next time you pay something off, whether it's a small credit card balance or a car payment, continue making the payment. Only now, make the payment to that rainy-day account. You likely won't notice anything other than the size of the pay-yourself-first account increasing.

To further inspire yourself, post a bar graph on your refrigerator to track your progress. Pat yourself on the back every day.

Manage Your Debt

By Rick DeChaineau, CSA, CRPC, CFP

Think of your lifetime income and earnings as a pipeline that flows from when you start making money to the last day of your life. Along the way, various faucets in the pipeline open and divert money to pay for needs (such as living expenses, a home purchase, furniture, and transportation) and wants (like big-screen TVs, vacations, a fishing boat, and more). For items you buy using debt — mortgages, loans, credit card purchases — the faucet opens wider and runs longer because you're paying not only for the item but also for interest. The result is that you have to either work longer to earn more money to repay the debt or scale back on your goals.

During uncertain economic times, the amount of debt you're in can magnify the threat to your financial well-being. After you sign on for a debt, you no longer control that faucet. If the unexpected occurs, you have less cash flow and fewer options. This tip explains how to close those faucets and keep the pipeline from running dry.

Avoid Bad Debt

The best way to keep your income pipeline filled is by avoiding unnecessary debt. Not only does setting aside money for future expenses save you the cost of debt interest payments, but it can also earn money for you if you invest your saved cash in an interest-bearing account. As you save, you help fill your pipeline instead of draining it!

Putting off purchases until you've saved enough also gives you an additional reserve beyond your emergency fund (see Tip #8). For example, if you're saving money for a new barbecue, you can instead use those funds to replace a clothes dryer that tumbled its last towel or any other unanticipated expense that exceeds your emergency fund.

But like most people, you can't afford to pay cash for everything. Buying your home most likely required a mortgage. Buying cars, furniture, and appliances may involve financing. When you can't pay cash for high-cost items, you need to borrow at least some of the purchase amount.

Four criteria determine whether debt is good or bad. Before taking on debt, ask yourself the following questions. If the answer to *all* four questions is yes, you're signing up for good debt:

- ✔ **Is it a need?** If dependable transportation is a requirement for your job, buying a car to replace one that's on its last legs is clearly a need. But if your TV works and those ads for big-screen flat-panel models are making your mouth water, that's a want — which leads to bad debt.

   Note: Where you live is important for your quality of life, so although you can live in an apartment, you may choose to buy a home to provide a more desirable environment, which would qualify as a *need* on the scorecard.

- ✔ **Do you need to buy it before you can save up for it?** Consider the timing. You're looking at good debt if your car is beyond repair and you need dependable transportation to keep your job. If the big-screen TV is on sale this weekend, you can wait. It'll almost certainly be cheaper six months down the line.

- ✔ **Can you afford the payment?** If the payment fits your budget, you won't have to cut back on other needs. That's good debt. If you can't afford it, you'll have to cut back on some newly defined extras — like gas, food, and braces for the kids.

- ✔ **Are the financing terms okay?** Check the

   - Rate

   - Terms

   - Prepayment penalties (which should be none)

With good debt, you may have checked with your bank, credit union, or trust company, so you know the interest rate is competitive and the length of the car loan isn't longer than 48 months. You're into bad debt if you use the in-store financing to buy that new couch. The danger: If you don't pay off your purchase within the allotted time, the finance company generally applies interest retroactively, effective from the date of purchase at rates as high as 35 percent! So that $1,000 sofa could suddenly cost you at least $1,350, and interest continues to accumulate until you pay it off.

Saving up for a future expenditure keeps you in control of your money. By signing up for debt, you give away that control. Avoiding bad debt keeps more money in your income pipeline going towards your needs, wants, and other goals.

Dump Debt Sooner

Few things both make you feel good *and* improve your financial situation as much as paying off debt! The sooner you can shut off those debt faucets, the longer your income pipeline will stay filled.

Pay more than the minimum

 When the economy is shaky, expensive credit card debt can take you down fast. Consider this: If you have a credit card with a balance of $1,500 at an interest rate of 21 percent, you will need over 14 years to repay the balance if you make the minimum monthly payments of 3 percent. That's $1,800 in interest, for a total bill of $3,300. Think a 21 percent interest rate sounds exorbitant? Department store interest rates can run as high as 28 percent!

Reduce your rates

Your first step in dealing with existing debt is working to reduce your interest rates. Here's how:

- ✔ You may have gotten your home mortgage when rates were much higher — check on the rate you can get by refinancing.

- ✔ Call your credit card companies and ask for a lower rate. Tell them about lower-rate offers you've gotten in the mail. Do this at least once a year.

- ✔ Check with your bank, credit union, or trust company to see whether you can refinance your car loan at a lower rate. Consider the cost of refinancing and whether it's worth the lower payment you may get.

When checking on lower-rate refinancing, ask the same questions about terms and prepayment penalties that you would when looking for good debt.

Accelerate your payments

As soon as you're paying the lowest rates available, you want to start accelerating debt payments to get out of debt sooner.

Whether you have old bad debt from before reading this book or good debt, the less interest you pay, the better. The order in which you eliminate your debts depends on the type of account and how the interest is calculated.

Here's the usual priority order for paying off debt:

1. Credit cards and other revolving consumer accounts

2. Auto, furniture, and appliance loans

3. Boat and RV loans

4. Home equity loans

5. Home equity lines of credit (HELOC)

6. Student loans

7. Home mortgages

You can pay off your debts most efficiently by applying any extra cash to just one account at a time (usually the one with the highest interest rate and smallest balance). As soon as that first account is paid off, accelerate payments on account number 2 by applying the full amount you'd been paying on account number 1 (basic payment plus the extra amount). As each debt is paid off, keep rolling the full amount being paid to the next debt account.

Free online debt-reduction calculators can help you see how much interest you'll save and help you choose which debt to pay off first. (Visit www.steps-2-wealth.com and go to the Debt Reduction section to try one.)

Don't bury your head in the sand. If you're having debt problems, contact a *free* credit counselling service in your community. These nonprofit agencies can help you come up with a realistic budget. In some cases, they even contact creditors for you to negotiate a break on interest. To find one in your area, do an Internet search or check the Yellow Pages under "credit counselling" and the name of your city or province.

As soon as a credit card account is paid off, don't close it — just cut up the card. Closing an account you've paid off hurts your credit score by reducing the total amount of credit you have available.

Improve Your Credit Score

By Derek Lenington, CFP

Your credit score is a factor in determining your mortgage rate, and it can influence the interest rates you get on credit cards and car loans. It can also affect your homeowner's and car insurance rates and may even be considered when you apply for a job! Here are some tips on improving your score.

Get a Free Credit Report

Your credit score is only as good as your credit report, and getting a copy is easy and free. You can get a copy of your credit report once a year totally *gratis*. Contact one of Canada's credit bureaus to receive a copy by mail:

- ✔ **Equifax Canada:** 1-800-465-7166; www.equifax.ca
- ✔ **TransUnion Canada:** 1-866-525-0262; www.transunion.ca
- ✔ **Northern Credit Bureaus, Inc.:** www.creditbureau.ca

If you need your report fast, you can view it instantly online for $15. For around $24 you can get your credit score — the three-digit number that lenders use to make decisions about whether to loan you cash. Your credit score ranges roughly between 300 (you never paid a bill in your life) and 900 (you borrow often, pay your bills on time religiously, and don't carry hefty balances on your credit cards).

To get your credit information, you need to provide your name, address, Social Insurance Number (SIN), and date of birth. Also be prepared to give previous addresses if you've moved in the last two years, and at least one piece of personal information only you would know, such as a regular monthly payment amount on a mortgage or auto loan.

Take a Good Look at Your Credit History

CBC's *Marketplace* program once asked 100 people to go over their credit reports for mistakes. More than 40 people spotted errors, and 13 of the errors were serious enough to affect their credit status. When you receive your credit report, look it over carefully for the following red flags:

- Addresses of places you've never lived or visited

- Aliases you've never used, which may indicate that someone is using your SIN or the credit reporting agency has mixed someone's data with yours

- Multiple SINs, which could mean that the information for someone with the same name as yours has made it into your credit report

- Wrong date of birth (DOB)

- Credit cards you don't have

- Loans you haven't taken out

- Records of unpaid bills that you either know you paid or had good reason for not paying

- Records of late payments that you know weren't late

- Inquiries from companies that you've never done business with (When you apply for a loan, the lender typically runs a credit inquiry, and that shows up on the report.)

 Addresses of places you've never lived or records of accounts, loans, and credit cards you never had could be signs of identity theft. Gak! Contact the credit reporting company immediately and request that they place a fraud alert on your credit report.

 Whether you're single, married, divorced, or separated, your credit history should include information about *you only*. Spousal information should be included only when you're both legally obligated to pay on a listed debt or if you're both permitted to use a particular account.

Keep the Good, Fix the Bad

If you have a credit score of 700 or higher, pat yourself on the back. You're above average and qualified to borrow oodles of cash at the lowest available rates. Anything below about 680 sounds the warning sirens. This is the point at which lending institutions get out the magnifying glass and begin raising rates and denying credit. If your credit rating dips below 700, take steps to improve it, such as the following:

- ✔ **Dispute any errors and omissions on your credit report.** Disputing a claim doesn't always result in a correction, but you can ask to have a paragraph explaining your side of the story added to your report.

- ✔ **Apply for fewer loans and credit cards.** When you apply for a loan or credit card, the lending institution typically orders an inquiry that shows up on your credit report. Evidence that you're applying for a number of loans or credit cards in a short period of time can make you appear as if you're grasping at financial straws. Have no more than two credit cards per spouse.

- ✔ **Pay off your credit card balance, or at least part of the balance.** Your balance should be 50 percent or less than your available credit limit.

To correct negative or incorrect information, you can send a dispute form, along with supporting evidence. Forms are available online, or by calling the credit bureau. Never send original documents and always track your submissions using certified mail or a similar service. If you don't get a satisfactory or prompt response, contact the creditor directly (and copy the credit reporting agency) to demand that they investigate your claim. When the reinvestigation is complete, the credit bureau must give you the results in writing. If the dispute results in a change, they also must send you a free copy of your report. After your file is corrected, the agency has to notify anyone who has received the old report within 60 days of the correction.

Avoid credit repair clinics. At best, they don't do anything you can't do yourself. At worst, these firms charge outrageous fees and suggest potentially illegal practices. Free credit counselling agencies (which we discuss in Tip #9) are a good resource.

You're allowed a brief statement (100 words or less) to explain any information in your report that you dispute. Your statement can't explain information that is negative but factually correct; this statement is only to dispute errors. However, these statements are rarely effective. Personally explaining negative information directly to a potential creditor is usually best.

Your credit score

Credit reporting agencies use statistical models to figure out your credit score. One of the most popular models is the Fair Isaac Company (FICO) rating system. The credit company assigns numerical values to specific pieces of data in your credit history, such as the length of your credit history and the types of interest you're paying. They then plug these numbers into the statistical model, which spits out your credit score. It's basically a numbers game that determines your credit score in the following manner:

✔ Thirty-five percent is based on your payment history.

✔ Thirty percent is based on your outstanding debt (how much you currently owe).

✔ Fifteen percent is based on the length of your credit history (how long you've been borrowing).

✔ Ten percent is based on recent inquiries on your report (whenever a lending institution requests a report).

✔ Ten percent is based on the types of credit you have (such as mortgage or credit card interest).

Add good information to your report

Yes, you can request that each of the three agencies add information to your file. Although they're not required to do so, they often do if they can verify the information. Focus on missing positive account histories, even if the account is closed. Also add information that explains or corrects potentially negative information.

Creditors care most that you have a proven history of paying credit responsibly. Account diversity matters, too, as does the length of your credit history. So adding an old credit card payment history to your report is well worth the effort.

Often, you find an account's positive credit history missing from only one of the three credit reporting agencies' records. Send that agency a copy of the correct reports. Include a brief cover letter explaining your request. Copies of monthly statements from the missing creditor make it more likely that they'll add the information.

Missing or incomplete information about your current and previous employers or residences can make it difficult for potential creditors to check your information. Without your full profile, they may not assess your credit history favourably. This is particularly important if the job or address change has happened in the last two to three years.

Don't assume that credit reporting agencies will add or permanently correct information on your report. Sometimes your corrections inadvertently disappear. Review your report at least annually, and more frequently if you plan on applying for a large amount of credit.

#11

Set and Prioritize Financial Goals

By Abigail Pons, MBA, CFP

If you don't take time to set financial goals, you tend to deal with issues haphazardly, addressing whatever happens to bubble up at the time. For example, without a plan, a leaky roof can easily liquidate your vacation prospects; however, proper goal setting can allow you to visit Niagara Falls without ending up with your own private waterfall in the living room.

Consider the following reasons to invest some time in setting financial goals:

✔ You achieve financial peace of mind.

✔ You gain the ability to live within your means.

✔ Time is your ally, enabling you to put away less money over longer periods of time.

✔ You're free to change your goals over time.

This section helps you put your goals in place and begin working toward them.

Get Started

Although setting personal financial goals isn't rocket science, it takes some thought (and maybe a cup of coffee). Most people have limited resources and have to be honest about what's most important in life. Become your own Personal Finance Project Manager, and start by getting it all down on paper:

1. **List all your goals.**

   Write it *all* down — new refrigerator, new roof, new car, vacations and travel, retirement, university funding, and so on. Don't forget the goals that you take for granted. For instance, if you have a five-year loan for your car, you committed to the goal of owning the car at the end of five years by taking out that loan. Take the time to make sure your list is complete.

2. **Attach a price tag to each goal.**

You need to know how much each goal costs in light of your budget and other goals. Sometimes the cost of a goal becomes a deciding factor in setting priorities.

Short-term goals are easier to address because the costs are more predictable. For example, if you aim to buy a new car outright in two years, you can assume that the current cost of the vehicle, plus a reasonable inflation adjustment, will provide a realistic estimate.

For longer-term goals, such as retirement and college or university savings, setting a price tag can be tricky. The Web site www.canadianbusiness.com has useful calculators for tuition fees, retirement savings, and mortgage costs. Check out Tip #51 and Tip #52 for good information about accumulating adequate funds for retirement.

3. **Prioritize your goals.**

When you have a good feel for the cost of your goals, list them in order of importance to you. Prioritizing allows you to focus on the goals you value most. You may decide that some goals are unimportant and remove them from your list altogether. Or you may make some important lifestyle decisions, such as buying a used car instead of a new one, to have enough money for RRSP contributions (see Tip #30). Don't be discouraged by cost (for example, the cost of retirement) — just realize that planning now is crucial so you can consistently chip away at the goal over time.

4. **Assign a tentative timetable to your goals and visualize how much they'll cost at various points in your life.**

Consider the scale of a big, long-term goal, such as retirement, against smaller goals, such as vehicle purchases and travel. And don't forget the effect of inflation over time.

Compare Short-Term and Long-Term Goals

Some big differences exist in how you handle and invest for short-term and long-term goals. This section lays them out for you.

Short-term goals

Generally, you want to achieve *short-term goals* in the next five years. They may include the following:

- ✔ Saving for a down payment on a new home
- ✔ Paying off credit card debt
- ✔ Buying a car
- ✔ Taking a vacation

Keep your savings for short-term goals in liquid investments. You can easily convert *liquid investments* to cash; examples include

- ✔ High-interest savings accounts
- ✔ Money market accounts or mutual funds
- ✔ Short-term GICs with staggered maturities

Don't invest in anything that may significantly drop in value, such as an individual stock, leaving you with less cash at the very time you need it.

Leave some money in your emergency cash reserves. The money you're directing toward short-term goals should be on top of your rainy-day fund, an in-case-of-emergency account that can support you for three to six months. Like savings for short-term goals, invest your emergency cash reserves in highly liquid, easily accessible investments. (See Tip #8 to make sure you're covered.)

Long-term goals

Long-term goals are usually more than five years away. Most people have just a few long-term goals, such as retirement, saving for a child's college or university education, or starting their own business in ten years.

Several factors make long-term goal planning tricky:

- ✔ **Inflation:** It happens, but you can't possibly know at what rate.
- ✔ **Investment returns:** You can't be certain how much your investments will make over long periods of time.
- ✔ **Taxes:** They can go up or down.
- ✔ **Changing costs of your goal:** The price tag of a long-term goal can be a moving target. Will you qualify for the maximum Old Age Security and CPP or a pension payment during retirement? Will your workplace pension fund thrive or dive?

You may not know exactly how these factors will play out, but you can make reasonable assumptions about them with current information, such as your CPP Statement of Contributions or the annual information return on your workplace pension plan. Generally, with long-term goals, erring on the conservative side is best — assume that inflation and taxes will be higher and investment returns will be lower than those in the last few decades.

The good news? Because your long-term goals are far into the future, you can take more risk to pursue higher returns with these investments. And here's even better news: Uncertain economic environments can present long-term investment opportunities. The important thing is to stay the course with your investment plan.

Put Your Plans in Motion

After you set your goals and know what you want to do with your money, actually putting that cash to work toward your goals is the essential next step. Here are some tips:

- ✔ **Pay yourself first.** You've no doubt heard it before, but it's good, reliable wisdom: You have to pay yourself first, or your money will find someplace else to go, without fail. If you want to achieve a financial goal, you have to make a payment toward that goal.

- ✔ **Keep the money separate from spendable funds.** One of the added benefits of RRSP accounts is that they're set aside from your everyday household funds. Accessing your retirement accounts is a hassle, and if you do it too early, you may pay a penalty. For other goals, keeping money mentally separate from your disposable funds may be harder. Consider keeping funds for other goals in a separate earmarked account to make it less tempting to raid.

- ✔ **Automate.** One of the great things about the modern, high-tech financial world is the ability to automate money transfers. Not only is it easier to pay your mortgage and credit card payments on time, but you can also set up automatic monthly transfers to your savings or investment accounts. Doing so removes the decision-making process from the picture and enables you to pay the most important person first — you!

After you define your goals and have a plan to achieve them, revisit and re-evaluate them on a regular basis. Give special attention to those moving-target long-term goals. If your current spending on short-term goals is maxing out your budget, you may be sabotaging progress toward your long-term goals. Make sure you review your priorities regularly.

Don't Let Your Money Beliefs Sabotage Your Goals

By Diane Blackwelder, CFP

Self-knowledge is power. To avoid sabotaging your financial goals, particularly in tough times, self-awareness and flexibility are essential. You're not likely to change your money personality, but by acknowledging your strengths and weaknesses, you can change your tactics and achieve financial success.

Know Your Money Personality (And Its Weaknesses)

Some finance professionals may say, "Who needs a financial plan? All you need to do is spend less than you make and invest the rest." Simple, right? So why is it so hard to do? Most of us know how to get ahead financially, but our own counterproductive ideas can hold us back.

Attitudes toward money and spending are often deeply ingrained. And they can have long-term implications, for both your relationships (money is a common source of conflict in marriage) and your financial health. Some people mirror the beliefs of their parents, while others adopt completely opposite attitudes. Identifying your money personality is the first step in understanding how your beliefs may be affecting your bottom line.

Here are three basic money personality types:

- ✔ Spenders
- ✔ Savers
- ✔ Procrastinators

Don't worry — no money personality is better than the others. Most people have a little of each. But when facing uncertain times, idiosyncrasies can rear their ugly heads.

Spenders

You've likely heard the saying, "Keeping up with the Joneses." Well, spenders *are* the Joneses. They live in the right house in the right neighborhood, drive a shiny new car, and are most likely buried under a mountain of debt.

Spenders live by the mantra, "I deserve it." They live in the moment and consider money a measure of success. Ironically, spenders feel frustrated because they have no money in the bank. And during uncertain times, spenders may feel the crunch from their overexuberance.

If the following describes you, you could be a spender:

- ✔ You often reward yourself by buying new shoes or a new toy.

- ✔ You're always waiting for your next paycheque.

- ✔ You think a budget is a brightly coloured bird beloved by pet owners . . . or wait, is that a budgie?

Everyone splurges once in a while. But when spending undermines your financial security, today or in the future, you need to get a grip. Consider the following tactics:

- ✔ **Freeze your credit cards — literally.** Take your credit cards and freeze them in a cup of water. It may sound silly, but waiting for your credit card to thaw will take the spontaneity out of splurging. If you prefer a less extreme measure, adopt a cooling-off period: Don't allow yourself to buy a single item over a preset limit, say $50, without waiting 24 hours.

- ✔ **Think about tomorrow.** Preparing a financial to-do list helps to prioritize spending. Suppose your goal is to have $5,000 in the bank by year-end. Set up automatic drafts from your chequing to savings, and invest in yourself. Before you buy that designer purse or another pair of high-end sneakers, ask yourself, "Will this purchase mean something to me in a year?"

Savers

The term *penny pincher* comes to mind when describing a saver. Savers clip coupons, live on strict budgets, feel guilty when making major purchases, and get a thrill out of watching their bank accounts grow.

Savers, unlike spenders, have a hard time living in the moment. A saver often refrains from taking a vacation or replacing his 10-year-old car. The saver's motto is, "Safety is king." A saver would rather bury his money in the backyard than risk losing a penny. Negative economic news is particularly worrisome to the saver.

If the following describes you, you're probably a saver:

- ✔ You can account for every penny you spend in a month, right down to the 75-cent late fee from the library (drat!).

- ✔ You bought a DVD player for $30 off the back of some guy's truck, only after the very last VHS tape was removed from your local video store.

- ✔ You're still wearing the same suit you got married in (after all, '80s fashions are back, aren't they?).

As far as financial security goes, being a saver isn't so bad. However, a little moderation never hurts. If you're a saver, try to remember the following:

- ✔ **Risk is not a four-letter word.** Take more risk with your money in exchange for greater rewards. Investing your cash in a diversified portfolio makes your money work as hard as you do. Investing is a long-term proposition. Don't let hiccups in the market distract you from your goals.

- ✔ **Relax.** Review your financial goals. After you establish your needs and find ways to make your money work harder for you, give yourself permission to enjoy the rest. Instead of researching bargain prices on toilet paper, plan a much-deserved vacation.

Procrastinators

Spenders and savers are on the extreme ends of the money personality spectrum. Procrastinators, on the other hand, live with their heads buried firmly in the sand. Walk into a procrastinator's house and you're likely to find stacks of unopened mail. Procrastinators are overwhelmed by financial matters and will do almost anything to avoid them.

Procrastinators do worry about money, but they're unable to act. They put off paying bills, enrolling in their company's retirement plan, setting goals, and even filing their taxes. During uncertain times a procrastinator will justify putting off any financial decision.

If the following sounds familiar, you could be a procrastinator:

✔ You miss the tax deadline every year.

✔ You wait until a collection agency calls before you pay your dentist's bill.

✔ You'd rather have a root canal than balance your cheque-book.

Many people put off today what they can do tomorrow. When it comes to money, procrastinating can harm not only your credit, but also your financial security. If you find yourself going this way, take the following actions:

✔ **Install safety nets.** Automate as much of your financial affairs as possible. Setting up automatic bill payments and regular transfers to your investment accounts will ensure that you get it done.

✔ **Feather your nest.** Make an effort to learn more about financial planning. Enroll in a personal finance class at a community college or read personal finance books. By investing in yourself and building knowledge, you'll be better able to weather financial storms.

Work to Improve Yourself

After you know what kind of money personality you have, and you understand where that type of personality may fall short, you can begin to make improvements. In addition to addressing the specific personality-related shortcomings we mention, try the following:

✔ **Find an accountability partner.** Share the responsibilities of managing your money with your spouse, significant other, or a professional. Having an accountability partner will keep your weaknesses in check and build on your strengths.

✔ **Think small.** Don't expect an overnight reversal of your belief system. Start with small steps, like taking a class or preparing a to-do list. Minor changes often bring big results.

#13

Avoid Common Mistakes in a Down Market

By Warren McIntyre, CFP, and Richard Weimert, MBA, CFP

Investment markets don't always go up. In fact, historically, over a one-year period, only about a 65 percent chance exists that a diversified stock portfolio will outperform the rate of return from a bank deposit, according to York University finance professor Moshe Milevsky. Seeing the value of your investments go down can be emotional. But if you stretch your time horizon to 10 years down the line, an 89 percent chance exists that your stock portfolio will outperform the bank interest rate. Wait 30 years, and you've got a 99 percent chance of reaping a better return. The fact is that the markets have consistently increased in value over very long periods and through all kinds of challenges. This tip gives you some things to focus on during the inevitable down periods.

Keep Cool

Don't let a market slump make you do something you'll regret later or derail your investment program. When the going gets tough, the urge to bail out of stocks can be strong. But panicking can wreck an investment plan faster than anything. Being out of the market won't allow you to keep up with the rising cost of living. In addition, franticly repurchasing later to avoid missing out on market gains could mean you're buying high and selling low. If you haven't developed a long-term investment plan, do it now. If you have, review it to make sure it still reflects your financial goals (refer to Tip #11).

Consider the following when markets are rocky:

✔ **Communicate with your financial advisor, if you have one.** Financial advisors earn their keep in turbulent times, and a good one can talk you through your panic, walk you through the holdings in your portfolio, and reaffirm your investment strategy.

✔ **Do nothing.** Sometimes doing nothing is preferable to taking action. Try leaving your account statements unopened for a while. When you look at them (every three months or so), you may find the account values are higher than you thought, especially if you're adding to them regularly.

✔ **Don't watch, listen to, or read too much commentary.** During a downturn, the news media has plenty of disheartening stories. The talking heads and bloggers are for *infotainment,* not to make you money.

✔ **Act less like a day trader and more like legendary investors Warren Buffet and Peter Cundhill.** They see market madness as normal and transitory and take advantage of opportunities in the hard times. Check your stomach for risk. If a big dip invokes too much anxiety, consider putting a larger proportion of your portfolio in less risky assets, like bonds and even cash. But be sure that doing so doesn't jeopardize your long-term goals.

Stick to the Basics

Market turmoil causes investors to question their own judgment and seek different approaches. But all investors really need to do is follow some fundamental principles. Consider the following:

✔ **Invest in securities and use time-tested strategies you can easily understand.** The subprime mortgage crisis in the United States and the collapse of Nortel are examples of strategies that failed because some very smart people couldn't control their complex schemes. Be sure you understand your investments, including risks, fees, and other costs.

✔ **Make sure you're well-diversified globally.** Canada isn't the only market in the world — it represents only about 4 percent of the total global stock market, and every day we become more dependent on a global economy. See Part III for strategies and asset allocations that will make your portfolio less risky.

✔ **Use mutual funds and exchange-traded funds.** Unless you have at least $100,000 to invest and the time and expertise to monitor individual securities, you're better off with well-chosen mutual funds or exchange-traded funds (ETFs). (See Tips #18 and #20 for the ins and outs of these investment vehicles.) The value of an individual stock or bond can go to zero, but a mutual fund is usually so diversified that losses are temporary. To reduce risk, limit any single stock or bond to no more than 5 percent of your portfolio. Be conscious of too much overlap in individual securities or in styles of funds in your portfolio. Your advisor or online tools can help you analyze the portfolio.

Limit yourself to 10 percent of employer stock. Be aware of how much company stock you hold in your various portfolios. With your employment and potential retirement benefits already aligned with the fortunes of your company, limiting personal exposure to your company's stock is best.

✔ **Keep costs in mind.** High costs are magnified when returns are low. Self-directed investors can minimize costs by using index funds and ETFs. If you need or want an advisor, don't be afraid to ask how the advisor is paid and about the fees and expenses of the mutual funds and other products used.

Uncertain economies and markets make adjusting your portfolio even more important. Many proprietary products handcuff investors by imposing heavy surrender charges or exit fees. Annuities are the most common offenders, but other hard-to-cash investments, such as limited partnerships, can keep you from making the necessary changes.

Be Savvy

Beyond the basics, a smart investor can use a variety of strategies to cope with adverse market conditions. Give some of the following a try:

✔ **Pay down debt.** The return on investment from paying off a loan is equal to the interest rate charged — but unlike other investments, the return is guaranteed. Even paying down a mortgage (often considered good debt) may be the best investment you can make in a down market.

✔ **Invest for *total return* (the combination of growth and income), not just income.** Down markets often coincide with sluggish economic conditions. Income investors feel the squeeze when rates on GICs and other income investments drift lower and lower. Invest for the highest total return consistent with your risk tolerance and then withdraw funds as needed.

✔ **Continue to invest the same amount of money on a consistent basis, be it weekly, monthly, or quarterly.** By sticking with the program in good times and bad, and increasing the amounts of your contributions when you can, you can build wealth regardless of market conditions.

✔ **Automate your savings program.** Participants in workplace group RRSP plans enjoy both automatic investing and dollar-cost averaging. But most financial institutions will arrange similar systematic investing in other types of accounts.

> ✔ **Use target maturity and lifecycle funds.** These *funds-of-funds* provide a complete portfolio rebalanced automatically, ensuring broad diversification and effortless investing.

Take Advantage of the Turmoil

You can't control what happens in the markets, but you can spin market turbulence into opportunities. Consider actions like these during market declines:

> ✔ **Buy more.** A decline in prices means investments are on sale. If you're saving and adding to your accounts, you should be delighted with a down market. You want the value of your holdings to be higher when you retire or when you need them —what they're worth now doesn't matter so much.

> ✔ **Rebalance your portfolio at least annually.** Market declines can cause your allocations to stray far from your target. To get your portfolio back in line, you buy what's gone down and sell what's gone up. Buy low, sell high.

> ✔ **Harvest your tax losses.** *Tax-loss harvesting* (selling assets in which you have a taxable loss and replacing them with other nearly identical securities) is a great and legal way to take advantage of the tax code. Just be careful to watch the *superficial loss rule* — basically, the Canada Revenue Agency will disallow your loss if you buy back the same security within 30 days of selling it. This includes mutual funds. You can, however, buy similar mutual funds; for example, if you sell a large cap value fund, you can buy another large value fund immediately, as long as it isn't the same fund you just sold.

Don't fixate on income taxes. Fear of paying taxes has prevented more people from taking necessary actions than just about any other reason. If your analysis suggests that you dump those stocks, don't let the tax consequences stand in the way. Besides, with special rates for capital gains, the tax bill may be lower than you think.

Part II

Using Investment Vehicles and Accounts throughout the Economic Cycle

The 5th Wave   By Rich Tennant

That's the Harrisons. Never have I seen an investment portfolio start so strong and go south so quickly.

In this part...

The investment marketplace is overflowing with choices, not to mention "expert" opinions on how to use these options to best meet your needs. In this part, you get an overview of the scads of investments and accounts that are available to you as well as an explanation of each investment vehicle or account and when it may work for you.

Include Cash Reserves: Savings, GICs, and Money Market Accounts

By Paul Dolce, MBA, CFP

*Y*ou may think of cash as the comfort food of investing. When things get dicey, you feel like pulling your money out of investments and moving it somewhere safe. Maybe you simply can't stand the thought of watching your investments decrease in value, a frequent problem in times of economic uncertainty. Having an investment strategy that holds up in good times and bad can help you overcome those concerns. And cash is one component of every good investment strategy.

You can use cash for a variety of things, including the following:

- **Your emergency fund:** Use emergency funds to cover unexpected expenses like car repairs or a leaky roof.

- **Short-term goals:** These include goals that are less than five years away, such as saving for a car or a down payment on a home.

- **Investment stability:** Include cash investments in your investment strategy as a *core investment* (primary holding) and to reduce *volatility* (a measure of how rapidly the value of your portfolio goes up and down).

- **Temporary component:** You can also use cash as a temporary component of portfolios earmarked for long-term goals. You may hold cash in these portfolios for a variety of reasons, including the following:

    - You've sold an investment and can't find a suitable replacement.

- You want cash on hand so you can take advantage of an anticipated investment opportunity.

- You need to draw income from your account, so you have to keep a portion of it in cash for safety. You don't want to have to sell an investment in the midst of market mayhem just because you need the cash to pay bills.

Your Cash-Equivalent Savings Options

Savings accounts, GICs, and money market accounts are three vehicles that you can use to ensure that your cash is working for you. Generically called *cash equivalents,* each of these investments has one key feature: safety. In other words, their value remains relatively stable.

Savings accounts

Savings accounts offered by banking and trust companies are safe, very safe. The Canada Deposit Insurance Corporation (CDIC) insures savings accounts at member institutions up to $100,000 per depositor. (Visit www.cdic.ca to make sure your financial institution is a member of CDIC.) Some provinces even have unlimited deposit guarantees for their credit union customers.

Savings accounts are liquid, too. This means you can haul your money out whenever you need it without worrying about early withdrawal fees, gains, losses, or other complications.

Savings accounts also have a downside: They pay low interest rates. When interest rates in the general economy decline, interest rates paid on savings accounts can be downright pathetic and may not even keep up with inflation. If inflation is increasing the cost of the things you buy by 3 percent each year and your savings account is paying you only 1 percent in interest, the purchasing power of the money in your savings account is actually declining by 2 percent per year. Plus, you pay tax on your interest earnings. So keeping your funds in a safe account can actually cost you big.

Online savings accounts, such as those from ING Direct (www.ingdirect.ca) and Citizens Bank of Canada (www.citizensbank.ca), offer CDIC-insured savings that typically yield a bit more interest than regular bank savings accounts. Because these institutions don't have physical branch buildings and staff, and they do business online or over the phone, their expenses are lower. To use them, simply open an account on their Web site and fund the account by transferring money electronically from your regular savings institution to your new account. You can transfer money back whenever you want to in the same manner. You can also pay many of your bills electronically from these online savings accounts, saving you money on postage!

 Set up a Tax-Free Savings Account. This new investment vehicle allows you to shelter up to $5,000 a year in investments tax free. Unlike an RRSP, you won't get a tax credit for the money you invest, but you *can* withdraw cash as needed — say for a new car or home repairs — without paying a tax penalty. (See Tip #32 for more.) Otherwise, keep money in savings accounts only for ultra-short-term needs. You have better options available for long-term investments.

Guaranteed Investment Certificates

The same institutions that offer savings accounts also offer Guaranteed Investment Certificates, or GICs. GICs are CDIC-insured, so they're safe like savings accounts. However, they generally pay slightly higher interest rates.

GICs can offer both safety and higher rates because they aren't as liquid as savings accounts — they have predetermined maturity terms, typically ranging from six months to two years or longer. When you buy a GIC, plan to keep it until the end of its term. If you redeem it before it matures, you may have to pay an early with-drawal penalty or forfeit a portion of the interest you earned.

 A bank's GIC rates may be negotiable. Banks and credit unions often offer special rates to attract funds. Shop around online (try the "Rates" section of `www.money.canoe.ca`) or by phone to find the best rates in your area. If they're better than your bank's rates, talk to an investment specialist at your bank and see if they'll match the higher rate — asking can't hurt. Just like any other business, banks hate to lose customers, and they sometimes do what it takes to keep you from taking your money elsewhere.

Money market accounts

A money market fund is an ideal place to hold money that you'll need soon or to park cash while you're seeking better investment opportunities. Although they aren't CDIC-insured, money market accounts combine some of the best features of savings accounts and GICs.

Like savings accounts, money market accounts are liquid. In most cases you can get your money out by the next business day. Some funds even offer chequing privileges with higher balances. But check the prospectus if you want cheque-writing privileges — the account may have restrictions on the minimum amount you can withdraw and on the number of cheques you can write.

Money market accounts are extremely safe because of the short-term nature of the investments they hold, and yet they offer better interest rates than savings accounts. Sometimes the rates aren't quite as attractive as those for GICs, but you have access to your money anytime; you don't get that with a GIC.

You can open a money market account at most banks and institutions that offer savings accounts and GICs. Many mutual fund companies also offer money market accounts. Money market mutual funds frequently offer even better rates than bank money market accounts, so check before you invest.

When investing in money market funds, know that the performance of various funds doesn't vary widely. Usually only about a 1.5 percent difference exists between the best and the worst returns. The upshot? The funds with the lowest management expense ratios (MERs) and no sales fees tend to perform the best, so avoid buying funds that charge a sales commission.

So Which One Is Right for You?

When you're choosing which type of cash account to use, consider the following:

- ✔ Your investment strategy
- ✔ When you may need your money
- ✔ The current rate of inflation and whether the interest rate will keep up with inflation
- ✔ Your comfort with using Internet institutions versus your local bank
- ✔ Your familiarity with mutual fund companies
- ✔ How easily you can access your money
- ✔ The restrictions and limitations associated with each type of cash account

When times are tough and markets are down, keep your short-term money needs in mind. If you know you're going to need cold hard cash sometime in the next couple of years, keep that sum in a nice, safe cash option. Keeping short-term money in long-term securities like stocks and bonds is flirting with disaster.

Government Bonds: Loaning The Government Your Money

By Michael Oswalt, CPA

Governments borrow money just as companies do. Although companies can raise cash by selling their own shares as well as by outright borrowing, governments can't. Their money comes from us, either through our taxes or through government debt instruments like Canada Savings Bonds, treasury bills, and bonds. Essentially, these investments are IOUs from the government with a bit of interest tacked on to reward us for our trouble.

During tough economic times, part of your portfolio should be dedicated to investments that offer predictability, safety, and liquidity (meaning they're easily accessible). For these objectives, government securities are a pretty good bet.

Canada Savings Bonds: Tried and True

The first Canada Savings Bonds (CSBs) were issued in 1946 as a successor to the wildly popular War Savings Certificates and Victory Bonds that helped finance our war efforts. When you buy a CSB, you're basically lending money to the feds for a specified period of time. The bonds are *non-marketable,* meaning they're registered in your name, and you can't sell them to other people.

On the upside, CSBs are easy to buy, come in small denominations (as little as $100), and provide enviable security and safety. On the downside, they pay interest rates that haven't kept pace with money market accounts or GICs. The result: They're popular ways to provide for kids and grandkids without giving cash, but frequently investors don't bother with them.

CSBs go on sale from early October to April 1 each year. The best way to purchase CSBs is through the federal government's Web site (www.csb.gc.ca). You can find out about rates, buy bonds, or sign up to purchase bonds through a payroll savings plan. You can also buy CSBs through your investment advisor.

These bonds have two basic flavours:

- ✓ **Canada Savings Bonds** come with either regular interest (paid annually) or compound interest (reinvested throughout the year) and can be cashed any time.

- ✓ **Canada Premium Bonds (CPBs)** are cashable once a year on the anniversary of the issue date and pay a slightly higher interest rate.

A Registered Retirement Savings Plan (RRSP), a Registered Retirement Income Fund (RRIF), a Registered Education Savings Plan (RESP), or a Tax-Free Savings Account (TFSA) can hold CSBs and CPBs.

Gimme a "T!": Treasury Securities

Most government debt in Canada is made up of *marketable* (tradable) securities in the form of treasury bills, or T-bills. These are short-term bonds issued by the federal government as well as some provinces. Government of Canada treasury bills offer investors attractive interest rates with the full backing of the government. They're considered pretty much risk-free if held to maturity. In fact, T-bills are regarded as the safest Canadian investment available with a term of under one year. Here's what you need to know:

- ✓ T-bills are issued in terms of one month to one year and are sold in large denominations. Investment dealers and banks then repackage the T-bills into smaller amounts, such as $5,000, $10,000, or $25,000, depending on the term, for individual investors.

- ✓ T-bills' return is called the *effective interest rate.* That's because in reality T-bills don't pay interest. The return is actually the difference between the price you pay for the T-bill (which is always less than face value) and its worth at maturity. Banks and investment dealers often translate this into a percentage return in the form of an interest rate so you can comparison shop with other investments.

- ✓ T-bills are highly liquid. You can sell them at any time and usually get your cash within one business day.

- ✓ An RRSP, RRIF, RESP, or TFSA can hold T-bills.

Government of Canada Bonds

As well as T-bills, the federal government issues marketable bonds in denominations as low as $1,000. You don't pay a commission to buy or sell these bonds; instead, investment dealers take their cut by building a commission into the price of the security.

The prices of bonds, in general, don't move in tandem with stock prices, so including a mix of bonds in an investment portfolio gives you powerful tools in an uncertain economy: diversification and liquidity. A mix of short-term treasury bills with medium- and long-term bonds provides a steady stream of risk-free income.

Government of Canada T-bills and bonds provide a superior alternative to bank or credit union GICs. Unless you really shop around for a GIC, they'll probably earn you a slightly lower return than a T-bill or government bond.

Does Government Backing Equal Risk-Free?

Because Government of Canada bonds and T-bills are fully backed by the Canadian government, they're considered to have essentially no credit risk. Only a monumental event or combination of events —war, government scandal, or an economic collapse — would prevent the Canadian government from repaying its debts. If these events occur, the government has the power to increase taxes and print additional money if the need arises. So you have almost no credit risk, but you do have other types of risks, just as with any type of fixed-rate security. Here are the major risks:

- ✔ **Interest-rate risk:** This is the risk that a bond's value will fall when interest rates go up. By keeping your bond until it matures, you receive all the principal and interest you expect. However, if you need to sell your security before it matures and interest rates go up, you may have to sell it for less than you paid.

- ✔ **Inflation risk:** This is the risk that a bond's return won't keep up with inflation. This risk is a special concern for government bondholders; the longer the term of the bond, the greater the risk. Because lending the Canadian government money involves no credit risk, the return is lower than it would be on higher-risk investments. If the Canadian economy is experiencing a period of inflation, the purchasing power of the dollar declines and so does the real value of your bond. Ottawa does offer Government of Canada Real Return Bonds with interest payments adjusted for changes in the consumer price index (CPI).

#16

Decide Whether Fixed Annuities Are Right for You

By Buz Livingston, CFP

Does an income stream that lasts a lifetime sound appealing? Adding a fixed annuity to your investment mix guarantees you won't completely outlive your nest egg during uncertain times. An *annuity* is a promise from an insurance company to send you, the *annuitant,* payments for a specified period of time, potentially the rest of your life. If you live a long time, you win; if you kick off early, the insurance company wins.

Annuities are either fixed or variable. A *fixed annuity* payment remains the same throughout the coverage period, no matter what happens in the economy. Like RRSPs, annuities allow your investment dollars to compound tax free. The regular payments from the annuity are taxed as pension income by Canada Revenue Agency.

Weigh the Pros and Cons

A fixed annuity isn't right for everyone. Like other investments, fixed annuities have their share of pros and cons.

Good reasons to buy a fixed annuity

The perfect candidate for a fixed annuity is an older investor in good health who has a family history of longevity and who wants to spend his or her money rather than pass it on to heirs. If you want to spend your last dime, an annuity is just the ticket. Following are some other reasons to buy a fixed annuity:

> ✔ **Generating income:** One of the best reasons to buy a fixed annuity is it may give you more money to spend. In some instances, an annuity can generate more income than a bond portfolio. For instance, a $100,000 bond portfolio at 4 percent interest may give a single, 70-year-old female

an annual income of $4,000. But if she opts for a $100,000 immediate annuity, she may rake in $8,400 — more than twice as much per year. (However, if she dies with the $100,000 bond portfolio, $100,000 goes to her heirs. If she dies with the immediate annuity, the income stops and nothing is left for the heirs.)

✔ **Building your pension:** With the demise of those gold-plated, traditional, defined benefit pension plans, you may find the security of lifetime income attractive.

✔ **Freeing money for other investments:** Retirees can use fixed annuity payments to cover basic living expenses, investing the stock portion of their portfolios more aggressively.

✔ **Replacing your paycheque:** If you're concerned about no longer earning a regular paycheque, consider a fixed annuity as a way to replace that income.

✔ **Deferring taxes:** If you're already making the maximum contributions to your RRSP account, but you're afraid it won't provide enough income during retirement, a fixed annuity is an option for tax-deferred growth.

✔ **Having an alternative to a Registered Retirement Income Fund (RRIF):** Funds in an RRSP or a Locked-In Retirement Account (LIRA) come from registered pension plans. That means, unless you want to pay heavy-duty tax on the withdrawals, they have to be transferred to an RRIF or an annuity. If you don't want the temptation of being able to withdraw a lump sum (as you can with RRIFs), and you want a steady fixed monthly income during retirement, consider the annuity option.

✔ **Supplementing an RRIF:** If you're looking for both income flexibility and security, you may consider supplementing your RRIF with an annuity. The RRIF allows you to take out as much money as you wish annually, providing you take the mandatory minimum withdrawal. The annuity offers the security of knowing you'll get a set amount of cash monthly no matter what happens in the market or the economy.

Never put all your assets into a fixed annuity. Make sure you're buying an annuity from a highly rated insurance company, and compare fees and surrender charges.

Reasons not to buy a fixed annuity

High commissions can inspire zealous salespeople to tout the benefits of fixed annuities and gloss over the limitations. Here are some of the risks:

✔ **Conservative returns:** Fixed annuities are conservative investments. In today's low-interest-rate environment, you'll be locking in at the bottom. So if you don't *have* to buy an annuity right now, you should probably delay the purchase. Another caveat: Be suspicious when someone touts an above-average return.

✔ **Relatively young age:** Fixed annuities generally work better for older folks; you should be in or near retirement. The older you are, the higher your payment.

✔ **Heirs:** Buying an annuity leaves less for your heirs to inherit. Payments stop after your death unless you purchase a rider, but the rider results in a lower monthly payment.

✔ **Inflation risks:** Purchasing an annuity means you're locking in for the rest of your life, so unless you purchase an inflation rider, which reduces your payments, the payments from a fixed annuity remain the same. Many years of high inflation can erode your purchasing power.

✔ **Chance of outliving the benefits:** If you purchase a term annuity and live past the term (often 90 years), the payments stop.

✔ **Health:** If you're in poor health, a fixed annuity is a bad idea. Remember, an annuity is "living insurance" because it pays more the longer you live. If you die shortly after buying an annuity, the insurance company wins.

✔ **Withdrawal penalties:** Withdrawals before you reach age $59^1/_2$ trigger a penalty. Also, annuities often charge a fee for any redemption during the beginning of the contract (called the *surrender period*). Don't buy an annuity unless you're absolutely certain you won't need the funds as a lump sum.

✔ Make sure you understand how surrender charges are calculated. Generally, surrender fees decline the longer you own the annuity. For example, a five-year surrender charge may levy a 5 percent penalty in year one, 4 percent in year two, and so on.

Choose a Payment Schedule

In terms of payment schedules, you can choose from two types of fixed annuities:

✔ **Immediate:** Payments can start anytime within 13 months. You can transfer a lump sum of money into an immediate annuity and turn on the tap to start receiving guaranteed income for life.

✔ **Deferred:** The payment start date depends on your contract. The longer you delay, the greater the payment. Deferred annuities don't work for most investors. The only reason to have a deferred annuity is to shelter income taxes, and you can do that in many less expensive ways. However, if you're planning to annuitize soon but not quite yet, a deferred annuity may make sense.

Choose the Policy That's Right for You

Fixed annuities come with a number of different features. As a general rule, the features that make it likely the insurance company will have to pay out more money come at a price. Here are some of the policies you can choose from:

✔ **Defined-term annuity:** Payments continue for a specified number of years, such as 5, 10, or 20.

✔ **Guaranteed annuity:** This annuity ensures that if you die before a certain number of years go by, the payments will continue and will go to your beneficiaries.

✔ **Life annuity:** Guarantees you'll get payments for the rest of your life.

✔ **Joint-life annuity:** Payments continue as long as you or your spouse are alive.

✔ **Indexed annuity:** Monthly payments increase every year to keep up with inflation.

If you invest primarily in fixed-income instruments such as bonds or GICs, consider an inflation-protected annuity. Otherwise, a diversified stock portfolio offers a better choice for inflation protection.

Unlike RRSP contributions, or payments to an employer pension plan, your annuity contributions aren't tax deductible. You should only consider an annuity once you've maximized your contributions to RRSPs and your employer pension plan.

#17

Simplify with Target-Date Funds

By Derek Kennedy, CFP

When you're choosing the investments in your retirement account, you may feel you're in for a tough decision — almost as if you had to choose only one kind of ice cream for the rest of your life. The usual reaction to the ice cream question is to respond with your favourite flavour. But like the clever kid who chooses Neapolitan — chocolate, vanilla, and strawberry in a single carton — you can choose a fund that's the Neapolitan of the investment world, allowing you many flavours of funds within a single package.

Target-date funds — also known as *life-cycle funds* — are mutual funds in which the assets change based on your age, providing the ultimate no-fuss investing approach. The products have only been available in Canada since 2005 and have already attracted millions of dollars in investments. Because a target-date fund invests in other mutual funds, including exchange-traded funds (ETFs), it's known as a *fund of funds*.

One-Stop Shopping for a Diversified Retirement Portfolio

With target-date funds, your one big investment decision is how long it will be before you need the money. Target-date funds typically invest in a mix of other mutual funds to create an asset allocation consistent with the length of time an investor has until retirement, as designated by the date in the fund's name, such as XYZ Target 2030 Fund.

These funds are generally offered by large mutual fund families and banks that manage the underlying funds, including Bank of Montreal (BMO) and Canadian Imperial Bank of Commerce (CIBC), as well as companies like Fidelity and IA Clarington. Managers automatically rebalance your mix of funds over time so the asset allocation reflects how close you are to retirement. The target date could be anywhere from 5 years to 30 years or more. The mix of funds within the target-date fund is more aggressive for younger investors and becomes more conservative for older investors.

Don't confuse a life-cycle fund with an *asset allocation fund,* also known as a *target-risk fund.* These funds are also typically a fund of funds, but the asset mix doesn't change. Although automatic rebalancing does occur, the mix doesn't become more conservative as you approach retirement. Target-risk funds usually come in three varieties: aggressive, moderate, and conservative. They're intended to correspond with an individual's risk tolerance.

The Upside of Target-Date Funds

Target-date funds can be useful in uncertain times, even if you're an experienced investor and even if you don't plan to use them as your core retirement savings. For instance, with small accounts, the automatic rebalancing feature may help save on the trading fees you'd pay to rebalance individual funds yourself. For modest investors, these fees can be a big drag on a portfolio. Also, target-date funds are diversified in accounts not large enough to hold multiple individual mutual funds.

Target-date funds can be an important investment tool in the midst of a market meltdown. They keep you focused on saving rather than stressing over investment choices. They allocate and maintain your investment with your retirement date in mind. Maintaining an appropriate asset allocation and avoiding emotional reactions to uncertain market conditions may be the most important things you can do for your investment portfolio over the long haul.

Great Isn't Necessarily Perfect: The Downside of Target-Date Funds

Like any investment, target-date funds have tradeoffs and issues. Here are some to be aware of:

- ✔ Target-date funds are off-the-rack investments. The asset allocations are designed to be generally appropriate for people of a certain age or distance from retirement. That allocation may not fit your own risk tolerance or financial situation. If you expect to retire in 2032, should you choose the target 2030 fund or the target 2035 fund? Most target-date funds target age 65 for your retirement, but what if you plan to work longer? What if the fund's assets hold mostly stock (because retirement is many years away), but you're more comfortable with GICs?

- ✔ Target-date funds can be difficult to integrate with other parts of your investment portfolio.

Target-date funds are already diversified. You may be tempted to add other investments to your account because you want greater diversification and having just one mutual fund feels wrong. Don't give in to the lure. You can undermine your asset allocation and defeat the purpose of using a target-date fund.

- ✔ Fees can be high for target-date funds. On top of the management fees you pay for the mutual funds they hold, you may pay an additional fee to the portfolio manager.

- ✔ Most target-date portfolios invest only in the sponsoring company's proprietary funds, so you may not get access to the entire range of asset classes, top-performing managers, and investment styles as you'd like.

However, for ease of use and the potential to get it mostly right, target-date funds can be a fantastic option.

Evaluate Your Options

A target-date fund may be a one-stop shop, but it's not a no-brainer. To know if a fund is right for you, ask the following questions:

- ✔ Is the internal asset allocation and progression consistent with your needs? Funds with the same target dates offered by different companies often have different initial allocations. They may also change allocations over time differently, or have different allocations after they reach their target at retirement.

- ✔ How high are the fees?

✔ What is the track record and performance of the underlying funds? Some target-date funds use index funds, and others rely on actively managed mutual funds. Which suits you best?

✔ Does it have lock-in features? Some funds allow you to lock in returns at their highest. Explore whether a target-date fund offers this feature and what it will cost you.

No matter which fund you choose, monitor the asset allocation and compare it to your own evolving preferences over time. And as with any investment, keep an eye on the fees and performance of the underlying funds at least annually to make sure all is on track.

#18

Invest in Mutual Funds

By Bruce Sneed, MBA, CFP

Mutual funds are an established way to invest in an uncertain economy. At their core, mutual funds are simply a collection of shares of individual companies' stock, possibly corporate or government bonds, and maybe some cash. By owning shares in a mutual fund, you actually own a few shares in dozens or possibly hundreds of different stocks or bonds.

For more about mutual funds, check out *Mutual Fund Investing For Canadians For Dummies* (Wiley).

Reap the Benefits

People invest in mutual funds for four basic reasons: professional management, diversification, convenience, and marketability. The following sections outline these benefits, which make mutual funds most attractive when capital markets are unusually volatile.

Professional management

Mutual funds offer professional management of your money. These managers have the training and resources to stay abreast of and adjust to market changes. Unfortunately, fund managers don't have a crystal ball; they can't keep you completely out of harm's way.

By law, fund managers have to choose and manage fund holdings in accordance with the investment objectives and policies described in the fund's prospectus. These objectives may be designed to minimize your risk exposure.

Diversification: Spreading the risk

Mutual funds help eliminate some of the risk of investing in individual stocks and bonds by giving you shares in many different assets. Remember Nortel and Briex? How did that work out for employees who based their futures on company stock? Mutual funds also reduce your cost of diversifying by sharing transaction costs with other shareholders.

Although every mutual fund buys many securities, the funds themselves come in many styles and classifications. Some mutual funds specialize in growth, some in value. Some invest in Canadian markets, others in foreign markets. Some invest only in bonds, others in a blend of stocks and bonds. A well-diversified portfolio invests across many styles and types of mutual funds. See Tips #36 through #43 for information about asset allocation and diversifying your overall holdings.

 Read the prospectus summary and annual report. Sometimes the titles of mutual funds can be misleading. A fund with the word *growth* in its title doesn't have to be fully invested in growth stocks. Also, your mutual fund manager's investment style can drift, especially in turbulent markets.

Convenience

The convenience of mutual funds begins with the initial purchase and continues with investments, withdrawals, reinvestment of dividends and capital gains, record-keeping, and tax reporting. Mutual funds make it easy and inexpensive to *dollar-cost average* (invest regular amounts of money at regular intervals). This tip is especially helpful when markets are up and down like a roller coaster — you end up buying more shares when costs are low. You can usually find everything you need to read, see, or do at a fund's Web site; otherwise, call the fund company.

Marketability

Marketability means you can easily buy or sell mutual funds. Unlike owning a house, you may be able to quickly exchange a mutual fund for another investment or cash. Marketability gives you the flexibility to create and maintain a diversified portfolio.

Choose from Types of Funds

Two major types of funds exist:

✔ **Open-end funds:** These are the most common type of mutual funds. You purchase and redeem the shares of open-end investment companies each day at their current *net asset values* (NAV) plus sales charges or minus redemption fees, if any. The NAV is calculated at the end of each day based on the value of the fund's underlying securities (stocks and/or bonds). The number of shares that can be issued is unlimited.

✔ **Closed-end funds:** Like open-end funds, closed-end funds buy many different stocks or bonds. But these make an initial public offering (IPO) of a *specific number of shares* and then trade on the stock exchange — similar to common stocks — at either a premium or discount to their NAV. Their market price fluctuates throughout the day based on supply and demand. Closed-end funds can be more volatile because they may have less trading volume than a similar open-end fund.

Because the initial offering price of a closed-end fund includes a sales commission, the shares are issued at a premium over the invested assets. However, after the IPO is completed, closed-end funds often trade at a discount. So passing on buying new offerings of closed-end funds makes sense. Instead, consider purchasing shares when they become available on the stock exchange at a discount from their net asset value. Table 2-1 summarizes the differences between closed-end and open-end funds.

Table 2-1	Comparing Open-End and Closed-End Mutual Funds	
Feature	*Closed-End Funds*	*Open-End Funds*
Shares sold	At IPO	Continuously
Shares sold to/ bought from	Stock exchange	Fund company
Share price	Market price	NAV
Share price changes	Continuously	End of day
Transaction costs	Commissions	Sales/redemption charges

Choose the Level of Management: Trying to Meet or Beat the Market

Mutual funds may be either index funds or managed funds. *Index funds* buy a set collection of securities and mostly leave the portfolio alone, earning you investment returns as the underlying values of the stocks or bonds you hold appreciate. They're basically managed by a computer. *Active fund* managers select securities in an attempt to beat the market or achieve a better risk-adjusted return than the market. However, they put a dent in your earnings by charging higher annual management fees.

Index funds

Index funds are popular because they're inexpensive, easy to understand, and give you a return similar to the market your index fund is designed to track. Over ten years or so, index funds typically outperform about 75 percent of more actively managed funds. Because of their popularity, mutual fund companies continue to bring several varieties of index funds to market. Funds are indexed to all types of assets and subsequently have all kinds of investment styles, expected returns, risks, and expenses.

Stock index mutual funds invest in a particular segment of the financial market. S&P/TSX Composite Index is an example, intended to represent the Canadian equity market by including the largest companies listed on the Toronto Stock Exchange. S&P/TSX Canadian Dividend Aristocrats Index is another, which includes only companies that pay dividends. They aim to match the market returns of that index by investing in the securities in the index. Index funds typically have very low expenses.

Common stock index funds can take you on a rough ride in a volatile market. Because the fund is usually fully invested and doesn't maintain substantial cash reserves, it's fully exposed to market ups and downs. However, over the long term, stock indexing is a sensible investment strategy.

Bond index funds work a little differently, but the basic objectives are the same: Try to match market returns and keep expenses low. Bonds aren't as liquid as stocks, so transaction costs are a bit higher and matching the benchmark is more difficult.

Actively managed funds

Actively managed funds aim to give returns greater than those of the overall market or aim for lower returns with less volatility. Fund managers use many factors to analyze the economy, industry sectors, and specific companies. Some managers consistently outperform the market on a risk-adjusted basis, but studies show that the majority don't. Managed funds have higher costs than index funds because of the cost of maintaining research staff and more frequent trading.

Some managed funds have low correlation to the market (maybe because they have substantial cash). Therefore, they hold up pretty well in a downturn but don't do so well when the market rebounds. Others use leverage to magnify the volatility both on the upside and the downside. Most actively managed funds fall somewhere in the middle.

Pick the Funds That Meet Your Needs

After you decide to invest in mutual funds, check out these tips on choosing the right funds for you:

- **Understand your investment objectives, time horizon, and risk tolerance.** If you're investing for retirement or your kids' education more than ten years away, you want to use common stock funds, which can outpace inflation. For shorter-term objectives, less volatile short-term bond funds or money market mutual funds work well. Regardless, never assume more risk than is necessary to meet your objectives. See Tip #37.

- **Decide whether you want to be an active or passive fund investor (or both).** You have thousands of fund choices and loads of variables to consider, including the fund company, portfolio manager, portfolio characteristics, cost of ownership, and past performance relative to peer groups. If looking at all these variables seems like too much work, then passive investing through common stock index funds may be for you.

- **Be sure you want to buy bond funds, not individual bonds.** A bond fund has a substantially fixed maturity, so you're always exposed to a certain level of principal risk no matter how long you hold the fund; the maturity of a bond, however, declines steadily, and your principal risk declines each year you hold the bond. Here's how to decide what's right for you:

  - If you want to maintain a fixed stream of interest income payments, buy individual bonds.

  - If you can't afford to buy a diversified portfolio of bonds (Tip #24), you're better off with a bond mutual fund.

  - If you don't want to analyze bond fund criteria, choose a bond index mutual fund.

- **Pay attention to the fund fees.** Some funds have upfront fees, called *front-loads,* which are really commissions that go to the sales force or companies. Others have redemption fees, called *rear-end loads,* charged when you sell your fund. Still others nick you for a small percentage every year that you own the fund as an additional load.

Hedge Your Bets with Segregated Funds

By Cheryl Krueger

Take a mutual fund and add a guarantee that you'll get a certain percentage of your investment back no matter what happens in the stock market. What do you have? A segregated fund. Seg funds are a form of *individual variable annuity* sold by life insurers and by mutual fund companies that partner with insurers to provide the contract guarantees. Think of them as mutual funds with an insurance policy wrapper.

Seg funds are attractive in uncertain times because they're an insurance product and provide guarantees that aren't available in mutual funds. Many of these guarantee features appeal to clients who want to benefit from stock market returns with little risk of losing money.

Understand the Basics of Seg Funds

A *segregated fund* essentially looks like a mutual fund account. When you buy a seg fund, you select from a limited list of investment funds provided by the company. Your seg fund account value reflects the gains and the losses of the selected investment funds, so you can end up with losses in your segregated fund account. What sets seg funds apart from mutual funds is that they carry the following two guarantees:

> ✔ **The maturity guarantee:** On maturity (usually after ten years or more), you can cash in your investment. Even if the market is tanking and the value of your investment is low, the insurer will pay back at least 75 percent of your original investment and sometimes as much as 100 percent. If your account value has grown, you get the benefit of that rise. The upshot: You profit when markets rise, and you reduce your risk of loss during a bear market.

✔ **The death benefit guarantee:** If you die, your beneficiary receives either the original principal investment or the market value, whichever is highest. In Quebec, the beneficiary must be your spouse, parent, child, or grandchild.

Here are some other common features of seg funds:

✔ They mature at least ten years down the line or at 90 years, when the contract is finished.

✔ Management expenses are deducted from your account periodically to cover the cost of their guarantees.

✔ Because they're legislated as insurance products, creditors can't seize seg funds as long as you designate a beneficiary. (Note that RRSPs are creditor-proof, too, but non-RRSP mutual funds are not.)

✔ As designated insurance products, upon death seg funds pay out to the named beneficiary and don't go through probate.

The downside of seg funds is that they're expensive compared to mutual funds, although some investors may feel the additional security is worth the cost. Nonetheless, be aware of the various fees that segregated funds sometimes charge:

✔ **Initial sales charge:** You pay a sales commission on seg funds, similar to the sales charges for mutual funds, and it may be either a front-end or deferred sales charge. Less commonly, seg funds can be sold on a no-load basis where the issuer pays the sales commission directly to the financial advisor.

✔ **Surrender charge:** If you cash out within the first several years of your payment, the company keeps a certain percentage of the initial premium as a surrender charge. These charges generally start at around 7 percent and decrease for each year of ownership.

✔ **Management expense ratios (MERs):** These fees can be as high as 4 percent or more per year, considerably higher than the 2 to 2.5 percent that most mutual funds charge and many times more than an index fund. The additional 0.5 to 1 percent covers the guarantees.

✔ **Additional fees:** As with mutual funds, segregated funds frequently have embedded trailer commissions and switching fees. These fees all reduce returns, of course.

Look into Features Designed to Reduce Risk

To make these investments more attractive, some insurers enhance seg funds to protect against declines. Here are some of the more interesting features:

- ✔ **Resets:** With some seg funds you can choose to *reset* the maturity and death benefit guarantees, usually up to 90 years. What that means is that you get to lock in the profits when the market value of your seg fund is higher than the original investment amount, ensuring that you get at least the enhanced amount upon death or when the fund matures. The following scenarios explain how this feature works to your advantage:

  - Scenario 1: Five years ago you invested $100,000 in a seg fund. Today it's worth $120,000. You can choose to reset the maturity and death benefits from today's date. The result: You or (in case of your death) your beneficiaries can't receive any less than $120,000 when the fund matures ten years down the road or you die.

  - Scenario 2: Three years ago you invested $100,000 in a seg fund. Today it's worth $70,000. Obviously you're not going to reset your maturity and death benefits at this point, because the market value of your fund is lower than your original investment.

- ✔ **Guaranteed Minimum Withdrawal Benefit (GMWBs):** After you're retired, you can withdraw income from a seg fund in the form of a traditional life annuity (refer to Tip #16), or you can withdraw cash monthly and continue to profit from the markets. But what if you choose the latter option and then the markets plummet? Some companies offer GMWBs that return your original investment to you in the form of regular monthly payments for the life of the plan. If your funds go up in value, your monthly payments go up, but you're guaranteed that they will never go lower than the agreed-on amount.

These guarantees appeal to investors who aren't comfortable with loss, and variations are likely to continue to appear. The bad news: Seg funds that offer these risk-reducing features often cost you 4 percent or more per year. Keep in mind that with any of these riders, you're buying insurance — and you probably won't collect, just as you won't collect on your auto insurance if you're a good driver. Rather than fully benefiting from increasing markets, you're paying an annual fee to get a floor on your losses.

If you have money to invest, don't get sold on the appeal of seg funds alone. A series of seg funds may have only a small group of mutual funds to choose from, so the selection of individual mutual funds likely offers better opportunities for diversification. If you do buy, be prepared to have your money invested for at least ten years. In most cases, you should keep RRSP and other retirement plan money out of segregated funds. Read your contract and prospectus carefully.

Finally, note that the insurance company provides the guarantees, even though your assets are in a separate account of the insurance company. Make sure you're dealing with a highly rated company. For insurance company ratings, go to www.ambest.com; make sure your insurer is rated excellent or higher.

Manage Your Segregated Fund

When you bought your segregated fund, did you decide to just let it accumulate and not look at the balance? You need to review a seg fund periodically, just like any investment. A seg fund's value fluctuates the same as the market fluctuates. Here are some tips for managing your segregated fund:

- ✔ **Choose segregated versions of mutual funds with solid track records and successful management teams.** You obviously hope to do better than just getting back your principal after ten years, so the basics of investing still apply: Pick a winner!

- ✔ **Don't forget to include your segregated fund as you consider your portfolio allocation.** When you allocate your investments, pick the best funds available in your seg fund and then see how they fit within your overall portfolio. Tell your financial planner or investment advisor what investments you have in a seg fund so he or she can consider them in the overall allocation.

- ✔ **If you're not rebalancing your seg fund to keep your allocations in line, check whether your insurer offers an automatic rebalancing program.** These programs are usually free — you just sign up and choose whether to rebalance quarterly, semi-annually, or annually.

Are you a candidate for a seg fund?

You pay for the insurance benefits of seg funds, so make sure this product is right for you before handing over your hard-earned cash. You might consider a seg fund if any of the following apply to you:

✔ You're an older investor interested in the guaranteed death benefit that refunds 75 to 100 percent of your investment to your heirs.

✔ You're a conservative investor who's appalled by today's low fixed-income investment rates and finds the estate planning features attractive.

✔ You're a businessperson or someone who wants to protect your assets from creditors.

#20

Invest in Exchange-Traded Funds (ETFs)

- -

By Charles Levin, CPA

- -

Exchange-traded funds, also known as ETFs, have been available in Canada since 1990, but their popularity has mushroomed in the last several years. An *ETF* is simply a basket of stocks or bonds that you purchase just like shares of stock. However, with a single investment in an ETF, you own a piece of dozens, if not hundreds, of different stocks (or bonds). Unlike index mutual funds, ETFs trade on a stock exchange, so you can buy and sell them just like you buy and sell stocks.

The oldest and most popular ETFs track very broad, well-known indexes such as the S&P/TSX Composite Index. However, a wide variety of methodologies has emerged for creating new indexes in narrower market sectors such as financial, energy, or gold stocks.

During uncertain economic times, when financial markets some-times hurtle upwards or downwards with the dizzying speed of a rollercoaster, maintaining discipline takes on even greater impor-tance. ETFs can make it easy for you to keep your seat, so to speak. What's more, they avoid the high management fees that can chew up a whopping 30 percent of your earnings when you invest in a mutual fund. Those fees are probably the major reason that over five years, about 75 percent of all actively managed funds can't out-perform their market index.

And yet, according to a recent survey by Barclay's Global Investor Canada, only about 7 percent of Canadians have ETFs in their portfolio, and only 11 percent even know about ETFs. To use ETFs wisely, you need to know enough about them, and this tip gets you started. (This part has several tips to help you understand risks associated with investing, assess your risk tolerance, and allocate your assets to minimize risk.)

ETFs versus Index Funds: Which Should You Buy?

Index mutual funds and ETFs, especially ETFs that track broad indexes, have many similarities. However, their structural differences — where they're traded, how they're priced, and so on — can mean that one or the other is a better choice for investors in different situations. (See Tip #18 for more on index funds.) Table 2-2 lists the key structural features of ETFs and index funds.

Table 2-2	Exchange-Traded Funds and Index Funds	
Category	*ETFs*	*Index Funds*
Where bought and sold	Traded on the stock exchange	Bought and sold directly from the mutual fund company
Basis of pricing	Based on supply and demand; may be higher or lower than the actual value of the securities held in the fund, though over time they should closely follow the tracked index	Based on the prices of the securities held inside the fund (equal to the fund's net asset value, or NAV)
Timing of pricing	Trading and price quotes are available throughout the day	Priced once per day at the close of trading; you place your order before market close at a price that isn't known until the end of the trading day
Commissions	Paid on each trade based on the commission rate your broker charges	Commission-free if purchased directly from a mutual fund company; can be charged if purchased through a brokerage account

So should you invest in ETFs or index funds? Here are some guidelines:

✔ If you're going to be making smaller, periodic investments, such as when you have an amount regularly withdrawn from your bank account or withheld from your paycheque for your company's group RRSP plan, you're likely better off using an index fund purchased directly from a mutual fund company to avoid paying commissions every time.

✔ If you're going to be making a single or occasional investment, then the commissions won't matter much over time. The next priority then is to compare the fees being charged by ETFs and index funds following the same index. ETFs often have lower fees, which can make a difference over time and is especially important when the economy is shaky.

In the end, the decision can come down to how often you'll be adding to or withdrawing from your investment.

Evaluate ETFs

Do your research before investing in ETFs. A great resource is *Exchange-Traded Funds For Dummies.* You can also find a great deal of information about ETFs on the Internet. Here are some useful sites:

✔ **Canadian Business Online — My Money:** www.canadian business.com/my_money

Search for "coach potato portfolio" to find *MoneySense* magazine's no-fuss approach to putting together a diversified portfolio with ETFs.

✔ **Yahoo! Canada Finance:** www.ca.finance.yahoo.com/etf.

✔ **TMX Money:** The PR arm of the TSX offers a comprehensive list of ETFs, as well as an FAQ section and information sheets. Just do a search for "ETF" at www.tmxmoney.com.

In addition, brokerage firm Web sites and some mutual fund company Web sites provide a wealth of information on ETFs.

When evaluating ETFs, focus on these areas:

✔ **The index the ETF tracks:** Understand what the index consists of and the rules it follows in selecting and weighting the securities it holds.

✔ **How long the ETF and/or its underlying index have been around:** You want to buy an ETF that has a track record. If possible, review the performance in both good times and bad.

✔ **The company that manages the ETF:** Review how long the company has been managing ETFs in general and how long it's been managing the ETF you're looking at.

✔ **How accurately the ETF has tracked its underlying index:** Seek out reports that show the performance of the ETF over various time periods versus its index. With an effectively run ETF, the only difference between its performance and the underlying index should be the fees charged by the ETF.

✔ **The ETF's expense ratios:** The greater the ETF's assets, the more straightforward its investing strategy, and the more prominent and well-known its underlying index, the lower the expenses are likely to be. Compare the expense ratios of ETFs that follow the same index. Some have lower fees than others.

Develop an ETF Strategy

Especially in difficult economic times, you need to stick to the basics when investing. Develop an asset allocation that makes sense based on your financial goals, your time horizon for investing, and your capacity for risk. Using ETFs that track broad market indexes gives you wide diversification. The following providers lead the market in Canada:

✔ **Barclays Canada:** The major provider of ETFs in Canada, it offers 24 funds in total. Some track Canadian stock and bond indexes, and others track the performance of U.S. and global companies. Visit the Web site at www.ishares.ca.

✔ **Claymore Investments:** Claymore offers 22 exchange-traded funds that cover the Canadian, U.S., and global core equity markets, sector strategies, dividend- and income-based strategies, and fixed-income-based strategies. See www.claymore-investments.ca.

✔ **Horizons BetaPro:** This company offers 27 alternative ETFs that track very specific sectors such as gold bullion, crude oil, and emerging markets. See www.hbpetfs.com.

Some newer ETFs are much riskier than index funds and ETFs that invest in broad market indexes. The following types of ETFs are too risky for most investors, especially in these uncertain times:

✔ A number of the newer ETFs follow much narrower indexes. For example, they may track the stocks of a single country, industry, or commodity (such as the price of oil). These ETFs tend to have much higher fees than those that track broad indexes, and these fees can reduce the value of your portfolio over time. In addition, the more narrowly focused ETFs often seek to capitalize on a recent hot segment of the market, and you may find yourself investing at exactly the wrong time.

✔ Some ETFs magnify the positive and negative returns of an index. For example, one U.S. ETF uses *leverage,* or borrowing, to generate twice the yield of the S&P 500. When the market is going up, this ETF greatly increases your gain. But if the market is down, your losses are magnified as well. If you choose to invest in one of the leveraged ETFs, be prepared for a wild ride through the ups and downs of its performance. Although the gains can be huge, so can the losses.

✔ You can also find ETFs that are structured to generate a gain equal to the amount the market or market segment has *lost.*

Diversify with Real Estate Investment Trusts

· ·

By Brian R. Smith, PhD

· ·

You don't have to be a real estate tycoon or a well-heeled investor to benefit from real estate. Many people first invest in real estate when buying their first home. For some, a next step may be buying another residential property or house.

But managing tenants, property, and cash flow can be a headache. In addition, you have to be savvy when choosing properties and negotiating terms and conditions. Furthermore, the cost and complexity of commercial real estate put it out of reach for most investors. If investing in bricks-and-mortar real estate sounds daunting, real estate investment trusts (REITs) may be right for you. REITs are a common asset class in plenty of diversified portfolios.

Get to Know REITs

REITs are corporations that invest in real estate and pay out at least 90 percent of their income in dividends. Some offer the potential for large dividends and trade on the stock exchange. REITs are more liquid than traditional real estate investments in which you're the landlord. In addition, investors don't need to worry about negotiating, repairing, advertising, pricing, or selling.

Here are the three types of REITs:

- ✔ **Equity:** These REITs own and operate income-producing properties — such as apartment buildings, offices, shopping centres, hotels, seniors' homes, and warehouses — and they may lease, develop, and manage property. They're the largest and most widely known type of REIT.

- ✔ **Mortgage:** These REITs lend money directly to real estate owners and operators or extend credit indirectly through loans or mortgage-backed securities.

Changes in interest rates and the possibility of defaults make mortgage REITs more volatile than equity REITs, particularly in an uncertain economy.

✔ **Hybrid:** These REITs both own properties and make loans to real estate owners and operators.

Table 2-3 describes the characteristics of publicly traded REITs.

Table 2-3	How Publicly Traded REITs Measure Up
Characteristic	*Description*
Performance	The dividends are generally competitive compared to those of investment-grade corporate bonds and stocks. REITs can provide strong capital appreciation.
Taxation	Payouts come in the form of dividends and capital gains; both receive favourable tax treatment.
Liquidity	REITs trade like stocks on public exchanges. Discount brokers can result in low transaction costs.
Diversification	REITs have low correlation to other asset classes. You can purchase them in mutual funds of REITs, indexes, or as focused exchange-traded funds (ETFs). Geographic diversity is an added advantage.
Transparency	Analysts and auditors monitor REITs regularly.
Leverage	You can buy REITs, ETF REITs, or mutual fund REITs on margin in taxable investment dealer accounts.

Refer to Tip #20 for more on exchange-traded funds (ETFs).

 When public exchanges don't offer REITs, investors may be restricted from selling shares (or units) in accordance with stated terms and conditions. These privately held REITs may offer higher dividends and the possibility of significant capital appreciation. But they may require high minimum investments, lack transparency, and have diversification risks that are more difficult to understand.

Fit REITs into Your Portfolio

REITs can help diversify your portfolio because they often perform better during periods of high inflation, when stocks and bonds are apt to tank. For that reason, they should make up 3 to 10 percent of your total portfolio. You may already own REITs in your stock portfolio. For example, the TSX/S&P Composite Index includes REITs.

For greater diversification, use mutual funds that own several different REITs. Some good no-load REIT funds include CIBC Canadian Real Estate, Dynamic Focus Plus Real Estate, and Sentry Select Real Estate.

REITs also offer an advantage that traditional rental real estate doesn't: You can include REITs in your retirement fund (for example, an RRSP or RRIF) or in a Tax-Free Savings Account.

Prices for REITs have dropped recently, but their income potential — which is what really counts — hasn't dropped dramatically. These REITs may be invested in shopping malls, apartments, and office buildings with long-term tenants and steady returns. Low prices for REITS may represent buying opportunities for you.

So how do you value a REIT? Look at its net asset value (NAV), adjusted funds from operations (AFFO), and cash available for distribution (CAD). If you want to compare REITs to stocks, the price divided by the AFFO is roughly equivalent to the Price-Earnings Ratio (P/E ratio) for a stock:

REIT value = Price ÷ Adjusted funds from operations

For more information, contact the Canadian Association of Income Funds (www.caif.ca).

#22

Consider a Wrap Account

By Thomas Arconti, CFP

For most investors, a well-diversified portfolio of mutual funds and/or exchange-traded funds (ETFs) serves them well. However, you may want a professionally tailored portfolio.

Plenty of studies show that low-cost, passive investing frequently outperforms active investment management over the long haul. But during shaky economic times, you may have a specific investment strategy that you think will perform better under current conditions. Or you may simply take comfort in having a professional money manager at the helm. In that case, a wrap account can provide an alternative to or complement mutual fund investing. Read on to discover more about these customized accounts.

Understand Wrap Accounts

A *wrap account* is an investment portfolio that one or more professional money managers control on behalf of an individual or institution. Most often, large financial firms like banks, full-service investment dealers, or fund companies are the ones who offer wrap accounts.

The account manager provides model portfolios based on selected investment criteria (such as large cap value, small company growth, and so on). But you can get a customized portfolio to meet your particular needs, such as minimizing taxable distributions and generating income. A wrap account can be made up of stocks, bonds, cash, or other securities, and the account manager has discretion — the ability to buy or sell securities on your behalf — as long as the investment choices conform to the stated investment strategy.

Similar to hiring other professionals (such as an attorney or CA), you hire an account manager to oversee and manage, on a day-to-day basis, either a portion of or your entire investment portfolio. You may discuss what to do about your investment account with the account manager, and at times you may direct the manager to take certain actions. But generally, you hire the manager for his or her expertise, and you expect the manager to make investment decisions about the managed account.

Weigh the Pros and Cons of Wrap Accounts

Like any type of investment product or service, wrap accounts have advantages and disadvantages. On the plus side, here's what you get:

- ✔ **Tax efficiency:** Unlike mutual fund fees, investment manager charges for wrap accounts may be tax deductible. (Consult your tax advisor to find out.) In addition, the account manager minimizes your taxable gains. With other taxable investments, you have to do it yourself.

- ✔ **Professional management:** Professional money managers conduct the research and analysis to make informed decisions on your behalf. Doing so is their full-time job — and probably not yours.

- ✔ **Manager access:** You can discuss the details of your investments and express your concerns or constraints with the account managers.

- ✔ **Transparency:** You always know what you're invested in because your account statements list each individual holding, with number of shares, cost basis, and current values.

- ✔ **Customization:** You can include or exclude certain securities or entire sectors. For instance, if you've accumulated a concentrated position in your employer's company stock, such as Research In Motion (RIM), you can exclude RIM and similar technology stocks from your holdings.

- ✔ **Liquidity:** You can buy and sell individual securities as needed, as opposed to trading shares of a single fund (as is the case with mutual funds or ETFs).

Here are some of the disadvantages:

- ✔ **High fees and minimum investments:** Wrap accounts typically charge high fees to provide a more personalized service. The fees are usually a percentage of assets under management (AUM) and can range from 1 to 3 percent. As a rule, the more assets you have under management, the lower the fee. A minimum investment is generally required as well.

- ✔ **Manager options:** Numerous asset managers are in the marketplace — investment dealers, mutual fund companies, financial planning firms, and banks all offer wrap products. You have to narrow the field and select the manager(s) who can provide a good fit for you and offer the best chance to achieve your financial goals.

> ✔ **Need for ongoing monitoring:** Monitor the performance of your manager(s) to determine relative performance to the market: Are the managers worth their fees? Are they staying true to their philosophy and approach? Does their style drift, such as buying growth companies in a value portfolio? What's their trading frequency and compliance history?

Compare Wraps to Mutual Funds

The primary difference between a wrap account and a mutual fund is that in a wrap, you may own individual stocks, bonds, and other investments. With mutual funds, you don't individually own any of the underlying securities in that fund. Instead, the mutual fund company owns the shares and the investors share the benefits in common.

Table 2-4 provides a side-by-side comparison of the key features of wrap accounts and mutual funds.

Table 2-4	Features of Wrap Accounts and Mutual Funds	
Features	*Wrap Accounts*	*Mutual Funds*
Access to professional managers	Individual investors may have direct access to the account manager.	Individual investors have no direct access to fund managers.
Portfolio structure	Individuals can have a customized portfolio to meet their specific needs.	The portfolio is structured to meet the fund's written investment strategy. No customization is allowed.
Full investment capability	Investors can fully invest the account for maximum potential gain. The manager isn't required to hold cash in the account.	Mutual funds usually hold cash to meet redemption requirements. If short on cash, managers may be forced to sell holdings to meet the redemption demand.

Features	Wrap Accounts	Mutual Funds
Taxation	Can be tax efficient; by choosing when to buy or sell individual securities in the account, investors can harvest tax losses.	Generally not tax efficient for individual investors because buying and selling decisions are made on a global basis. (Note: Some funds are designed and marketed as tax-managed funds. Others, such as index funds, tend to be inherently tax efficient.)
Minimum investment requirements	Wrap accounts have much higher minimum investment requirements than mutual funds. Minimums vary but often begin at $100,000.	Most mutual funds have low minimums. They vary from as low as $50 to $10,000 or more on the high end.
Fees	Management fees vary but are often significantly higher than those of mutual funds. Total fees include the management fee, brokerage costs, and account service fee. These can range from 1.5% to 3% per year.	Management fees can range from as low as 0.2% for no-load index funds to around 2% for actively managed funds. Brokerage fees and other costs must also be included. These additional fees can result in total costs of about 0.3% to 3% per year.

Exchange-traded funds (ETFs) have many of the same features as mutual funds, except ETFs are fully invested. They offer great tax efficiency and liquidity, with no minimum investment requirements and at a much lower cost than wrap accounts. For more on ETFs, refer to Tip #20.

Examine the Types of Wraps

Just like mutual funds and ETFs, you can obtain wrap accounts in many flavours. Providing you can meet the investment minimums, you may want a narrowly focused wrap account that specializes in one asset class or style (such as Canadian growth equity, global equity, large cap value, or bonds). The following scenarios show you how you might benefit from wrap accounts:

✔ **Single-style wrap accounts:** Suppose you've accumulated a good core portfolio through your group RRSP or pooled plan at work. You also have a sizable taxable investment account. After reviewing your overall asset allocation, you realize you're too invested in growth company funds and have little exposure to large cap value companies. You'd like to manage capital gains and losses in your taxable account, and you believe that in this market environment, an experienced asset manager could find good value investment opportunities. You research account managers who specialize in large cap value portfolios and choose one to manage your account.

✔ **Unified wrap accounts:** You're a detail-oriented person who doesn't want or have time to manage your investments directly. But you like the ongoing personal service that wrap accounts offer. You decide to put your full portfolio in the hands of experts with whom you can confer. To get a diversified, balanced portfolio, you need a wrap account with a broader focus. Here are two approaches:

 • You hire an account manager who serves as the general contractor and then hires sub-account managers, each with his or her own style and sector expertise. This type of multiple-style managed account often requires higher minimum investments (perhaps in the $250,000 category) to achieve proper diversification.

 • You find a single account manager who offers a broad-based, diversified portfolio of varying asset classes.

Invest in Wrap Accounts Wisely

If you think wrap accounts may be a viable investment option, do the following:

✔ Define your investment goals and guidelines (refer to Tip #11).

✔ Compare wrap investing to ETF or mutual fund investing to make sure wrap accounts are the right choice for you. (In other words, do you need a custom tailored suit, or is off-the-rack just fine?)

✔ Conduct due diligence to find the right managers for you. Be sure to review the wrap account's prospectus, which describes its objectives and expenses.

If you look hard, you can find lower cost alternatives to traditional wrap accounts by hiring asset managers that use low cost, no-load mutual funds and/or ETFs in the portfolio instead of individual stocks. These managers may charge a fee of 0.25 to 0.50 percent. When combined with the expense ratios of the individual holdings in the portfolio, the total overall management fee could still remain at about 1 percent, depending on the amount of assets under management.

✔ Monitor the performance of your investment managers regularly to confirm they're meeting your objectives and providing benefits in excess of their fees.

Although you can direct the account manager to make changes to your wrap account, second-guessing or micromanaging the investment decisions is a bad idea. After all, you're paying for the manager's expertise and assuming that he or she can produce better results than you. Agree on the investment strategy upfront and indentify your constraints. Then let the account manager make decisions within those parameters.

#23

Invest in Individual Stocks

By Herb Montgomery, CFP

Investing in individual stocks can be fun and profitable, but remember that the level of risk can be high. A slow economy may present you with bargains as stock prices go down with consumer pessimism. But be careful: Start out small, don't invest more than you can lose, and do your research!

Do Some Serious Soul-Searching

If you're going to take the plunge and begin investing in individual stocks, a question-and-answer period with yourself is in order. Write down these questions as well as their answers to avoid any finger pointing if things don't go as planned.

Are you willing to be an investor rather than a trader?

An *investor* buys shares in a company that he or she knows something about and plans to hold these shares to reap the benefits of a successful company. An investor expects both long-term growth in share value as well as the payment of dividends along the way. A *trader* buys shares of stock in a company, expecting the price of the stock to rise rapidly so he or she can cash out with a quick gain.

Historically, investors are more successful than traders over long periods of time. An investor isn't hit with short-term capital gains, trading commissions, or most importantly, the inability to successfully time the market. When markets are volatile, investing on a whim or on a hot tip in hope of a big payoff is tempting. But that isn't investing; it's gambling. Save the gambling for casinos, not your stock portfolio.

Investors also need discipline, which includes a systematic approach to taking profits and realizing losses. Don't get caught up in the emotion of the moment. Don't fall so in love with a stock on the rise that you refuse to sell when it starts to drop. Be willing to admit your mistakes and sell a loser before it becomes next to worthless. Remember some of the darling stocks of the past that plunged rapidly while their investors stubbornly held on to them — stocks like Nortel and Bre-X.

How much money are you willing to lose?

Without diversification you could lose everything in the stock market. If you have a certain amount of cash that will only be invested in the speculative section of the stock market, then identify the amount, write it down, and don't go over it.

Always remember the importance of diversification. One argument for investing through mutual funds and index funds is that they pool their money into a wide variety of stocks and/or bonds. You need to invest in a wide variety of stocks as well. Avoid having more than 10 percent of your total portfolio in any one stock and avoid buying too many similar stocks. If you own only technology stocks, for example, and technology goes through a rough patch, like it did during the "dot-com bomb," you could lose most of your investment. If you can't diversify sufficiently, consider mutual funds. See Tips #38 through #44 for more on diversification.

How much time and money can you commit to research?

A full-time job, spouse, children, elderly parents, house, and yard may all compete for your time. Because the time you spend researching companies directly affects your success in the stock market, make sure you can spend time away from your other activities.

Stock Investing in Turbulent Times

When the economy's in the dumpster, holding stocks can be nerve-racking. Keep these points in mind when investing in turbulent times:

- ✔ **Opt for blue-chip equities in defensive sectors like telecom, health care, and consumer staples.** Invest in things that people need even in a down market.

- ✔ **Buy stocks that pay dividends.** Regular income can be calming in the midst of market volatility, and when stock prices go down, some dividend yields go up. Most calming during uncertain times is the fact that Canadian dividends give tax credits to taxpayers.

✔ **Seek out bargains.** Seasoned investors often look out for bargains when others are deserting the stock market in droves. The stock screeners on the Web sites of most discount brokerages can help you separate the wheat from the chaff.

✔ **Weed out the equity "dogs" in your portfolio.** Selling off consistent underperformers can free up cash to pick up bargain-priced stocks or to even out the volatility in your portfolio. Why not use those losses to offset your capital gains, reducing your tax bill? The good news: You can carry them back to the previous three years.

Research Before and After You Invest

If you've got the time and the inclination to invest in stocks, this section guides you in choosing and managing those investments.

Spend some time with annual reports

Think about the following characteristics of the companies you're interested in:

✔ **Free cash flow:** What's left after the bills are paid

✔ **Returns on equity:** How much the company made on the money invested in it

✔ **Returns on assets:** How much the company made by using the assets it owns

✔ **Net margins:** How much the company made from every dollar of sales

Each of these items is readily available in the *financial results* section of the company's annual report. These days, annual and quarterly reports are available on almost every company's Web site. Or you can call a company's headquarters and have them mail you annual reports for free. But don't get carried away by the pretty pictures. Look closely at the financials.

Follow some general research advice

Here are rules to consider when doing your own research:

- ✔ Use an *independent research firm,* someone with absolutely no financial interest in any of the companies you're thinking about investing in.

- ✔ Look at the competition. Who's growing faster? Who has better financials? Who has more new products in the pipeline?

- ✔ Calculate how much the company is worth. Buy a stock only if you can get it at a discount to its fair value; you need some wiggle room if the stock price begins to slide.

- ✔ Pick companies for the long term. Remember that you're an investor, not a trader. Look for companies with solid financials and good growth prospects for a couple of years at least. Traders are hoping for that one big inning. Investors are looking for a championship.

- ✔ Sell at the right time. The right time depends on the company. If the fundamentals have changed and you probably wouldn't purchase the stock presently, sell it. Perhaps the stock has performed well, but its price is now too high to justify further growth. Or maybe the economy has changed and the company's products aren't as desirable as they once were, or maybe competition has stepped in. Any of these factors could trigger a sale. However, if all the reasons you purchased the stock in the first place still apply, keep it. Sometimes even the best companies experience temporary setbacks.

Don't let any one stock position grow to more than 10 to 12 percent of your entire portfolio.

Know where to find good information

Numerous free and paid services can help you decide whether a company is suitable to invest in at a given time. Are these sources always right? No, but if you're not willing or lack the time to do the research, their picks will undoubtedly be better than just shooting from the hip. Here are some sources:

- ✔ Your investment dealer account, whether it's with a large firm or a discount broker, has several offerings, either paid services or free with your account. Many have stock screens where you enter your criteria and eliminate companies that don't interest you.

- ✔ TMX (www.tmxmoney.com), the PR arm of the TSX, has loads of info available and will send out annual reports *gratis*.

- ✔ Yahoo! Finance (finance.yahoo.ca) has mountains of free information about companies.

- ✔ *The Globe and Mail*'s financial Web site (www.globeinves-tor.com) provides accurate, unbiased information to the public. You'll find company reports, charts, and snapshots as well as info on market winners and losers and tools that allow you to track your portfolio.

- ✔ Morningstar (www.morningstar.ca) is a favourite research site for professionals and do-it-yourselfers. Their free site is a good place to start, though a membership (which is quite reasonable) gets you into the screens and gives you a more in-depth analysis. They also have several different newsletters both in print and online.

"Expert stock pickers" also put out paid newsletters. Some of them have pretty good track records; some are legends only in their own minds. Most of them probably generate more income from selling newsletters then they do from picking successful stocks. (If they're so good at picking stocks, why do they need to sell newsletters?)

The Five Rules For Successful Stock Investing, by Pat Dorsey, Director of Stock Analysis at Morningstar (Wiley), and *The Ultimate Dividend Playbook,* by Josh Peters, CFA Editor of Morningstar Dividend Investor (Wiley), may be helpful when you're researching and choosing individual stocks.

Invest in Individual Bonds

By John Vyge, CFP

In uncertain times, reducing the ups and downs of your investment portfolio should be your top priority. Adding individual bonds to your portfolio is a great way to minimize volatility. Although stocks and stock mutual funds can fluctuate wildly every time a TV commentator announces "what's going to happen next," individual bonds can be your portfolio's Rock of Gibraltar.

Understand Bond Basics

A *bond* is a debt obligation from an issuer, usually a government or corporation. Governments and corporations issue bonds to raise money to build bridges, schools, hospitals, and new factories. They're borrowing money from you, the bond investor. If you hold an individual bond until it matures, you'll receive the face value of the bond along with fixed interest payments — as long as the issuer doesn't default.

The less likely the borrower is to default on payments, the less risky the bond; and the less risky the bond, the lower the interest rate the borrower is willing to pay you. In the case of corporate bonds, usually the riskiest of all bonds, bondholders still have priority over the shareholders of the company. In other words, if a company goes out of business, any assets of the company are used up in the following order:

1. Creditors

2. Bondholders

3. Preferred shareholders

4. Common shareholders

Bond types

Bonds are issued by local, provincial, and federal governments; federal agencies; and corporations. You can typically invest in the types of bonds Table 2-5 shows. (Refer to Tip #15 for more about bonds issued by the Canadian government.)

Table 2-5	Bond Types and Risks	
Bond Type	*Issuer*	*Risk/Interest*
Canada Savings Bonds	Canadian government	Pay interest annually and are credit-risk free.
Treasury bills	Canadian government	Sold in terms of one month to one year and considered pretty much risk free.
Government of Canada bonds	Canadian government	Slightly lower returns than GICs and backed by government, so considered risk free.
Government of Canada agency bonds (usual minimum investment is $5,000)	Canadian government	Issued by Crown corporations like the Export Development Corporation, Canada Mortgage and Housing Corporation, and the Business Development Bank of Canada. Sold in terms of 2 to 10 years. Extremely high quality.
Provincial bonds (minimum investment is $5,000)	Provincial governments	Sold in terms of 1 to 30 years, they pay a guaranteed level of fixed income (usually higher than that offered by the federal government) and are considered extremely high quality.
Municipal bonds	Municipal governments	Pay higher yields than other government bonds and considered very high quality but liquidity is lower. Should be held to term.
Corporate (minimum investment is $1,000)	Corporations	They attract investors who seek higher yields in exchange for a higher risk of default.

Some corporate, municipal, and government agency bonds offer additional risk in that they can be *called*, or redeemed, by the issuer at full face value prior to the due date. You therefore miss out on some interest payments.

So how do you decide which type of bond to hold? In a nutshell, if you're looking for the highest level of security, Government of Canada bonds are for you. Want security, with a slightly higher yield? Municipal bonds might be just the ticket. Looking for the highest income? Corporate bonds are usually your best bet.

You need to be earning a yield that's higher than inflation. To combat inflation, the government offers Government of Canada Real Returns Bonds. The interest rate fluctuates with the cost of living as measured by the Consumer Price Index. You get a lower interest rate on real return bonds compared to traditional Government of Canada Bonds, because the other portion of your return comes from the inflation adjustment to the principal. That means no matter what happens with the rate of inflation, you earn a decent return above and beyond that rate. With governments printing off money at a record pace, Canada could be in for an inflationary environment.

Your return on investment: Yields, yields, and more yields

Why buy a bond when you can just put your money into a savings account or money market account? Well, savings account interest can fluctuate up and down, but bond interest is fixed. Here are four ways of looking at the return you get from a bond:

- ✓ **Coupon payments:** Bonds pay you a stream of semi-annual interest payments, called *coupons*.

- ✓ **Current yield:** The return you get paid annually, in the form of coupons, based on the current market value, is called the *current yield*.

- ✓ **Face value:** Face value, or *par*, is the dollar amount that is returned to you when your bond matures. Most bonds are issued with a face value of $1,000. However, you may purchase a bond for more or less than its face value. The bond matures at face value, so any extra premium you paid reduces your yield to maturity; but if you purchased the bond at a discount, your yield to maturity is higher than the coupon rate.

- ✓ **Yield to maturity (YTM):** *YTM* is the actual rate of return you receive on a bond investment, if you hold the bond until it matures.

Yield to maturity is frequently the most important number to pay attention to — it allows you to compare bonds of different coupons and maturities. Yield to maturity is the total return, made up of interest and repayment of principal, if you hold the bond to maturity. Never buy a bond solely on the coupon alone.

You can purchase marketable bonds that don't pay any interest until they mature. These bonds have had their interest coupons removed or *stripped* off, hence the name. With strip bonds, the yield is compounded semi-annually and paid at maturity. Generally only government and high-quality corporate bonds are stripped.

One drawback to stripped bonds is that you have to report the interest as income annually, even though you haven't received any payments. Your best bet is to purchase them inside an RRSP or RRIF because you won't have to pay tax on the interest.

Climb the Bond Ladder in Uncertain Times

When interest rates rise, bond prices fall; and when interest rates fall, bond prices rise. Longer-term bonds are more sensitive to interest rate changes, but as a bond maturity date gets closer, it fluctuates less in price.

Changes in interest rates can wreak havoc on the value of your bonds. Furthermore, tying your money up for long periods of time at one interest rate means you may miss out on higher rates when interest rates are on the rise. One strategy to combat this problem is to use a *bond ladder,* which consists of short-term, medium-term, and long-term bonds. As each individual bond matures, you invest the cash you receive from the maturing bond into new long-term bonds or the highest-yielding bonds available at the time.

Buying bonds

Bonds are available individually through discount brokers and full service investment dealers. To build a diversified bond portfolio, you should probably have at least $50,000 to start. Otherwise, stick with a low-cost bond fund from a discount broker. For more on building a diversified bond portfolio, see Tip #43.

For commission-free trades, you can buy Canada Savings Bonds directly from the government (www.csb.gc.ca).

Reviewing bond ratings

Just as you get a personal credit rating, municipal and corporate bonds get a rating, too. Bond rating services, such as Dominion Bond Rating Service (DBRS) and Canadian Bond Rating Services, analyze and rate the financial security of the issuing company or agency. Even though bond ratings can be wrong (even some of Air Canada's bond ratings were investment grade in the months leading up to its rescue), they're a starting point. Choose from two categories of bonds:

- ✔ **Investment grade bonds:** Bonds rated at this level have a relatively low risk of default. DBRS, for example, rates investment grade bonds at BBB or higher.

- ✔ **Speculative grade bonds:** Bonds rated at this level have a relatively high risk of default. They're also called junk bonds. DBRS uses BB or lower.

If a bond's rating changes for the worse due to the company's profitability or credit rating, the bond's market value may go down. This doesn't change the amount you receive if you hold the bond to maturity or the amount of interest you're paid, because these amounts are based on the face value of the bond. But it can be a problem if you need to sell the bond prematurely.

The coupon component on bonds is considered interest income. You should probably hold investments that generate interest income within a registered account, such as a Tax-Free Savings Account (TFSA) (see Tip #32), RRSP, or RRIF. For more on getting the most from your RRSP accounts, see Tip #30.

#25

Hedge with Options

By Gigi Turbow Marx, MBA

How many times have you heard the mantra that stocks outperform all other asset classes in the long term? Unfortunately, many retiree wannabes are finding out the hard way that the long term can be really long.

The most important reason to hedge is that waiting for the long term isn't always an option. Investment success comes from careful risk management, which means minimizing losses, not being a genius stock picker. Broad diversification among asset classes should be your first line of risk management defence (see Tip #37). But hedging provides you with a Plan B, and having a back-up plan is definitely the best plan in uncertain times! This tip explains how to use options to hedge.

Know the Options Basics

Options are a *derivative* product. Very simply, that means their value is derived from something else. If you buy or sell options on an asset such as a stock or exchange-traded fund (defined as the *underlying* asset), the price of the option is going to move with that stock or index in a fairly well-defined relationship. That relationship allows you to use options to track price changes in the underlying asset for a fraction of the cost, but with a great deal more risk and very high commissions.

Understand how options work

Here are some useful options-related terms:

- **Premium:** The price of the option.
- **Strike (exercise) price:** The price at which you agree to buy or sell the underlying asset if the option is exercised.

✔ **Expiration:** The date on which the option ceases to exist; all rights and obligations conferred by the option contract terminate when the option expires.

✔ **Contract size:** One contract is equal to 100 shares of the underlying asset.

Any options contract gives rights to the buyer and commits the seller to obligations. Options also come in two varieties, calls and puts, depending on whether the buyer wants the right to purchase or sell the underlying asset. Table 2-6 shows how these rights and obligations break down.

Table 2-6	**Rights and Obligations of Options Contracts**	
Buyer or Seller of the Option	**Calls**	**Puts**
Option holder (buyer)	By buying a call option, the holder purchases the right to buy the underlying asset at a set price by a set date (the expiration).	By buying a put option, the holder purchases the right to sell the underlying asset at the strike price by a set date.
Option writer (seller)	By selling a call option, the writer commits to selling the underlying asset at the strike price by a set date.	By selling a put option, the writer commits to buying the underlying asset at the set or strike price by a set date.

Perhaps the single most important concept about options is the following: Options have a limited life.

Unlike your core portfolio holdings, options expire, and when they do, they no longer have value and no longer exist. That may actually be your goal. If not, you can liquidate an option position or roll it over to another strike price or another time period. The important point is that you must do it *before* the expiration. This underscores the point that hedging requires an economic point of view and active oversight.

Look at how you can use options to hedge

You can use options for the following reasons:

- ✔ To protect your portfolio
- ✔ To generate additional income
- ✔ For speculation/leverage

A 2008 Charles Schwab study of options trading found that, contrary to popular perception, only one in four traders surveyed indicated market speculation was their leading reason to trade options. Three-quarters of the respondents used options with the goal of generating income or hedging for risk management.

Okay, but how do you actually use this stuff? In this limited space, we can barely scratch the surface of useful ways to apply options, but the following example may give you some ideas. Consider the unpleasant situation in which one of your ETFs has fallen 20 percent over the past year. In theory, you know that you should try to buy more to reduce your average cost and rebalance your holdings. In reality, you have little cash and even less stomach for further losses.

If you have only $5,000, you could use the whole amount to buy 50 shares of your now-$100 stock today. Alternatively, you could purchase call options — the right to buy that stock — for less money and buy yourself some time to see whether the situation worsens or improves before you commit to buying more stock.

Say you already own 400 shares. You decide to buy four call contracts at a $95 strike price to reduce your cost basis more effectively. You see that you can buy options that expire in four months for a premium cost of $7 a share, costing a total of $2,800 ($7 per share × 100 shares per contract × 4 contracts).

If you're right and the stock recovers to $105, you've locked in the right to buy up to 400 shares at the strike price ($95) plus the premium ($7), or $102 per share total — $3 less than market price.

But what if you really want to add only 50 shares to your position? By selling 350 shares in the stock market at $105 and exercising your contracts to buy 400 shares, you'll get your 50 shares. You'll also get a $1,050 gain on the stock you don't want to keep ($3 × 350)! That's a gain you can use to replenish your cash account or to repair another investment. (And *that's* why they call them *options,* Virginia!)

What if your analysis is wrong and the stock keeps dropping? Again, the value of your options will move in tandem with the underlying asset — that is, down. But you've limited the potential loss on your investment strategy because you can't lose more than the ($2,800) premium you paid, and you've still got some cash left to consider a new strategy.

Do Your Homework

Options trading is a game of strategy similar to competitive chess or sports. It's versatile but complex, so do your homework and research the risks and returns of any strategy you want to pursue.

You could just be committing financial suicide if you start dealing in options without at least reading a book on the subject or taking a course offered by major brokerage houses and discount trading firms. Some even offer online demonstrations that start you off with play money. Check out www.m-x.ca, where the Canadian Derivatives Exchange offers futures and options quotes, a rundown of the rules, information, and tools.

Newsletter vendors, whether covering options or any other investment, aren't regulated. They can consequently make all sorts of groundless claims about potential investment returns without fear of scrutiny or sanctions. You need to know enough to evaluate which newsletters are reputable.

Take Your First Steps

You can't just decide one day that you'd like to try a little options trading and go place an order. You first have to apply to your brokerage firm for trading authorization. Multiple levels of authorization are required, and you have to graduate through the ranks. Demonstrate financial capacity and reasonable care using conservative strategies, and they'll approve you for more complex strategies. They're doing you a favour because they've seen the road kill. Here are some other important rules of the road for novices:

✔ **Start with the asset or market you understand best.** Options trading is complex, so make sure you're familiar with the underlying assets.

✔ **Start small.** Just because you have $5,000 doesn't mean you should spend it all in one place! Options provide a lot of leverage for a wee bit of cash, but it works both ways — gains *and* losses.

#26

Invest in Commodities

By Robert Friedland, PhD

Any resource whose quality is easily measured can be, and most likely is, a *commodity*. Common commodities include the following:

- ✔ Non-renewable energy such as oil or natural gas
- ✔ Agricultural products such as cocoa, coffee, corn, cotton, orange juice, soybeans, sugar, and wheat
- ✔ Livestock such as cattle or hogs
- ✔ Timber
- ✔ Metals such as copper, gold, nickel, platinum, silver, and zinc

Commodity values tend to have cycles different from those of stocks and bonds. They also provide protection from inflation, particularly unexpected inflation. Unexpected or accelerating inflation tends to reduce the value of stocks and bonds. But when the primary source of this inflation is the cost of raw inputs — that is, commodities — the value of commodities also rises.

Although commodities themselves are traded in both local and global markets, the global trading of commodity derivatives plays a huge role in commodity pricing. *Derivative* is a fancy name for a contract that derives its value from something tangible. Common types of derivatives are futures contracts, forwards contracts, options contracts (refer to Tip #25), and swaps. (For more information on derivatives, see the latest edition of *Investing For Canadians For Dummies,* by Eric Tyson and Tony Martin [Wiley].) Although handling a contract is less smelly than handling a pork belly, the real purpose of derivatives is to reduce business risk.

When you buy stock, you're buying part of a company. When you buy a bond, you're buying part of the debt issued by that company or government. When you buy a commodity, you're buying the raw input into the production of everything being produced. Including commodities in your portfolio enables you to diversify your risks in a unique way. You can share in the growth of the global economy and hedge against inflation. A key factor in deciding if or when to invest in commodities is whether you think the world economy is getting stronger. When the world economy shows little growth, little need exists for the raw materials that become products later.

Lock In a Price with Commodities Futures

Commodities markets are essential for those who grow, raise, or extract commodities and for businesses that use these resources in their production. For instance, a farmer decides which crops and/or livestock to raise, in part, by comparing anticipated costs to expected market prices. Although the farmer can reasonably estimate production costs in advance, he or she has no way of knowing what the sale price of the crop will be at harvest. Buying a futures contract allows the farmer to get someone to commit to a purchase price well ahead of time.

How do commodities futures work?

A *futures contract* is an obligation to either sell or buy a particular commodity at a specific price on a specific day. For instance, a farmer can go to the commodities exchange and purchase a contract to sell wheat at a specific price and date in the future. This contract reflects both the farmer's willingness to deliver the wheat at a specific price and the buyer's willingness to pay that price. A likely buyer is a company that mills wheat into flour. The company needs to plan its production and market the flour to its customers, such as bakeries, so the company wants to lock in the price it'll pay for the wheat it'll need in the future.

If, by the time the crop comes to harvest, the market price *(spot price)* is lower than the contractual price, the farmer will be glad he or she entered into this contract. The miller, however, won't be so happy, because that company will be obligated to buy the wheat for more than the market price.

This contract eliminates some risks to each business, but the derivatives market helps further. If the miller can anticipate a drop in the wheat price below the contractual price, it'll try to sell its contract ahead of time. If, on the other hand, the market price for this crop turns out to be higher than the contractual price, the tables turn and now the farmer may try to sell the contract in advance. However, the miller and the farmer wouldn't be able to find buyers without a larger marketplace. This is where investors like you come in.

Most commodity investors aren't interested in or capable of taking possession of or delivering the commodity. After all, where would you store 20 tons of frozen trimmed pork bellies or 1,000 barrels of crude oil or 25,000 pounds of copper? Investors are, however, interested in making a profit, and they consider many factors when deciding how much to pay the farmer or miller for the contract. The investor makes judgments concerning weather, infectious disease, accidents, fire, supply, political changes (such as nationalization, revolution, or democratization), currency exchange rates, and the actions of other buyers and sellers. Successful commodity investors have to make buy/sell decisions based on all these factors and perhaps more, including the future trend of inflation.

Why invest in commodities?

Assume that a barrel of sweet grade light crude oil is $60. What if you purchased a contract six months ago for $10,000, allowing you to buy 1,000 barrels of oil for $30 per barrel today? You could use this contract to purchase the oil for $30,000 and turn around and sell it for $60,000, pocketing $20,000 ($40,000 minus the contract price of $10,000 — before taxes, shipping, handling, and storage charges). Moreover, if you were savvy enough to have used your margin account, you may have used only $5,000 of your own money to increase your wealth by $30,000 for just one contract. Not bad!

You probably don't want to take delivery of the oil, but someone in the market does, and that person would be willing to pay you for your contract to get the better oil price. The closer you get to the contract date, the more likely someone will be willing to pay close to $100,000 for your contract.

How to Invest in Commodities

You can invest in commodities in multiple ways:

- ✔ **Purchase or sell futures contracts.** This is the purest way to gain exposure, but volatility can be high. (Refer to the preceding sections for details on futures contracts.) Some investors try to mitigate some of this volatility by buying and selling commodity futures indexes, which bundle related commodities.

- ✔ **Buy shares in *royalty trusts*, which are special trusts that receive income or profits from the commodity.** These trusts can pay high dividends, particularly because the trusts don't pay corporate income taxes. The trust also offers tax advantages by distributing proportionate shares of its depreciation and depletion allowances.

✓ **Buy commodities through mutual funds and exchange-traded funds (ETFs).** These funds often have different investment strategies, so read and understand the prospectus before investing. Using a mutual fund (refer to Tip #18) gives you professional investment managers, dramatically increases your diversification for a small price, and gives you the convenience of one mutual fund purchase rather than an array of futures contracts.

ETFs (refer to Tip #20) have similar advantages but are more likely to simply mirror a particular index of commodity futures. As a result, the ETF's management costs may be less than those of a mutual fund. ETFs, however, can be traded just like stocks.

✓ **Buy traditional stocks or bonds of companies in the business of growing, raising, or extracting a commodity.** A popular approach is to purchase shares in a mutual fund or ETF — often called a *specialty fund* — that focuses on companies that fit a particular commodities theme. But holding the stock of a group of companies in a specialty fund isn't the same as buying the commodity. Odds are the company stock will move in concert with the rest of the stock market and, depending on what else the company does or owns, won't be a strong hedge against inflation.

Although you want exposure to commodities, this exposure — either pure or indirect — should be a relatively small share of your investment portfolio. If you own Canadian stocks or mutual funds, chances are good that you already have a pretty heavy weighting in commodities, because the TSX has more than its share of natural resource stocks. Don't invest in commodity futures, or index-commodity futures, unless you're willing to put in the time and effort to study and follow that specific commodity market closely.

An estimated 90 percent of amateur commodity traders lose money. Keep in mind the words of Bernard Baruch, a U.S. stock speculator and presidential advisor to Woodrow Wilson and Franklin D. Roosevelt. He said, "Whatever failures I have known . . . have been the consequence of action without thought."

#27

Consider Short-Selling

By Neil Vannoy, MBA

As of this writing, Nortel Networks shares have fallen to levels not seen since the early 1980s, which is rather sad for what was once Canada's largest company. What does these mean to you? It means that if you hold Nortel stock, you've probably lost money — even if you held the stock for 25 years!

Maybe you saw it coming, so you sold all your Nortel stock. Selling would have kept you from losing money, but what if you wanted to make money instead of just protecting yourself from losses? After all, what happened to Nortel could happen to another company, especially during difficult economic times. *Short-selling* is a strategy that can help you make money when a company, or the economy as a whole, faces uncertainty.

Sell High and Buy Low

Short-selling involves selling a stock you don't actually own in order to profit from a price decline. When you short a stock, you want the value to drop.

Here's how it works: You borrow shares from your investment dealer through a margin account and immediately sell them on the open market. The proceeds are then deposited into your account. Eventually you repurchase the shares and return them to the dealer to close out the short position. If you pay less to buy back the shares than you received from selling them, you keep the difference! For example:

1. XYZ stock is trading at $25 per share. You think the true value is around $15 per share. You speculate that the price of XYZ will decline, so you sell short 100 shares of XYZ stock at $25 per share.

2. Your investment dealer loans you 100 shares, you sell them on the open market, and the $2,500 in proceeds is deposited into your account. (100 shares × $25 per share = $2,500).

3. Two weeks later, XYZ stock declines to $19 per share. You purchase 100 shares to return to your investment dealer at $19 per share.

Your profit from the transaction is $600 ($2,500 from the sale of XYZ – $1,900 to repurchase XYZ).

This example doesn't account for the commissions that apply in the real world!

You don't have to master short-selling yourself to incorporate it into your portfolio. Some mutual funds, called long-short funds, use short-selling as a part of their strategy. Make sure you understand and agree with both the strategy and fees.

Now for the Bad News: It's Not So Easy

Sounds easy, right? Well, before you start short-selling your way to untold fortunes, you should know a few things.

Short-selling is a speculative strategy with high risks and is probably not right for most investors. You can only guess that the price of a stock is going to fall. If it rises instead, you lose money.

History shows that stocks appreciate

Using history as a guide, the long-term trend for stocks is positive. Although the market drops or trades *sideways* (moves up and down within a limited range) at times, stocks have appreciated more than any other asset classes over long time periods. Although you have no guarantee that this trend will continue, be aware that short-selling involves going against this powerful trend!

You risk unlimited loss for a limited gain

The potential gain from short-selling is limited to the cash you receive from selling the stock, but the potential loss is unlimited. Recall the $2,500 you received from selling XYZ in the example earlier in this tip. The most you could make from the transaction is $2,500, but XYZ would have to go bankrupt for you to be able to keep the entire amount.

So what happens if the price of XYZ stock begins to skyrocket after you sell the shares short? You're responsible for purchasing the 100 shares of XYZ stock to close the short position, no matter the price!

Although an unlimited loss is possible only in theory, be aware that the price could easily *double* or *triple* before you have the chance to repurchase the shares. This is especially true for stocks of small companies, or stocks that are *thinly traded* (which means they don't have a high volume of shares that are regularly traded).

In this scenario, if the price of XYZ stock doubles after you sell short, you have to buy back 100 shares at $50 per share. You spend $5,000 to buy the same stock you sold for $2,500. You lose $2,500 *before* you add in commission fees and the interest you have to pay for the time until you close the short position.

Selling-short in Canada is subject to provincial securities laws and marketplace rules. Make sure you know the rules!

You pay interest on losses

You're required to open a margin account with your dealer before you can short-sell. Margin levels for short-selling are much higher than typical margin borrowing, because of the risk involved with using borrowed shares. If you sell a stock short, and the stock price begins to increase, your investment dealer will move money from the cash balance of your account to cover the losses. A margin balance will be created if you don't have sufficient cash to cover the position, and you'll accrue interest charges on the margin balance. So you could not only suffer a loss from your short position, but also end up paying interest for the privilege of losing money!

Learn the Lingo

This section covers the lingo you need to dabble in short-selling, or to impress your buddies at cocktail parties!

Selling, shorting, selling short, going short, short

These terms are used interchangeably to describe an investor who's engaged in short-selling. *Selling, shorting, selling short,* and *going short* are used before an investment position is established, and *short* is used to describe the position after the fact. (Note that *buying, going long,* and *long* are the opposite of these terms.)

Again, assume you think XYZ is overvalued. You could say you're considering "selling XYZ," "shorting XYZ," "selling XYZ short," or "going short XYZ." After you establish a short position in XYZ, you simply say you're "short XYZ."

Bull and bear markets

The terms *bull market* and *bear market* are commonly used to describe the stock market, but they can describe any investment market (such as the bond market, commodity market, or currency market). Security prices in bull markets are increasing or expected to increase; prices are falling or expected to fall in bear markets. Likewise, a *bull* is an investor who's betting the market will rise. A *bear* is an investor who expects it to fall. Short-sellers are *bearish* because they expect the price of the security to fall.

Short interest

Short interest refers to a specific security's total number of shares that have been sold short. When short interest increases, many investors believe it's a bearish indicator. For example, if the short interest in XYZ stock increases from 2 percent to 6 percent of outstanding shares, it would appear that more investors are expecting the price of XYZ to fall.

Covering

Investors who sell a security short eventually have to *cover,* or buy back, their position. For example, if you short 100 shares of XYZ stock, you later cover the position by purchasing 100 shares.

Short squeeze

A *short squeeze* occurs when a rapid stock price increase leads short-sellers to cover their positions. This increased demand, combined with a lack of supply, causes the price of the stock to continue upward, compelling more and more short-sellers to cover their positions.

Days to cover (short interest ratio)

Days to cover (also known as *short interest ratio*) gives you an idea of the future buying pressure on a stock from short-sellers who will eventually have to cover their positions. This ratio measures the short interest in a stock relative to its *average daily volume* (the average number of shares that exchange hands in a day). The longer the days to cover for a security, the greater the chance of a short squeeze. This formula determines days to cover:

Days to cover = Current short interest ÷ Average daily share volume

Called away

You establish a short position using borrowed shares of a security. Your investment dealer has the right to redeem those shares at any time. If the original owner redeems the shares, and your dealer can't find replacements, the shares may be *called away* from you. You'll have to cover your position immediately, despite market price. Gack!

Use Caution When Buying on Margin

By Neil Vannoy, MBA

Buying on margin is similar to buying a home. In home-buying, borrowing money increases your purchasing power and allows you to buy a larger home than you could otherwise afford. Margin is basically a loan from your investment dealer, and buying on margin allows you to purchase more of a security — such as a stock or a bond — than you could on your own. The interest on loans to fund investments in a non-registered or a taxable portfolio is tax deductible.

Know How It Works: Everything's Bigger with Margin

Investors buy on margin to increase their returns. Because margin gives you the ability to buy more stock with less money, an increase in the price of the stock leads to a larger gain than if you hadn't used margin. Here's an example: Assume you pay cash for stock worth $5,000 and that stock appreciates to $5,500. That represents a 10 percent return on your $5,000 investment. Not bad. Now assume you make the same investment by using $2,500 of your money and $2,500 that you borrow from your investment dealer. The same $500 appreciation would be a 20 percent return on your $2,500 investment ($500 gain ÷ $2,500 investment = 20 percent). Much better! But keep in mind that you have to pay interest to your investment dealer for the privilege of borrowing its money.

 Margin is a double-edged sword. Buying stocks on margin is great when prices go up, but stocks don't always appreciate. Any loss on a stock purchased on margin is magnified just like gains are magnified. Buying on margin in a volatile market is risky business!

Understand the Details

To buy securities with borrowed money, you need a *margin account* with your investment dealer. That means you have to qualify and your investment dealer has to approve the account.

Minimum and initial margin

Before trading on margin, you have to meet margin requirements set by the Investment Dealers Association and the exchanges. These are the minimums, but your dealer firm can have stricter requirements.

When you buy on margin, you're basically borrowing cash to invest by using your existing investment assets as collateral. You can usually invest only up to 50 percent of your equity holdings, although that percentage sometimes narrows depending on the volatility of the market or the stock you're pledging as collateral. No margin may exist, for example, for equities trading under $3. You can meet the minimum and initial margin requirements by depositing cash or securities into your margin account.

Maintenance margin

After you purchase a security, you're required to keep a minimum amount of equity in your account. This is called the *maintenance margin.* You can meet the maintenance margin requirement by depositing cash or securities into your margin account.

For example, assume you purchase $10,000 of XYZ stock on margin by depositing $5,000 in cash into your account and borrowing $5,000 on margin. Your equity in the account is $5,000 ($10,000 market value of XYZ – $5,000 margin loan = $5,000 equity). If the value of XYZ falls to $8,000, the equity in your account falls to $3,000 ($8,000 market value of XYZ – $5,000 margin loan = $3,000 equity). If your firm has a 25 percent maintenance margin requirement ($2,000 in this example), your account would still be in good standing. However, if your firm has a 40 percent maintenance margin requirement ($3,200 in this example), you wouldn't have enough equity in your account; you'd need to deposit more cash or securities to increase the equity to, or above, the maintenance margin.

Margin call

You may receive a *margin call* from your dealer firm asking you to deposit more cash or securities if the equity in your margin account falls below the maintenance requirement. Ignore the call, and your firm will sell enough securities in your account to meet the maintenance requirement.

Your investment dealer doesn't have to notify you that your account has fallen below the maintenance requirement or contact you before selling your securities!

Margin rate

The *margin rate* is the interest rate you pay to purchase securities on margin. Margin rates are based on the investment dealer's call rate, which is the interest rate that dealer firms pay to banks for financing margin loans. Be aware that margin rates are variable, so they can change at any time!

Recognize the Risks

Consider these issues before buying on margin:

- ✔ **Stocks don't always increase in value.** Buying on margin will magnify your loss if a stock declines in value.

- ✔ **You can lose more money than you deposit.** If the securities you purchase on margin decline in value, you may be required to deposit additional funds or sell some of your securities.

- ✔ **Your investment dealer can force the sale of securities in your account.** If you can't deposit more money to meet a margin call, your investment dealer can force you to sell securities to meet the maintenance margin.

- ✔ **Your investment dealer can sell your securities without contacting you.** Your investment dealer has the right to sell your securities to meet the maintenance margin without contacting you first. And you may not get a chance to decide which securities are sold.

- ✔ **You're not entitled to more time to meet a margin call.** Your firm *may* extend the time to meet a margin call under certain circumstances.

✔ **Your investment dealer can increase the maintenance margin at any time.** Changes in the maintenance margin take effect immediately and may cause a margin call if you don't meet the new requirements.

✔ **You'll pay interest even if you lose money.** Interest is charged on your margin balance whether or not you make or lose money on the trade.

Get the Most Out of Your Taxable Accounts

By Kevin Sale, ChFC, CFP

So you've maxed out the RRSPs (and RESPs, if applicable), invested the most you can in your workplace pension plan, and filled your TFSA to the gills. But given today's economic climate, you're still worried you won't accumulate the tidy little nest egg that will help you reach your financial goals. That's where taxable or non-registered accounts come into play. A *taxable account* is simply any account whose use doesn't give you a tax advantage. It can be a savings account, chequing account, investment dealer account, mutual fund account, or many others. The key is that income and gains generated by the investments held in the account are taxed.

Most people use taxable accounts almost daily for one main reason: They're flexible. Generally, using them involves no restrictions or penalties. Any restrictions or penalties that do exist are tied to your investment choice, not your account. Taxable accounts can help bolster pension, TFSA, and RRSP earnings. They also provide a parking spot for spending money or money for your short-term goals.

Stashing some cash away is an excellent idea, but it does you no good if you're losing money on your savings. And that could happen if you don't account for the taxes you pay on your earnings. Consider, for example, a $10,000 investment in unsheltered GICs returning 2.5 percent interest. If you're in the top marginal tax bracket, you pay 39 to 48 percent tax on your $250 in earnings, and with inflation rates at 1.5 percent to 2 percent, you'll be in the hole by the end of the year. When evaluating your investment choices, what really counts is how much cash you'll have in *after-tax* dollars.

Make Tax-Smart Investments

Research shows that ignoring the tax impact of investing can cost you between 1 and 5 percent per year in returns. That's nothing to sniff at in this era of low interest rates. Fortunately investments held in an RRSP aren't taxed, so if you have cash to invest after making your maximum RRSP and TFSA contributions, your open or taxable accounts are the place to keep the truly tax-smart investments. Good bets include the following:

- ✓ **Buy-and-hold stocks or mutual funds:** You're not taxed on capital gains until you sell your investment or the money manager sells and distributes the gains to unit holders. Consequently, the easiest way to avoid tax in the short term is to avoid selling any assets with accrued capital gains. *Remember:* A tax deferral is the next best thing to a tax deduction.

- ✓ **Dividend-paying stocks.** That 16 to 27 percent tax bite (depending on your province) in the top income bracket on dividend income still beats the 39 to 48 percent tax on interest income.

- ✓ **Potential money-losers.** Okay, nobody starts out thinking they're going to lose money on an investment. If, however, you're taking a flyer on a risky stock or specialized mutual fund, consider keeping those investments in a taxable account. The reason? You can't write off losses inside your RRSP. Outside the RRSP, you can at least use your capital losses to offset capital gains made in the last three years, or you can carry the loss forward indefinitely, lowering your tax bill.

Under Canada Revenue Agency's *superficial loss rules,* if you (or your spouse, or your business) buy back into an investment 30 days before or after selling it at a loss, you can't use the capital loss to offset current capital gains.

Time Your Investments Right

To make sure you're not paying unnecessary taxes in your taxable account, don't buy mutual funds just prior to their fiscal year-end. Mutual funds generally pay out all of their income and *net realized capital gains* — basically the profits on stocks traded within the portfolio — every year. Although the payout date can vary, many funds allow the income to accumulate all year long and then shell out in December to the unit holders of record. You, in turn, have to declare any gains distributed by your funds to the CRA, even if you simply reinvest them.

In real-person language, this means that if you bought into a fund on December 10, you may have paid an inflated price. Why? Because you forked out for the income and gains that were accumulating all year. And here's the clincher: You still have to pay tax on that distribution, even though you didn't really earn it and you're not benefiting from it. If, however, you wait until the beginning of the new year to invest, your fund will have probably already paid out its distribution, and the fund price will have dropped accordingly (again, depending on the fund's fiscal year-end and normal distribution dates).

Aim to sell off money-losing funds before the end of the year. Stock market or mutual fund sales have to take place no later than December 31 to count as a loss for the current tax year (which can then be applied against capital gains to reduce taxes). Most advisors recommend you have your redemption order in by December 24 to ensure it's processed in time.

Keep an eye open for unrealized capital gains. Longstanding funds with a buy-and-hold strategy may be sitting on a hefty load of profits (unrealized capital gains). But if a new manager comes on board and does a house cleaning or the fund gets caught in a downturn, the fund may have to sell off some of those stocks. Who ends up with part of the tax liability? *You* do, even if you just bought in and haven't actually earned all those gains.

#30

Invest in Registered Retirement Savings Plans (RRSPs)

Registered Retirement Savings Plans (RRSPs) are one of the best tax shelters left to Canadian investors. If you're not taking full advantage of them, give your head a shake! In these times of uncertain investment returns, tax-sheltering your investments is doubly important. Otherwise you risk seeing your earnings swallowed up by inflation and taxes.

Understand the Benefits of RRSPs

At the risk of stating the obvious, a *Registered Retirement Savings Plan* is a special account where you plunk a certain proportion of your income. RRSPs are a great complement or replacement for retirement savings at work. You get two main tax benefits from investing in an RRSP:

- ✔ **A tax deduction for your contribution:** For example, if you scrape together a $5,000 RRSP contribution, you can deduct that same amount from your earned income (salary, bonuses or commissions, self-employment earnings, or investment income) for the year. So if you're in the top tax bracket, paying tax at 48 percent (depending on your province), you would save about $2,400 in taxes right off the top! You could use that tax refund to take a trip to Cuba, pay off your mortgage, or — perhaps wisest of all — fund next year's RRSP contribution. (Sorry, but somebody has to be the wet blanket!)

- ✔ **Tax-free earnings on your contributions:** You pay no tax on the earnings of your RRSP contributions until you cash them in. Hopefully that won't be until you retire, when you're in a lower marginal tax bracket.

What to Hold in an RRSP

You can put just about anything into an RRSP — cash, GICs, mutual funds, mortgages, shares of small businesses or venture capital corporations, gold or silver bullion, and stocks or bonds. One very simple principle of tax-smart investing, however, is to shelter the investments yielding the highest amount of taxable earnings in your RRSP. Those may include the following:

- ✔ Interest-bearing investments like bonds, bond funds, cash, and GICs, because earnings are taxed at the same level as income (up to 48 percent in the top marginal tax bracket).

- ✔ Stocks or equity funds which you don't intend to hold for the long term, or mutual funds that are heavy traders, because you're forced to pay tax on the earnings when you sell.

- ✔ If you're a conservative investor and not a fan of heavy-trading stocks or mutual funds, you may want to hold stocks that regularly pay dividends, income, or other distributions in your RRSP. Although these investments are more tax efficient than interest-bearing investments, if you're in the top marginal income bracket, you still pay up to 28.5 percent tax on dividend income from Canadian stocks. However, you can't delay that payment until your income level is lower — after you retire, for example.

Figure Out Contribution Limits

The maximum RRSP contribution amount that can be deducted from your income is called the *RRSP deduction limit.* Your 2009 deduction limit is included on your 2008 Notice of Assessment or Notice of Reassessment from Canada Revenue Agency (CRA). If you haven't received your notice or simply can't find it (hey, it happens to all of us!), call the CRA at 1-800-959-8281 (English) or 1-800-959-7383 (French).

The RRSP deduction limit is calculated as 18 percent of your earned income for the preceding year, to an annual maximum of $21,000 for 2009 and $22,000 for 2010.

The amount you're allowed to contribute to an RRSP is reduced if you belong to a company pension plan. The government figures out the value of the contributions to the pension plan (called a *Pensions Adjustment*) and then deducts either the lesser of the maximum amount allowable or 18 percent of your earned income. The result is your *allowable contribution.*

You can keep contributing to an RRSP up to and during the year you turn 71. You can contribute to a spousal RRSP up to and including the year your spouse turns 71.

Contribute just a little extra

You can contribute up to $2,000 more than your allowable RRSP contribution. Although you won't receive a tax deduction for the excess contribution in the year you make it, you can claim it as part of your contribution limit in upcoming years without paying a penalty. If you go over $2,000, though, you could be assessed a penalty of about 1 percent per month.

Carry forward your contribution

Imagine that you're self-employed and this year was pretty dismal — your clients went belly up, and you made enough to pay the bills but not much else. Even if you can't scrape together an RRSP contribution, you can *carry forward* your RRSP contribution room to future years. That means that next year, when you're rollin' in the dough (which you will be — after all, you were smart enough to buy this book!), you can make a higher contribution. As a bonus, if you're in a higher income tax bracket, you get more money back from the government as a tax refund!

Make that RRSP contribution if you can. Weigh the advantage of holding off until you're in a higher income bracket against the disadvantage of getting the tax refund a year or more later — and the risk that you'll never actually get around to making up for that missed contribution.

Hang Tough in Hard Times

When times are tough, people sometimes resort to cashing in their RRSPs early to make ends meet. If you can avoid doing this, please do! You often end up paying more tax to withdraw the funds than you initially received in tax deductions. What's more, you lose the contribution room even though you've withdrawn the funds. So if you can't commit to leaving your cash in that RRSP until retirement, don't contribute. The two exceptions to this rule are paying for education or taking advantage of the Home Buyers' Plan (see the sidebar, "The Home Buyers' Plan").

If cash is tight and you're uncomfortable locking away your money in an RRSP with hefty penalties for early withdrawal, a Tax-Free

Savings Account may be for you. You can still save in a tax-advantaged manner, but you can withdraw your contributions (not your gains) at any time, penalty and tax free. See Tip #32 for more information on the TFSA.

Wait until at least age 65 and then convert RRSP funds into a Registered Retirement Income Fund (RRIF) before pulling out money. The RRIF income you receive at age 65 or older may be eligible to be split between you and your spouse. It may also qualify for the pension income tax credit of up to $2,000 or more per person, per year.

Endure Short-Term Pain for Long-Term Gain

Retirement may be decades away for you. So how do you resist that pair of designer jeans or that awesome new electronic gizmo in favour of socking money away in an RRSP? The following example might offer some incentive.

According to Lenore Davis, CFP, RFP, senior partner with Dixon, Davis & Co. in Victoria, British Columbia, if you start saving for retirement at age 26 and invest $100 a month until you're 65, you'll have invested $48,000 directly. But, given a 7 percent return on investment, you'll end up with $262,482! If you wait until you're 36 to start saving, however, you'll have to put away $200 a month (a direct investment of $72,000) to achieve $243,994 in savings given the same return on investment.

Forget the jeans and invest that money instead — you'll be glad you did in the long run.

Know That It's Never Too Late

Retirement is looming and you're petrified that you'll be eating dog food in your golden years. Gack! A retirement income calculator, such as the one at www.fiscalagents.com, can help you come up with a workable savings plan.

Can't meet that goal at your current level of savings? You've got a choice: You can save more dollars, take less income in retirement, work longer, or earn more on your investments. Although the latter option seems the least painful, stay away from investments that might pay off big, but involve a high level of risk. The fact is, as you get older you're less able to recover from failed investments.

The Home Buyers' Plan

The federal government's Home Buyers' Plan enables you to withdraw as much as $20,000 per person, or $40,000 per couple, from your RRSPs to put toward your first home without paying the usual tax penalty. That said, you're expected to pay back those RRSP contributions over a maximum of 15 years, starting on the second year after you make the withdrawal.

If you and your partner borrow the full $40,000, you'll have to repay a minimum of $2,667 a year. The amount doesn't count as an RRSP contribution, so it can't be deducted from your taxable income. If, for instance, you can only manage a $1,000 repayment, the $1,677 shortfall gets added on to your taxable income, which contributes to your tax bill. However, if you pay more than necessary, your payment amount in upcoming years gets reduced.

Making a withdrawal through the Home Buyers' Plan is simple — just fill out Form T1036 and submit it to your RRSP issuer. You can pick up the form from your tax services office, order it by calling, toll free, 1-800-959-2221, or print it from the CRA Web site (www.cra-arc.gc.ca).

The sheer amount you need to save may seem overwhelming, but don't give up in despair. Consider this: If you own a mortgage-free home and have already paid for your kids' education, you may be at a slight advantage financially over younger people when it comes to saving. Start by simply diverting the cash that once went to those fixed expenses to your RRSP, preferably by setting up an automatic withdrawal each month. If you never see that money in your account, you're not likely to miss it.

Lack the discipline to start a voluntary savings plan? You may be better off taking out an RRSP catch-up loan and then paying it back over a period of no more than two years. Often, those of us who don't have much discipline for voluntary savings have greater discipline for paying down debt.

Make the Most of Your Employer Retirement Accounts

Your eyes may glaze over at the thought of employer retirement plans. But for many people, a hodge-podge of private pension plans is crucial to accumulating enough for retirement.

This tip, which emphasizes the general rules rather than the exceptions, gives you a basic understanding of employer retirement plans and some ways to make the most of them. To ensure you have enough money during retirement, your best bet is to combine resources received from all sources. Tip #60 has more information on government sources of retirement income and how to combine your resources.

 You have investment risk in your retirement plans. Manage this risk by working these accounts into your overall asset allocation and monitoring the costs and performance of your plan investments.

Workplace Pension Plans

Each workplace retirement plan has its own rules. But these rules can really affect what you get when you retire. Keep that in mind, particularly if you're considering different job offers — the value of a better pension plan can really add up over the years. Workplace pension plans come in three basic flavours, which we look at in the following sections.

Registered Pension Plans (RPPs)

Registered Pension Plans (RPPs) are workplace pensions established by an employer or a union. If you have an RPP, lucky you. Only about 38 percent of all paid workers in Canada are covered by such a plan. When it comes to RPPs, you have a partner in saving because employers are bound by law to contribute to the plan. Contributions are tax deductible and earnings accumulate tax free. You pay tax only when you receive funds from an RPP as pension income. Another bonus: Assets held in RPPs are protected from creditors.

Most RPPs fall into three basic types.

Defined benefit pension plans

About 80 percent of Canadians covered by an RPP have a *defined benefit* plan, which is the type of plan that large companies and government employers usually offer. If you're covered by one of these plans, upon retirement you get a set annual income (your defined benefit) from the pension fund. Those payments continue for the rest of your life, and your employer is responsible for ensuring that the retirement fund has enough money to pay you.

Your employer usually calculates the amount of money you get using a formula that takes into account the number of years you worked and your salary.

Defined benefit plans have many permutations. Understanding how your plan works may have an impact on whether and when you choose to change jobs. Consider the following:

- ✔ Your plan may be set up to retain the most skilled people in the company. Consequently, it may implement generous pension increases after your fifth year of employment. Those increases may taper off again after your twentieth year because of the perception that older workers get too expensive. You may want to stay with the company at least until you get to that crucial fifth or sixth year or take a buyout after the twentieth year.

- ✔ Another plan may provide a pension benefit that is calculated by multiplying 1.5 percent of your average salary by the number of years that you've worked at your company to come up with a percentage of your last five years' salary. If you've worked at Company X for 40 years, for example, you'd have a pension of 60 percent of your earnings during the last five years before retirement. You'd want to maximize your earnings in those last five years.

Defined contribution pension plans

Defined contribution plans determine your pension benefit by tallying the contributions you've made to the plan and the growth of those contributions over time. Often your contribution comes right out of your pay, so you never get your hot little hands on it. Your employer must contribute at least 1 percent of your salary. Your pension will be based on the funds you've accumulated in your account by the time you retire — an amount that isn't set in advance (so your contribution is "defined," but your benefit is not). Some defined contribution plans offer you the option of deciding how you want your contributions invested.

Hybrid plans

Hybrid (or combination) plans incorporate aspects of both defined benefit and defined contribution plans. Basically, they arose out of the under-funding of defined benefit plans, which led employers to try to reduce their future financial obligations to employees.

As a general rule, if you can choose your plan, opt for the defined benefit plan first, the hybrid plan second, and the defined contribution plan third.

Group RRSPs

Employers sponsor group Registered Retirement Savings Plans (group RRSPs), although they may or may not choose to contribute. Group RRSPs are much like defined contribution plans, except they aren't regulated by provincial legislation. With *group RRSPs,* employees make regular payments to an RRSP through pre-tax automatic payroll deductions that are forwarded directly to the investment company on the employee's behalf. If you have a traditional group RRSP, your employer has probably limited your investment options within the plan — the investment equivalent of a *prix fixe* menu. If, on the other hand, you have a *self-directed group RRSP,* you may be able to choose your investments from a wide array of stocks, bonds, mutual funds, and other investments.

Deferred Profit-Sharing Plans (DPSP)

Deferred Profit-Sharing Plans (DPSP) are set up by an employer for employees. The employer makes contributions based on the company's profits up to a specified maximum. Like RPPs and group RRSPs, savings in a DPSP are tax assisted. The contributions and investment income remain tax sheltered until they're paid out. When you retire, you may receive a lump-sum payment, transfer the funds to an RRSP or RRIF, or use them to purchase an annuity.

Get Money into Your Accounts

So how do you invest money in your retirement plan? You have a few options:

✔ You contribute the funds through salary deductions.

✔ Your employer contributes the funds.

✔ You accumulate investment earnings in a retirement account.

✔ You roll another retirement account into the plan.

Employee contributions

If your workplace retirement plan is a *contributory plan,* your employer deducts from your paycheque any contributions you're required to make. The total contributions are reported on your T4 tax slip yearly and they're tax deductible.

Employer contributions

Many workplace pension plans have an employer match based on a formula or percentage. For example, perhaps an employer matches 50 cents for each dollar the employee contributes, up to a maximum of 6 percent of the employee's salary. This is free money, and you should take advantage of it. Here are a couple of tips:

✔ If your employer matches contributions, contribute at least as much as needed to get the entire employer match.

✔ Consider contributing enough to receive the match and then funding an RRSP. Continue contributions to the RRSP up to the maximum allowed, if you have enough income.

Investment earnings

The choices your employer made usually limit the investment options in your employer plan. Think of it as your menu. When choosing, consider the following:

✔ Don't put too large of a percentage of your assets into your employer's stock. Every stock you own is subject to company risk, which is compounded when the company is your employer.

✔ Look at your employer plan as part of your total portfolio. Choose plan investments that fit your overall asset allocation and complement investments in your RRSP and other accounts.

✔ Look for investments with low fees and operating expenses. Fees and other costs cut into your return.

Leaving a Company Before Retirement

If you have an employer-sponsored group RRSP, you can simply transfer your funds (including your employer's contributions) into an individual RRSP without tax penalty. Unless you actually cash in the funds, you won't pay tax. But funds held in RPPs are *locked in,* meaning they can't be paid out in a lump sum to you — they must be used to provide a lifetime retirement income. If you're planning to leave a company before retirement, you usually have three options:

✔ Take a pension from that company when you retire.

✔ Roll your RPP money over into your new employer's pension fund.

✔ Transfer your pension money to a Locked-In Retirement Account (LIRA), sometimes known as a Locked-In RRSP. You still can't withdraw that income until you're 50, when you can convert your LIRA into a Locked-In Retirement Income Fund (LRIF), a Life Income Fund (LIF), or an annuity and start receiving a pension. You can only withdraw up to a specified amount each year.

Payments from your RPP are subject to income tax and can be subject to a penalty tax unless they're qualifying distributions. Rules differ from province to province, but usually, you can take qualifying distributions only after about age 55, unless one of the following applies:

✔ Financial hardship

✔ Shortened life expectancy

✔ Non-residency in Canada

✔ The amount in the plan is too small to purchase an annuity; in that case, it may be cashed out or rolled over into an RRSP

You must apply to take early distributions from your plan and be able to back up your claims.

#32

Set Up a Tax-Free Savings Account

Canada Revenue Agency gave us all a little gift recently. As of January 2009, you can shelter up to $5,000 a year in investments in a Tax-Free Savings Account (TFSA). Unlike a Registered Retirement Savings Plan (RRSP), you don't get a tax deduction for the money you invest, nor do you get a government grant on your money, as you do with a Registered Education Savings Plan (RESP). The beauty of the TFSA, however, is that you can withdraw cash as needed — say for a new car, home repairs, or just to get you through a rough patch — and you don't pay a tax penalty.

The Ins and Outs of a TFSA

A government-implemented tax shelter with no rules sounds almost too good to be true. Here's what you need to know about the TFSA:

- ✔ You can start contributing to a TFSA at age 18 — all you need is a Social Insurance Number (SIN).

- ✔ TFSA contribution room accumulates even if you don't open an account. What that means is that, if you don't open an account or make a contribution this year, by next year, you'll have $10,000 in contribution room waiting and so forth.

- ✔ Over-contributions are subject to a penalty tax of 1 percent per month.

- ✔ Eligible investments in a TFSA run the gamut, from daily interest savings accounts to stocks, mutual funds, bonds, GICs, and, in some cases, shares in small business corporations.

- ✔ Income earned in a TFSA, including interest, dividends, or capital gains, isn't taxable.

- ✔ Unlike any other tax-advantaged savings vehicle, you actually recover contribution room the year after you make a withdrawal.

✔ If you die, the fair market value of your TFSA goes into your estate tax free, but any gain or income that builds up afterward is taxable.

✔ You can't currently name a direct beneficiary for a TFSA, but future amendments to provincial laws may allow that.

An All-Purpose Savings and Cash Management Tool

The TFSA is so versatile that you can use it in a number of ways:

✔ **Supplementing tax-sheltered money in RRSPs and Registered Retirement Income Funds (RRIFs):** After you maximize your RRSP and RRIF contributions, you can begin to invest in a TFSA, safe in the knowledge that your earnings will accumulate tax free.

✔ **Saving for your child's education:** After you've maximized the RESP contributions eligible for the 20 percent Canada Education Savings Grant paid by the government, you may well choose to put any additional contributions in a TFSA. If you're really not certain that Junior's headed for higher education, but want to set aside some money for his future anyway, the TFSA beats an RESP hands down.

✔ **Saving for your own education:** Right now, under the RRSP Lifelong Learning Plan, you can withdraw up to $20,000 from your RRSPs spread over four years to fund higher education. However, you have to repay that cash and the RRSP loses the benefit of the growth of those funds. With a TFSA, you could contribute up to $5,000 a year to cover educational expenses and leave the RRSP for retirement savings alone. Just like RRSP money, your TFSA earnings accumulated tax free, and you don't pay a tax penalty when you withdraw the funds. But you have no obligation to pay those funds back within a certain period of time, although you regain the contribution room.

✔ **Accumulating a down payment on a home:** Although the federal government's Home Buyers' Plan (see Tip #30) allows you to withdraw money from you RRSP to buy a home, you have to pay it back within 15 years. That can be tough if you're house poor. With the TFSA, you can withdraw as much as you need and don't have to worry about paying it back.

✓ **Keep an emergency fund:** Although contributions to a TFSA aren't tax-deductible, both earnings and payouts are tax free. If, for instance, your car breaks down and you need cash right away to fix it, you don't have to worry that you're going to trigger additional taxes when you withdraw the funds. What's more, you regain the contribution room the following year.

Incorporate contributions to the TFSA into your budget. The combination of tax-sheltered earnings and flexibility gives you additional options when times are tough.

Comparing TFSAs to Other Registered Investments

Okay, so you've got a limited amount of cash and you're swimming in alphabet soup, torn between making payments to your TFSA, an RESP, or your RRSP. What to do? Table 2-7 displays some of the pros and cons of contributing to each.

Table 2-7	Registered Investment Comparison		
Investment Vehicle	*Tax-Deductible Contributions*	*Tax-Free Earnings*	*Flexibility*
TFSA	No	Yes	Yes
RESP	No, but government grants are available	Yes	Not so much
RRSP	Yes	Yes	Not so much

Just like contributing to a spousal RRSP, you can make contributions for your spouse to a TFSA. You can also contribute for a child or other relative, even a friend, so that they, too, can reach their own annual contribution limit. The income earned on the contribution won't be attributed back to you.

Deciding Whether to Use a TFSA to Save for Retirement

The decision about whether to use an RRSP or a TFSA to save for retirement isn't easy. Read on for two separate scenarios that illustrate some of the factors to consider:

✔ If you expect your income in retirement to be lower than your income while working, use an RRSP as your primary savings vehicle. The main reason is that RRSP contributions are tax deductible. If you live in Alberta and your working wages total more than $38,832, for example, you'd get at least a 32 percent tax refund on your contribution. Assuming that your post-retirement income will be below $38,832, you'd only be paying tax on those earnings at about 25 percent.

✔ If you expect your retirement income to be more than $63,500, however, the decision isn't quite so straightforward. Why? Because that's the income at which Old Age Security is clawed back at a rate of 15 cents on each additional dollar of income. Talk to a financial planner to decide which option is right for you.

Part III

Demystifying Risk: Accumulating and Protecting Wealth

The 5th Wave   By Rich Tennant

Defining your investment risk with the:
TOAST RETRIEVING RISK TOLERANCE TEST

LOW RISK | Waits for toast to pop up even though it's burning.

MODERATE RISK | Goes after toast with wooden toast prongs.

HIGH RISK | Goes after toast with all metal butter knife.

ULTRA HIGH RISK | Goes after toast with metal butter knife wearing a wet swim suit and a stainless steel colander on head.

In this part...

*K*nowledge is comforting. The more you understand investment risks and how to minimize them, the better you're able to design a portfolio that'll allow you to accomplish your goals while sleeping well at night. In this part, you explore the types of financial risks, how to measure your risk-adjusted investment performance and your personal tolerance for risk, and how to design a portfolio that maximizes diversification so you can achieve attractive risk-adjusted returns in any market environment.

Understand Investment Risks

· ·

By Michael Knight, CFP

· ·

Some risks can certainly be avoided; others cannot. The only certainty in investing — and probably in life — is *uncertainty,* and if that scares you a little, you're in good company. Investing involves risk, which means that preparing for long-term goals like retirement can be an adventure. Like a Radisson and Grosseillier expedition — you can't anticipate every step of the way, but you'll reach your destination if you're prepared and you understand the risks of this long and exciting adventure.

With investing, you may think that the only risk involves watching your investments lose their value when the market goes down. However, other risks — emotion, inflation, outliving your assets, taxation, and holding investments that you don't understand — lurk in the shadows. These risks become less scary if you understand them and develop a plan to deal with them.

Emotional Risks

The biggest threat to your financial freedom may be *you.* When the market went through its painful three-year downturn beginning in 2000, many investors decided to run for the exits and then missed out on the solid returns of the next five years. Fear and greed tend to drive markets, and succumbing to either of these powerful emotions is easy. The worst thing that you can do is react to what happened in the market today or yesterday. You need a big windshield and a small rearview mirror.

Take a long-term, disciplined, and consistent approach to investing, and expect some market volatility.

If you know yourself and if you know how you've reacted in the past, you're in a better position to invest in a way that is right for you. Here's what to do:

- ✔ Understand your risk tolerance (see Tip #35).

- ✔ Know that the best plans are based on clear and specific goals. So use a financial advisor to help develop an investment plan that fits your financial and emotional needs.

- ✔ During times of uncertainty, look at your monthly statements, but don't check your investments daily and don't panic. Stick to the plan, Stan!

Threats of Inflation

One reason you invest is to keep pace with inflation and shield yourself from lost purchasing power. When you invest for a long-term goal, such as retirement, you need to think about the impact of inflation over 30 or 40 years.

The longer the time period, the more inflation erodes your buying power. With 4 percent inflation a year, one dollar today will buy just 30 cents worth of goods or services in 30 years. In other words, at an annual 4 percent inflation rate, $100,000 set aside today for retirement will be worth just $30,800 30 years from now. If inflation jumps to 5 percent, your $100,000 will be worth $23,000 in 30 years. Now that's scary.

Another negative effect of inflation is that it reduces the value of long-term bonds as interest rates rise. This includes government bonds that may be backed by the federal government but are subject to a decrease in value when interest rates go up.

Here are some ways to protect yourself from inflation:

- ✔ Remember that the best strategy is to invest for long-term growth and inflation protection with a diversified mixture of stocks and high-quality short-term bonds. For more information, check out Tip #38.

- ✔ Invest in a diversified mix of investments that includes Canadian, U.S., and international stocks.

- ✔ Use high-quality short-term bond funds and high-quality money market accounts when interest rates are rising.

- ✔ To protect against unexpected inflation, invest a small portion of your investments in Government of Canada Real Return Bonds (RRBs). They pay a rate of return that is adjusted for inflation. (Refer to Tip #24 for more information.)

Roller Coaster: Market Volatility

Volatility is a measure of how much a security rises or falls within a short period of time. Low volatility is best because the greater the volatility, the more difficult it is to achieve your goals.

Many investors felt the pain of extreme volatility when the technology bubble burst in 2000. For example, one technology mutual fund, the U.S.-based Janus Venture Fund, fell 60 percent between March 2000 and February 2001. This means that $10,000 invested on March 1, 2000, was worth just $4,000 a year later. Returning to the $10,000 original investment would require a 150 percent gain.

You can reduce the risk of big, volatile swings in the value of your investments through diversification. And because volatility seems to diminish over time, carefully consider how soon you'll need your money when making investment choices. Here are a couple of tips:

- If you'll need a certain amount of cash within the next five years, don't invest it in speculative stocks. Use money market funds, GICs, and high-quality short-term bonds as well as blue-chip dividend-paying preferred shares and balanced mutual funds.

- Avoid concentrated investments in any one company or market sector. This includes your employer's stock, which should be limited to no more than 10 percent of your investments.

The Risk of Outliving Your Money

One of life's greatest uncertainties is how long you'll live. Retire at 65, and you could live 30 years or more without a paycheque and risk depleting your nest egg. Consider a married couple, both age 59 and nonsmokers: A 50 percent chance exists that one of them will live to age 92 and a 30 percent chance exists that one of them will live to age 95.

One of the best strategies is to prepare now for a long retirement by saving more and spending less. Planning ahead and sussing out ways to generate income during retirement is also useful. Understand your current and future cash flow needs.

If your cash flow plan includes a way to separate the expenditures you *need* to make from the ones you *want* to make, you'll be able to adapt to the unexpected. Here's how:

- Expense control is crucial, so find a system for tracking expenses. Personal finance software programs like Quicken or Microsoft Money are good options. You can also use a free budget planner at www.practicalmoneyskills.ca (click on the "Consumers" section and then on "My Budget Planner").

✔ Be careful about withdrawal rates. One rule is that you shouldn't be withdrawing more than 4 percent from your savings and investments during the initial years of your retirement.

✔ Consider a fixed annuity with a portion of your savings, say 25 percent, but wait until you're approaching age 70 to invest in it. (Read Tip #16 to find out more about fixed annuities.)

✔ Delay collecting Canada Pension Plan (CPP) until at least age 65 or even 70 if possible.

✔ Plan ahead so you can generate some income in retirement. A part-time job can keep you fit, involved, and social. It can also take some pressure off your investments.

The Risk of Making Investments You Don't Understand

Investments are sometimes complicated because they're designed to be good for the company selling the product rather than for you. Make sure you research and know what you're buying. Find out what penalties you may face if you want to get your money back.

Understand the compensation policies for salespersons. If you're dealing with investment products sold by banks, investment dealers, mutual fund dealers, or insurance companies, watch out for a potential conflict of interest. The person representing the institution is receiving a salary and/or commissions from guiding you to a short list of products that generate income for the institution. To avoid this risk, follow these tips:

✔ Don't invest in products you don't understand.

✔ Be sure you know how the salesperson or advisor across the table is being paid.

✔ Use a fee-only advisor, if available, who's willing to provide you with a written statement that says that loyalty to you is the top priority.

Sort Through an Investment's Return

By Jean Keener

*E*ver looked at your RRSP statement and wondered, "Is this good?" Or looked at the sales commissions and other fees being charged each time you invest in your mutual fund and thought, "How are these affecting my retirement savings?" Unfortunately, we're betting that as soon as you start thinking about all the percentages, ratios, and math involved in answering these questions, your eyes glaze over, and suddenly tomorrow sounds like a much better time to get answers.

Well, in reality, you deal with return on investment in your daily life. It can be a question of how much effort you'd have to invest to lose 10 pounds. Or whether the time required to cut carrots and put them in baggies for lunches is worth saving the money on pre-assembled snack packs. You make these decisions constantly in a split second based on your priorities, knowledge, and resources of time, money, or energy.

Assessing financial return on investment really isn't much different. Figuring out your returns takes just a couple of minutes. This can mean a better retirement, an awesome vacation, or more money to spend on the things you really care about.

Calculate Your Return

The *return* is how much money you made or lost on an investment. You look at how much you invested and the total amount it's worth now, including dividends and interest. The difference in these amounts is your *profit* — either positive or negative.

Holding period return

Holding period return shows you the return over the entire time you owned the investment, whether that's three months, a year, ten years, or some other time period. Here's the calculation:

> Total value of investment – Money invested = Holding period return

With the holding-period-return formula, don't forget any dividends or other income received from your investment. If you reinvested the income, it's automatically included. If you didn't reinvest, you need to add the income to what your investment is worth now to calculate an accurate return.

After you figure out the dollar amount you made or lost (hopefully made!), you can convert it to a percentage. Percentages allow you to compare different investments regardless of the dollar amount invested in each. Here's how to calculate your percentage return:

> Holding period return ÷ Money invested × 100 = Percentage return

Annualized return

The rubber really meets the road with annualized returns. If a couple buys a house for $100,000 and sells it ten years later for $130,000, they may think they earned a really great return. They made $30,000, or 30 percent, according to the formula in the preceding section. But think about what that actually amounts to each year.

Calculating annualized returns takes more math than calculating holding period returns because of compound interest. Each year, your investment's increase in value is based not only on the original investment amount but also on all the interest or increase in value gained in earlier years. Financial planners use financial calculators to calculate annualized returns; no one does this manually. For the $100,000 house that sees a 30 percent holding period return over ten years, the annualized return comes out to 2.66 percent.

You can eyeball annualized returns with this shortcut:

> Percentage return (of holding period) ÷ Number of years = Ballpark annualized return

With the house example, the annualized return comes out to 3 percent when you use the shortcut method. (Just remember that this shortcut isn't exact.)

You can also use online calculators to get exact annualized return figures. If an online calculator asks for the *present value,* enter the value of the investment at the beginning. *Future value* is the value of the investment at the end. The following Web sites offer some good online calculators:

- **Bank of Canada** (www.bankofcanada.ca): Click on the "Rates and Statistics" tab and then scroll down to the investment calculator under "Related Information."

- **Citizens Bank of Canada** (www.citizensbank.ca): Click on the "Personal" tab and choose "Calculators" for the compound interest calculator.

For other options, type "compound interest calculator, Canada" into your favourite search engine.

Don't forget the effect of expenses when calculating your returns. Here are the most common expenses:

- **Real estate:** Take into account expenses such as commissions and closing costs, property taxes, mortgage interest, and repairs. If you're calculating returns on your primary residence, also take into account that you need a place to live, so you would've been paying rent if you hadn't been paying your mortgage.

- **Mutual funds, stocks, or bonds:** Include any commissions or management fees as part of the initial cost of your investment. If you're not sure whether you're paying commissions, you probably are. Ask for no-load funds if you want to avoid commissions, and be sure you're clear on how your advisor is compensated. Opting for a commissioned advisor? The downloadable disclosure form at www.investorism.com/disclosure.pdf pushes advisors to reveal all sources of income, including front-load or back-end load charges, trailer fees, and transaction and service charges.

Identify Good versus Bad Returns

After you calculate your annualized return, you're ready to determine whether your results are up to par. Three basic factors show you whether your returns are doing their job. The importance of each depends on your personal circumstances.

Achieving your goals

The first question to ask is whether this investment is returning enough to achieve your goals (refer to Tip #11 for info on setting financial goals). When you set a goal to retire in 15 years, you make several assumptions about how much money you'll be saving and what kind of return you'll be earning on your savings. In financial jargon, this is your *required rate of return*. A required rate of return varies by individual, depending on the following:

- The length of time the money will be invested
- Your tolerance for risk
- Other options available to you in terms of investment vehicles

If your investment is meeting your required rate of return, great! If not, you can adjust your goals, look for a better-performing investment, or take on more risk.

Beating the benchmark

How does your investment's return compare to its peers? In some years, a 2 percent return for a particular mutual fund is pretty good. In other years, a 2 percent return for the same mutual fund is terrible. It all depends on what comparable funds did that year.

To accurately compare an investment to its peers, determine the relevant benchmark. You can usually find data on the benchmark and the performance of similar funds on your brokerage's Web site. Here's how to define peers of various investments:

- **Stocks:** Compare with other companies of similar size in the same industry.
- **Bonds:** Compare with other bonds of similar maturity dates and credit ratings.
- **Real estate:** Compare real estate appreciation or depreciation in similar neighbourhoods in the same or other markets. Sites such as The Canadian Real Estate Association at www.crea. ca (see the MLS statistics) and Canada Mortgage and Housing Corporation at www.cmhc.ca are good sources to help you analyze the housing market.

✔ **Mutual funds:** Three industry standard benchmarks are based on the size of company a mutual fund invests in:

- **Large cap:** S&P/TSX 60 Index
- **Mid cap:** S&P/TSX MidCap Index
- **Small cap:** S&P/TSX Venture Composite Index

Look for choices that have consistently performed at or above their benchmark, but beware — don't jump to a fund just because it's had a really terrific year and wildly outperforms its comparison fund. Also, don't automatically dump a fund because of one bad quarter or year. A lot of investors chase returns, but when you do, you have a good chance of buying high and selling low rather than the other way around.

#35

Assess Your Ability to Absorb Losses

By Ben Jennings, CPA/PFS, CFP

*E*very investment exposes you to some type of risk, and the risk that often dominates during uncertain times is shrinking portfolio values — what most people call "losing money." But if you have a well-diversified, long-term portfolio, you should look at declines as temporary. The long-term reality is that you won't lose *all* your money, contrary to what it feels like during volatile markets.

Over time, you'll have investment experiences that differ from your expectations; the real issues are *how much* and *for how long*. If the temporary losses exceed your willingness to maintain your strategy, you're likely to take actions such as abandoning stocks in favour of cash; or you may fail to take actions such as rebalancing the portfolio. Both paths lead to worse long-term investment results than if you had a more stable, less anxiety-producing portfolio in the first place.

Knowing how able and willing you are to maintain your portfolio strategy during downturns is critical. Here are two primary considerations:

- ✔ Making sure your expectations are realistic
- ✔ Knowing what your likely response will be in various scenarios

This tip discusses how to develop realistic expectations and helps you gauge your risk capacity, risk tolerance, and risk requirements.

Line Up Your Expectations with Reality

Suppose you love the ocean, the mountains, the great outdoors, and salmon. You consider moving to Vancouver, but you've heard the rain is awful. You do some research and discover that Vancouver actually gets fewer inches of rain than Toronto in summer. So this means Vancouver's climate is about the same as Toronto's, right? Not so fast! Average rainfall in summer doesn't give the complete picture. To get a realistic view of Vancouver's climate, you have to take a closer look. In winter, the rain in Vancouver seems as if it will never end. You may love living on our West Coast — millions do — but you need to have realistic expectations before moving there.

In a similar way, looking at average returns in the stock market doesn't provide a reliable perspective on actual stock market behaviour. For example, you may know that the average return for the Canadian stock market over the last 30 years has been a little bit above 10 percent. However, since 1980 alone, investors have experienced six *bear markets* — temporary periods of loss for long-term investors.

Investing in stocks and simply expecting a 10 percent average return is like moving to Vancouver and expecting it to be less rainy than Houston: Although it may be technically true, your actual experience will differ. A well-diversified, long-term portfolio often shows declines in particular asset classes as well as overall declines.

Evaluate Your Risk Profile

When you have realistic expectations of market behaviour, you're ready to implement an investment strategy. When determining your portfolio allocations, consider at least three perspectives:

✔ **Risk capacity:** How much risk *should* you take, assuming a worst-case scenario? Take the following into account:

- Your age and how many income-earning years you expect to have left

- Your ability to insure against risks to your financial security

- Your net worth

- Your expenses covered by future incomes not related to investments, such as workplace pensions and Canada Pension Plan

- Your family situation

✔ **Risk tolerance:** How much risk *can* you take? Consider your ability to stick with your investment plan without lying awake at night. Your emotional reaction to volatility is much more of a *trait* (a long-term characteristic) than a *state* (a temporary response). Though your reaction to volatility may change as you gain investing experience, it's also related to how you're wired.

Free online questionnaires from mutual fund companies and investment dealers can help you assess this aspect of your personality. Alternatively, an Australian company, FinaMetrica, offers two Web-based assessments for a fee (www.myrisktolerance.com).

✔ **Risk required:** How much risk *must* you take? The answer depends on your goals and objectives and on how much time you have to achieve them. Remember, your objective isn't necessarily to earn the highest return but rather to have the greatest likelihood of accomplishing your goals. It makes no sense to tolerate more risk and volatility than necessary simply for the sake of potentially higher returns. Strive to plan for enough — not more — and your investments won't cause sleepless nights.

These three perspectives together make up your risk profile. Base your portfolio design on the lowest level of volatility that these three elements indicate.

In an uncertain economy, your ability to absorb losses should be driven by you and your comfort levels rather than by some product-pushing investment salesperson. Avoid their fancy charts used to convince you that the only way to achieve your goals is to crank up your risk tolerance. The investment world has many more safe investments available than risky investments — believe it or not. Choose what's right for you and your own risk tolerance.

Create a Portfolio You Can Grow and Consume

By Katherine Holden, ChFC, CFP

Creating a financial portfolio may feel daunting. A portfolio that's designed for both growing and withdrawing funds at the same time is challenging to build, but certainly possible. The key is to divide your portfolio into sections that are dependent on when you'll need the funds.

Develop Goals with Varying Time Periods

Investment goals are generally either short-term or long-term. For short-term goals, you save and invest money to be used within one to five years. That means you need to grow your savings, but you also need to protect what you're putting away because you'll need to spend it soon. Your investment choices should be less risky in this case.

Longer-term goals may be 10 or 30 years in the future, so you'll be setting aside money regularly, growing it, and then using it either all at once or over time. Your goal may be to save a sizeable down payment to buy a home; you'll use all your savings at one time in this scenario. You may choose to assume a higher level of risk because you have more time to reach your goal. But the closer you get to your goal, the less risk you want to take.

Perhaps your goal is to sock away money for the kids' university or college education. If so, you'll be saving over 18 to 22 years if you start at the birth of each child, and you'll likely spend those savings over four to ten years (depending on how many children you have).

Create the Portfolios

This tip offers four examples of short-term versus long-term goals to show you how investment choices may vary. Suppose you want to purchase a refrigerator, buy a car, save for a home, and fund a two-year trip around the world in 20 years. The time horizon you set for reaching each goal determines how you invest.

Start with a list of the items you want to purchase or fund and prioritize them. These are your goals. Prioritizing your goals helps you decide which goals to fund and which ones to put on the back burner during tough financial times.

Think about each goal's cost and your time frame for each. You may

- ✔ Use one account to save for all four goals.
- ✔ Use several accounts based on the time to complete your goals.
- ✔ Use separate accounts for each goal.

Consider the account and transaction fees that your investment dealer or bank charges. Using one account for all four goals may make it confusing to track which investments are linked to each goal.

Goal #1: Save $1,200 for a fridge in a year

For money you need soon, choose the savings vehicle carefully. Avoid stocks! If the stock market tanks, you won't have the funds you need for the purchase.

Consider a Canada Deposit Insurance Corporation (CDIC) insured account, such as a savings or money market account, at a bank or credit union. Accounts are insured up to $100,000 per depositor; individual and joint accounts are insured separately. Or you can use a money market mutual fund, which isn't insured (refer to Tip #14 for more information). To compare interest rates, you can pay one dollar for a real-time report at www.cannex.com.

If the refrigerator you want to buy in a year currently costs $1,200, how much should you save per month? Here's how it breaks down:

Ultra-Short-Term Savings

You need $1,248 ($1,200 adjusted for one year of inflation at 4 percent).

Save $100/month (assuming a return of 3 percent).

You're primarily saving for the fridge out of current income while earning just a small return on your savings. But your focus is on preserving your cash because you'll be using it up on this purchase.

Goal #2: Save $5,000 for a deposit on a car in three years

Because you don't need the money for your car for three years, you may be willing to accept a slight risk, although a higher return isn't guaranteed. After evaluating the current bond market, you could invest in a short-term high-quality bond mutual fund for the first two years. Then transfer your savings and contributions to a money market fund for the last 12 months. How much should you save per month?

Short-Term Savings

You need $5,624 ($5,000 adjusted for three years inflation at 4 percent).

Save $138/month (assuming a return of 4.45 percent compounded monthly).

Set up an automatic withdrawal from your chequing account into your car account. Doing so saves you time and ensures you put that cash away every month.

You're still funding most of the car down payment from current income, but you're also aiming for a bit of growth by accepting a small amount of risk. If economic uncertainty creeps in, you may want to transfer your savings to a money market account sooner.

Goal #3: Save $60,000 for a down payment on a home in ten years

Because the time period in this home example is longer than in the previous examples, you can take on more risk with diversified investments in large- and small-cap value equities, international equities (developed countries), short- and intermediate-term high-quality bonds, and real estate mutual funds. Be sure to diversify rather than limit yourself to one or two holdings.

Long-Term Savings

You need $88,815 ($60,000 adjusted for ten years of inflation at 4 percent).

Save $406/month (assuming a diversified portfolio with approximately 50 percent equity and 50 percent fixed income with an average annual rate of return of 8 percent).

As with the first two goals, you'll use all your savings at one time when making the down payment. So you may choose to get more conservative with your investment choices when you're two to three years away from your goal. Monitor economic forecasts regularly so you can move into a more conservative allocation if things become more uncertain.

Consider using the Home Buyers' Plan option with your RRSP (see Tip #30), which will shelter $20.000 of your down payment savings. Also, consider investing in a Tax-Free Savings Account (see Tip #32), which can shelter $50,000 of your $60,000 over ten years.

Goal #4: Save $300,000 for a two-year world trip in 20 years

Because you won't need the funds in this world-trip example for 20 years, you can assume even more risk. Opt for a diversified portfolio of large- and small-cap value and growth equities, international equities (developed countries), short- and intermediate-term investment-grade and government bonds, and Real Estate Investment Trust (REIT) funds.

Extra-Long-Term Savings

You need $657,337 ($300,000 adjusted for 20 years of inflation at 4 percent).

Save $755/month (assuming a diversified portfolio with approximately 60 percent equity and 40 percent fixed income with an average annual rate of return of 9 percent).

This goal differs from the first three because you'll be using your savings over two years to fund your travel and living expenses. As with Goal #3, you may opt for a more conservative allocation when you're within a couple of years of your trip. When you're consuming your savings, continue to pursue a conservative amount of growth and keep a certain percentage of your portfolio available as cash. Because this goal covers 20 years, you can be almost certain you'll experience economic ups and downs. Regularly track what's happening with the economy. Good, sound investing practices can help you ride out the down periods.

Altogether, the examples show setting aside $1,399 each month for the first year. As you achieve each goal, the monthly savings you need drop, allowing for additional goals.

#37

Allocate Your Assets to Minimize Risk

By Deidra Fulton, CFP

Building a portfolio is like cooking: You start with several basic ingredients, and the way you combine them can lead to something delicious or an inedible mess. You may use all your ingredients or only a few. Or you may use most of them but in varying amounts. This tip describes how to best allocate your assets for the most appetizing result: maximum returns with minimum risk.

Combine Asset Classes

Multiple asset classes in your portfolio can improve returns and decrease volatility. Large-cap Canadian stocks, real estate, and bonds are a few examples of different asset classes.

Keep these ideas about asset classes in mind:

- ✔ Different asset classes perform differently during the same time period. When large-cap stocks are performing poorly, performance results from bonds are sometimes stellar.

- ✔ You can't predict the best- and worst-performing asset class. Investment results are unpredictable — as is life! Over the last 30 years, all asset classes have had their day and then some.

- ✔ Combining multiple asset classes can help reduce risk within a portfolio; however, you can't totally eliminate risk. Losses do occur occasionally. The goal for a well-diversified portfolio is that losses be small and infrequent.

If you diversify by investing across multiple asset classes, you needn't worry about which asset class is the best performer this week or this month. The following tips help you to get the best combination.

Look for low correlation

Good investors seek asset classes with low correlation to each other. *Correlation* is a measure of the relationship, if any, between the returns of different asset classes. If they move in the same direction, they're positively correlated; asset classes that move in opposite directions are negatively correlated.

In Table 3-1, the higher the number, the stronger the correlation. You can see from this table that large-cap stocks are most closely correlated with small-cap stocks, because they generally move in the same market direction. Although the data comes from the United States, Canada shows similar patterns of correlation.

Note that large-cap stocks are positively correlated with every other asset category in Table 3-1. However, this isn't the case with all other asset classes. For example, international stocks and small-cap stocks are negatively correlated with intermediate government bonds and treasury bills, though in varying degrees.

Using combinations of asset classes that have low or negative correlation with most other holdings within a portfolio can improve performance and reduce volatility.

Watch out for asset class volatility

Some asset classes are more volatile than others. Their potential for higher returns can be appealing, yet those higher returns also bring greater potential for major losses. Think of this cooking metaphor: A little chili pepper can add a wonderful taste, but too much can ruin the dish. With investing, use the more volatile asset classes sparingly.

Table 3-1	Correlations of Historical Annual Returns (1970–2006)							
	Equity REITs	Internat'l Stocks	Large-Cap Stocks	Small-Cap Stocks	Long-Term Corp. Bonds	Long-Term Gov't Bonds	Intermed.-Term Gov't Bonds	Treasury Bills
Equity REITs (real estate)	1.00	0.31	0.46	0.75	0.26	0.18	0.13	0.08
Internat'l stocks	0.31	1.00	0.59	0.41	0.08	0.06	–0.07	0.13
Large-cap stocks	0.46	0.59	1.00	0.66	0.33	0.27	0.20	0.04
Small-cap stocks	0.75	0.41	0.66	1.00	0.13	0.4	–0.01	–0.02
Long-term corp. bonds	0.26	0.08	0.33	0.13	1.00	0.95	0.91	0.01
Long-term gov't bonds	0.18	0.06	0.27	0.04	0.95	1.00	0.91	0.04
Intermed.-term gov't bonds	0.13	–0.07	0.20	–0.01	0.91	0.91	1.00	0.31
Treasury bills	–0.08	–0.13	004	–0.02	0.01	0.04	0.31	1.00

Source: Stocks, Bonds, Bills and Inflation 2007 Classic Edition Yearbook by Morningstar, Inc.

Consider your time horizon

Generally, the shorter the time horizon, the more conservative the investments should be because you have less time to recover from a market downturn. For example, if your son will be entering university or college in two years and you've saved $50,000 for post-secondary education, you should keep the majority of that $50,000 in less volatile holdings, such as cash or bonds.

If you leave the majority of the $50,000 in aggressive stock holdings, your risk is much greater because your funds are subject to much higher volatility and declining values during that two-year period. The value of the funds could decrease just at the time you need the money.

#38

Rebalance Your Asset Allocation

By Deidra Fulton, CFP

Rebalancing is the process of modifying investments that have changed in value to keep your target investment weightings on track. In its simplest form, rebalancing involves selling some of the holdings in asset classes that have become overweighted and using the money you free up to buy additional holdings in under-weighted categories.

Reasons to Rebalance

Asset classes perform differently over given time periods, just as do individual investments. When the economy is purring along nicely and credit is easily attainable, smaller and mid-sized capitalized companies may perform especially well. Large-cap companies — with their stronger balance sheets and greater diversification — may have an edge during periods with tighter credit and greater economic uncertainty. Bonds may hold a distinct advantage during recessionary periods. And international stocks may have an edge during periods when the domestic economy is under pressure.

Consider rebalancing for the following reasons:

- ✔ **Distorted allocations:** The asset allocations you initially decided on may become distorted over time and need occasional adjustments.

- ✔ **Risk:** Balanced diversification can help minimize risk. Although letting a high flyer remain unbridled is tempting, you'll be increasing your risk in the long run.

- ✔ **Improved returns over time:** Rebalancing helps level out the major ups and downs in your portfolio and improve returns over time.

You can choose one of several criteria as a standard for rebalancing:

- ✔ **Time period:** This method uses some predetermined interval of the calendar as the trigger for rebalancing, typically quarterly, semiannually, or annually. Asset class allocations are adjusted back to the original target weightings at the predetermined time.

- ✔ **Absolute percentage weighting:** This method uses a simple standard for making future changes: Rebalance at any point in the future when the actual asset class weightings have shifted from the original target allocations. The only problem is that this method may have you almost constantly rebalancing your holdings — not to mention paying higher trading costs — due to the continual movement of markets as a whole.

- ✔ **Tolerance window range:** This method allows for some judgment in deciding whether to rebalance. For example, you may have a threshold of 3 percent as your criteria for a tolerance window. If the weighting is more than 3 percent above or below your target weighting, you rebalance.

- ✔ **Combination:** For example, you can combine both a percentage tolerance window and an annual calendar interval. In that case, you may rebalance once a year if any holding is more than 3 percent off the original target.

Ways to Rebalance

No single correct approach for rebalancing exists. Regardless of the rebalancing method you use, you should regularly review and adjust your portfolio's asset allocations to stay diversified and reduce risk. Here are some common methods:

- ✔ **Sell and purchase:** Sell your overweighted investments and purchase underweighted ones.

- ✔ **Withdraw or invest:** Take regular withdrawals from overweighted categories or direct future investments to underweighted asset classes.

- ✔ **Redirect:** Redirect payouts, such as dividends or capital gains distributions, from holdings in overweighted asset classes to investments in underweighted asset categories.

During an uncertain economy, thinking about rebalancing may be even more difficult. Your gut instinct may be to cut and run. But to make money in the long term, sticking to the discipline is crucial. When the stock market is falling rapidly, selling bonds and buying stocks may just be the right thing to do because, suddenly, your portfolio is more heavily weighted in bonds, and stocks are relatively cheap. Conversely, when the stock market is soaring, you may sell off some of your winners and buy bonds. Remember the old adage: Buy low and sell high. Sticking to the rebalancing discipline can help you accumulate wealth and keep it.

An Example of Rebalancing in Action

This section presents an example of rebalancing. Suppose your target asset class allocations are the following:

✔ **Large-cap stocks:** 30 percent

✔ **Small-cap stocks:** 15 percent

✔ **International stocks:** 25 percent

✔ **Long-term government bonds:** 5 percent

✔ **Intermediate-term government bonds:** 10 percent

✔ **Treasury bills:** 15 percent

Assume you invested $100,000 at the beginning of 2005 and you rebalance annually, using a 3 percent tolerance window. Table 3-2 shows your original asset category weightings and the amounts invested by asset class.

Table 3-2	Original Investments by Asset Class (Start of 2005)	
Asset Class	**Target Weighting**	**Amount Invested**
Large-cap stocks	30%	$30,000
Small-cap stocks	15%	$15,000
International stocks	25%	$25,000
Long-term government bonds	5%	$5,000
Intermediate-term government bonds	10%	$10,000
Treasury bills	15%	$15,000

Table 3-3 shows the original amounts invested, returns for the year, the amounts invested by asset class at the end of 2005, the end weightings, and the original target weightings. Although weightings have changed, no category exceeds the 3 percent tolerance window, and no rebalancing is needed.

Table 3-3 **Returns at the End of 2005**

Asset Class	Beginning Amount Invested	Returns by Asset Class	Ending Amount Invested	Ending Asset Class Weightings	Target Weighting	Adjustment Needed with 3% Window
Large-cap stocks	$30,000	4.9%	$31,470	29%	30%	0
Small-cap stocks	$15,000	5.7%	$15,855	15%	15%	0
International stocks	$25,000	14%	$28,500	27%	25%	0
Long-term government bonds	$5,000	7.8%	$5,390	5%	5%	0
Intermediate-term government bonds	$10,000	1.4%	$10,140	9%	10%	0
Treasury bills	$15,000	3.0%	$15,450	14%	15%	0
Total	$100,000		$106,805	100%	100%	

Table 3-4 shows the year-end results following 2006.

Table 3-4			Returns at the End of 2006				
Asset Class	Beginning Amount Invested	Returns by Asset Class	Ending Amount Invested	Ending Asset Class Weighting	Target Weighting	Adjustment Needed with 3% Window*	
Large-cap stocks	$31,470	15.8%	$36,442	30%	30%	0	
Small-cap stocks	$15,855	16.2%	$18,424	15%	15%	0	
International stocks	$28,500	26.9%	$36,167	29%	25%	–4	
Long-term government bonds	$5,390	1.2%	$5,455	4%	5%	1	
Intermediate-term government bonds	$10,140	3.1%	$10,454	8%	10%	2	
Treasury bills	$15,450	4.8%	$16,192	13%	15%	2	
Total	$106,805		$123,134	100%	100%		

* Applied to target asset class weighting for revised total portfolio value. Note that international stocks are now beyond the 3 percent tolerance window and have triggered the need for rebalancing. Notice further that three other asset classes are below their respective targets.

To rebalance, you sell international stocks and purchase intermediate government bonds and Government of Canada treasury bills. Table 3-5 shows the updated portfolio.

Table 3-5	Your Rebalanced Portfolio					
Asset Class	**Ending Dollar Amount 2006**	**Adjustment Needed with 3% Window***	**Adjustment (Dollars)**	**Revised Amount Invested**	**Revised Weighting after Rebalancing**	**Target Weighting**
Large-cap stocks	$36,442	0.0%	$0	$36,442	30%	30%
Small-cap stocks	$18,424	0.0%	$0	$18,424	15%	15%
International stocks	$36,167	–4.0%	–$5,384	$30,783	25%	25%
Long-term government bonds	$5,455	0.0%	$0	$5,455	4%	5%
Intermediate-term government bonds	$10,454	2.0%	$2,692	$13,146	11%	10%
Treasury bills	$16,192	2.0%	$2,692	$18,884	15%	15%
Total	$123,134			$123,134	100%	100%

* Applied to target asset class weighting for revised total portfolio value.

#39

Diversify Your Stock Portfolio by Size

By David McPherson

You can break down stocks into an almost endless number of categories. You can find growth stocks and value stocks, blue chips, industrials, and financials. The list goes on and on. But the basic starting point is market capitalization, or size; that is, how much is a company worth? How big is it?

Using the market-capitalization measure, stocks are categorized into three broad groups: large caps, mid caps, and small caps. These terms frequently appear in the names of mutual funds that focus on specific segments of the stock market.

This tip deals with one of the best ways to ease the uncertainty of investing in good times and bad: being sure your portfolio includes portions of large caps, mid caps, and small caps. This type of diversification can help you capture the strong performance in one category and offset the declines in another. For most individual investors, the best way to diversify by cap size is through mutual funds or exchange-traded funds (ETFs) rather than individual stocks. (Refer to Tip #18 for info on mutual funds; Tip #20 discusses ETFs.)

Know the Market Cap Categories

The *market-capitalization* measure that people use to categorize stocks as large caps, mid caps, or small caps is a simple calculation that multiplies the number of outstanding shares in a company by the price of a single share. For example, a company with 100 million shares worth $10 each has a market capitalization of $1 billion.

In defining market cap categories, different institutions use different standards that can change with market conditions. But in general, sizes are defined in the following manner:

- **Large cap:** These stocks represent the largest companies trading on the market. In Canada, they usually feature companies with market capitalization of $1 billion or more. In the United States, large cap is generally defined as having market cap of more than $5 billion. Examples include some of the best-known companies in North America, such as Rogers Communications, Research in Motion, General Electric, and Bank of America. They also include lesser-known companies such as Potash Corp., a Saskatchewan-based commercial producer of nitrogen, phosphate, and potash, and Avery Dennison Corp., a U.S.-based label maker. This category accounts for about three-quarters of the overall stock market in terms of value.

- **Mid cap:** This category encompasses stocks that fall within a market capitalization range of $500 million to $1 billion in Canada, or $1 billion to $5 billion in the United States. Though considered medium-sized by the market, a number of fairly well-known companies such as Laurentian Bank and CGI Group in Canada, and American Eagle Outfitters, and Netflix, Inc., in the United States, are mid caps.

- **Small cap:** This group encompasses publicly traded companies with market capitalizations of less than $500 million in Canada, or $1 billion in the United States. Though they account for only about 10 percent of the stock market in dollar value, small caps make up the majority of publicly traded companies in North America. You may recognize a few of the names on this list — they include Cogeco Cable, Inc., and Sierra Wireless, Inc., in Canada, and U.S. companies such as Kosan Biosciences, Inc., and Illumina, Inc.

- A subcategory of small caps known as *micro caps* makes up the smallest of the small in terms of market capitalization. The definition of a micro cap varies widely, with some people starting at a market capitalization of $250 million or less. Others use a $100 million starting point. Either way, these are the riskiest of stocks and most individual investors should avoid them. Many micro caps qualify as *penny stocks* because their shares regularly trade for less than one dollar.

Get the Right Mix in Your Portfolio

Different types of investors may be drawn to one category over another based on the traits of large caps, mid caps, and small caps, particularly in times of market turmoil. Table 3-6 shows how the stock categories compare.

Table 3-6		Comparing Large-, Mid-, and Small-Cap Stocks		
Size	*Makeup*	*Returns*	*Dividends*	*Ideal For*
Large caps	Older and better-established companies; in difficult times, they stand a better chance of surviving than young upstart companies	Less risk for investors also means less potential for future growth. The chances of seeing a stock price double or triple in a short period aren't great.	They typically feature higher dividend payments than mid caps or small caps, which can make large caps particularly appealing during periods of uncertainty.	Those who want the inflation-beating returns of stocks without taking on too much risk
Mid caps	Both companies on the way up and those unlikely to grow any larger	Though less risky than small caps, mid caps over the last ten years have delivered higher average annual returns.	They tend to pay investors little, if anything, in the way of dividends.	Investors who seek higher growth potential but can't stomach the volatility inherent in small caps
Small caps	Less-established companies that contain tremendous growth potential but also run a higher risk of failure	Historically, this category has featured the highest returns in exchange for higher degrees of volatility.	They tend to pay little, if anything, in the way of dividends; they may not have enough cash to go around, or the companies are hoarding it to finance growth.	Investors with appetites for risk who plan to buy into this category after prices fall and are ready to hold for the long haul

Under most circumstances, you should own a little bit of each category to counter the uncertainty of money and markets. The right mix of large caps, mid caps, and small caps depends on your risk tolerance, goals, and circumstances. Traditional asset allocation models call for higher portions of large caps and smaller portions of mid and small caps. Aggressive investors who seek higher returns and can withstand the volatility may want to allocate larger shares to mid caps and small caps.

Keep Trading Costs in Mind

When you're diversifying your stock portfolio by market capitalization, carefully consider the variable trading costs of large cap, mid cap, and small cap mutual funds. Often, your fund's *management expense ratio* (MER), which is the fee charged for managing the fund, pales next to its trading cost, which isn't even included in the MER.

As a rule, small-cap funds tend to have much higher trading costs than large-cap funds. In fact, one study in *The Journal of Investment Consulting* found an average trading cost of 0.65 percent for large-cap value funds, compared to a 3.12 percent cost for a small-cap growth fund.

The reason? Small-cap stocks are less liquid than large-cap stocks, meaning they trade less frequently and with lower volumes. Sometimes even a relatively small buy or sell order by your fund manager can cause a substantial blip in the stock price before the trade is complete, resulting in higher acquisition costs or lower proceeds from a sale.

#40

Diversify Your Stock Portfolio by Valuation

By David Anderson, CFA

In uncertain times, which is better — growth investing or value investing? Everyone agrees that the purchase price of an investment ought to represent good value; that is, the anticipated return should justify the risk. Unfortunately, *good value* doesn't have a universal definition; it becomes obvious only after the fact.

Undaunted, the intrepid consultants divide the universe of investment managers into three style categories: value, growth, and a combination of the two labeled *blend* or *core.* This tip explains how value and growth investing compare and advises you on how to protect yourself from manic changes in the market.

Value versus Growth: Taking Lessons from History

So what's the difference between value and growth investors?

- ✔ **Value investors generally look backward at history.** They study financial statements to estimate an intrinsic value of a stock and compare it to the current price. If the current price is significantly lower than the estimated intrinsic value, the value investor purchases the stock. He anticipates that other investors will recognize the disparity and *their* purchases will drive up the market price so that it equals or exceeds the estimated intrinsic value. The fly in the ointment is getting everyone to agree on the definition of *intrinsic value.*

- ✔ **Growth investors look forward.** They operate on the assumption that companies growing at above-average rates will provide above-average returns. Generally, the higher the anticipated growth rate, the more investors are willing to pay. The fly in their ointment is that the companies in which they invest don't always achieve the expected growth rate. Lower growth translates to a steady or — much worse — falling stock price.

> A growth investor's most disconcerting moment is discover-
> ing that a stock declined 10 percent in one day because the
> company's earnings missed analysts' forecasts by 5 cents.
> Wiping out 10 percent of the market value for such a minor
> shortfall seems awfully excessive. However, the strong
> reaction suggests that investors believe the company's
> growth rate has hit a turning point and will begin to slow.

A value stock's earnings typically fluctuate with the economy;
these stocks tend to do well when the economy is accelerating out
of a recession. Growth stocks are expected to be impervious to
economic fluctuations. However, what makes economic sense can
be trumped by the market's propensity for manias. Read on.

Growth manias

The stock market's mantra is "anything worth doing is worth
overdoing," and growth versus value is no exception. In the
uncertain times of the last 40 years, growth-stock investing has
twice been taken to extremes. In the early 1970s, the market
became enamoured with *one-decision stocks:* American multinational companies such as IBM, Xerox, and Polaroid were projected
to grow at above-average rates indefinitely, and analysts believed
that stock valuation was irrelevant. Investors merely had to
purchase and hold. Of course, they were blindsided by the 1970s
inflation that drove up expenses faster than revenues. Rather than
growing, profits declined and so did stock prices, as much as 80 to
90 percent in many cases.

A similar occurrence involved one-time stock market darling
Nortel Networks, which made up about 35 percent of the weight
of the TSE 300 at one point. Investors were happy to ignore
Nortel's impossibly rich valuation and focus on its past record of
impressive, sustained growth. The result was a stock price that
peaked at a ridiculously high $124 in 2000. Just a year later,
Nortel's stock had plummeted to $20, largely because the company
couldn't sustain enough financial growth to justify its valuation.
What's more, in Canada at least, the Nortel debacle spearheaded
a downward trend that affected the whole high-tech and bio-tech
growth sector. During this aptly namely "dot-bomb," many
companies saw price declines of 80 to 90 percent. (At the time of
publication, Nortel declared bankruptcy!)

Value manias

Value stocks aren't immune to manias. The value sector contains
a large percentage of bank and financial services stocks. The
inflation of the 1970s generated a lot of real estate lending by U.S.

banks and savings and loans. However, when the United States Congress shortened the real estate depreciation schedules in 1986, many real estate projects became untenable. Stock prices of major banks declined as much as 75 percent from 1989 to 1990.

Because value-oriented stocks sat out the growth stock mania of the late 1990s, they didn't have major gains to surrender in the bear market of 2000 to 2002. However, they made up for it by funding the U.S. mania in housing prices from 2004 to 2007. After the marginal buyers were sucked in with teaser adjustable-rate mortgages, no one was left to buy. Supply overwhelmed demand, which in turn started the decline in home prices. Financial panic ensued when bonds backed by shaky mortgages turned bad as housing prices declined. Again, stock prices fell dramatically.

However, one segment of the value-oriented universe did extremely well through the housing debacle of 2007 to 2008. Energy and commodity prices soared beyond anyone's wildest expectations, providing a boon to Canada. Ten years ago, the price of oil was scraping US$10 per barrel. The low prices of the late 1990s caused oil companies to de-emphasize finding new energy sources because of the low return on investment. But as demand from emerging nations such as China and India increased, supply couldn't keep up with demand, and energy and commodity prices skyrocketed along with their stock. But high energy prices sow the seeds of their own decline. More recently, the economic dislocations caused by higher energy prices overwhelmed the growth in demand for energy, and prices declined.

Find the Right Balance and Avoid Manias

Should you invest in growth funds or value funds in uncertain times? Fortunately, you don't have to choose one over the other. Managing your portfolio can be a matter of shifting the emphasis as you participate in growth and value funds as well as blended funds:

- ✔ Emphasize growth funds when economic growth is slowing.

- ✔ Emphasize value funds when the economy begins to accelerate. These periods are usually accompanied by a steep yield curve, when short-term interest rates are much lower than long-term rates. Banks are a large component of the value sector, so a steep yield curve usually precedes higher bank profits.

How do you approach the value-growth question and protect yourself from manias? Here are some guidelines:

- ✔ **When purchasing either kind of fund, examine how well the current portfolio manager navigated debacles of the past.** Keep in mind, however, that past performance doesn't guarantee future results.

- ✔ **Don't believe the hype.** Use common sense. Investment management is a closed world, and managers feed off of one another. When an investment theme looks extreme, head for the exits; if it looks too good to be true, it probably is.

- ✔ **Read a mutual fund's annual and semiannual reports to get a sense of the fund management's thinking.** Watch out for language that echoes some of the more hyperbolic language used by the talking heads on the business news channels.

- ✔ **Examine a fund's holdings for style drift.** In the late 1990s, value managers suffered because their funds were dramatically underperforming their growth counterparts. In desperation, value managers added growth stocks to improve performance. Unfortunately, many did this at the market peak, which caused their value funds to decline like a growth fund in the following bear market. Value funds that remained true to their style performed much better in the bear market of 2000 to 2002.

In all cases, develop your own investment policy with a target asset mix based on your tolerance for risk (refer to Tip #35 for information on assessing your risk tolerance). Rebalance your portfolio when asset-class weightings experience significant gains and declines. The decision to emphasize growth or value stocks or funds should be only a nuance in your long-term strategy of diversification that matches your investing goals with your risk tolerance.

#41

Diversify Your Stock Portfolio by Country

By Corry Sheffler, MBA, CFP, CFE

Today's investment world isn't the same as it was for your parents. You live in a global economy, as reflected in your investment options.

Domestic markets are the equity and bond investments in your own country, and *foreign markets* are all the equity and bond investments outside your country. This tip offers a number of ways to diversify your investment portfolio with foreign markets.

Get Your Feet Wet in Foreign Waters

A global portfolio is a more diversified portfolio, so over time, it tempers your overall volatility. Being globally diversified in troubled economic times is especially important, because Canada makes up only about 3 percent of the global equities market. When the Canadian market is struggling, other markets may perform better. For example, while Canadian stocks logged anemic performances in the 1990s, stock prices in China, Poland, Russia, and, to a lesser extent, the United States, soared. Portfolios that lacked foreign stocks often lagged behind those that were more international. Diversification and rebalancing are the perfect ways to ensure that, on average, you're buying low and selling high.

Here are several ways to gain exposure to countries outside Canada:

- ✔ Invest in multinational Canadian companies.
- ✔ Invest directly in the stocks of foreign countries.
- ✔ Buy mutual funds that invest in foreign stocks.
- ✔ Buy exchange-traded funds (ETFs) that specialize in U.S. or international markets. (For info on ETFs, refer to Tip #20.)

✔ Buy global funds that invest in domestic Canadian as well as international equities and bonds.

 For most people, investing in these markets through mutual funds and ETFs is best. If you don't have the time to research your mutual funds, consider hiring a fee-only financial planner to help you decide — or rely entirely on index funds. Also refer to Tip #37 for more on tempering risk.

Decide How Much to Invest

How much of your investment portfolio should be in non-Canadian equities? To make this decision, do the following:

✔ Determine what portion of your total portfolio should be in equities in general.

✔ Determine your personal risk tolerance.

✔ Accept that by investing in foreign markets, you'll be taking on more short-term risk.

✔ Realize that you're taking on some currency risk because the total return on foreign investments includes not only the underlying investment but also the foreign currency exchange gains or losses during the investment holding period.

 For the stock portion of your portfolio, experts vary in their opinions on how much of your investments should be domestic or foreign. Still, depending on your stage in life, a good rule is to invest between 20 and 30 percent of your portfolio in non-Canadian equities.

Diversify within Your Foreign Allocation

Just as in your domestic investments, you want to have the appropriate allocations between large-cap, mid-cap, and small-cap investments. Here are a variety of ways to go:

✔ Invest in funds that specialize in an individual country, such as the United States, China, or Japan.

✔ Invest in funds that specialize in regions like Latin America or Europe, Australasia, and the Far East (EAFE). (***Note:*** *Australasi*a includes Australia and New Zealand.)

✔ Invest in an investment fund or ETF that captures a good part of foreign markets, such as the S&P 500, or a total market index.

In foreign markets, investing in both developed and emerging markets is also important. Think of this as the difference between domestic large-cap and small-cap stocks:

✔ **Developed markets:** Like large-cap domestic stocks, developed markets are more established than emerging markets. Developed markets are considered less risky than emerging markets. Examples include the United States, Germany, Japan, and the United Kingdom.

✔ **Emerging markets:** Emerging markets are more like the rapid-growth domestic small-cap stocks. Emerging market stocks are newer to the global investing scene. Examples include Mexico, South Korea, and Taiwan.

Make the bulk of your foreign investments in developed markets, with a small percentage, perhaps 2 to 5 percent, in emerging markets. Like country-specific or regional markets, you can buy developed and emerging market stocks individually, through mutual funds, or through ETFs.

As a rule, avoid foreign funds that invest in just one country. The lack of diversification may defeat the whole purpose of investing internationally.

Diversify Your Portfolio by Industry

By Robert Friedland, PhD

When buying a share in a company, you buy into a particular industry. For a well-diversified stock portfolio, consider not only the size, valuation, and geographical coverage of the companies (refer to Tips #39, #40, and #41) but also the industries. A portfolio of large- and small-cap firms allocated nicely between growth and value stocks in the same industry does little to diversify a portfolio. Predicting which industries will best weather an economic storm is nearly impossible, so the best long-term strategy is a portfolio broadly diversified across industries.

Industry: A Concept of Shared Risks

An industry reflects the collection of businesses that make up a particular sector of the economy. The sector includes competitors of the firm in which you own stock and many related companies, such as companies that sell to and buy from the company whose stock you own.

An industry reflects a group of different businesses whose financial fortune or demise is likely linked. These links may be in shared labour markets, related regulations, a common purpose, or a shared technology. Hence, changes in technology, government regulations, or the marketplace may fundamentally change the business of the company you own.

Understand the Industry Life Cycle

Industries, as well as the firms in them, evolve and change. Major evolutionary leaps are often marked by a technological or scientific advancement. Rapid growth within the industry often follows.

Eventually, industry-wide growth may decline. Finally, the industry reaches a period of maturity and sometimes overall decline. Of course, firms enter the industry at different stages in the life cycle, so considerable diversification of size and valuation among different firms in the same industry can exist.

Products of some industries are vulnerable to the normal movements of the overall economy. Industries that move in the same direction with the economy are considered *cyclical.* Industries that move in the opposite direction are considered *countercyclical.* The extent to which an industry is cyclical or countercyclical creates a relationship between the stock price and the business cycle.

Use Sector Funds to Add Exposure to an Industry

Adding exposure to a particular industry sector is easier than ever. By purchasing either a mutual fund or an exchange-traded fund (ETF) that focuses on a specific sector (refer to Tips #18 and #20), you gain concentrated exposure to an industry through one investment. Often called *sector funds, specialty funds,* or *single industry funds,* they provide a cost-efficient and effective avenue for buying a large number of companies within a specific industry. Purchasing or selling sector funds enables someone with an already diversified portfolio to quickly add or reduce exposure to a specific sector.

Sector funds alone aren't well-diversified investments. A single event affecting the industry may quickly decrease the value of the sector fund. However, the volatility of a sector fund is likely to be less than the volatility of just one or two companies in that industry sector.

Know How Sectors Fit into the Economic Cycle

The inevitable contractions in the economy result in job loss and fear of job loss for many people. Fortunately, an expansion follows every contraction, which means new jobs, less fear of losing a job, and less anxiety about spending to replace durable goods or expand inventory or equipment. These contractions and expansions cause stock prices to rise and fall.

Many investors manage their portfolios by moving in and out of certain industry sectors based on their assessment of the economic cycle. Their goal is to buy at the low point of a contraction and sell at the high point of an expansion:

1. When investors believe the market has bottomed out, they buy in the financial and transportation industries when those industries are at their expected lows and expansion is on the horizon.

2. As the economy improves and heads toward a peak, the capital goods industries tend to appreciate.

3. Soon thereafter, the basic industries appreciate, followed by precious metals and the energy sector.

4. At the peak, the only way to go is down into a contraction! Now, noncyclical and consumer goods — such as food, cosmetics, and health care — look good.

5. As the economy moves deeper into contraction, utility and consumer cyclical sector goods look more attractive — until just about the time the economy hits the bottom and the cycle begins anew.

Unfortunately, knowing just where the economy is in the business cycle isn't easy. People can speculate, sound knowledgeable, and even be correct about it by accident. Knowing when the economy has hit the peak or the bottom is like driving on a road you've never seen before while looking in the rearview mirror. You can easily see where you came from, but knowing what lies ahead is impossible.

 If you buy individual stocks, buy companies in industries you understand. If you buy mutual funds or ETFs, pay attention to your portfolio's overall allocation to a given industry.

 Canada's resource-heavy economy gives you another reason to diversify your portfolio by country (refer to Tip #41). You get exposure to industry sectors that might not be available at home.

#43

Diversify Your Bond Portfolio

By Jennifer Luzzatto, CFA, CFP

Most investors can best buy the bond portion of their portfolios by purchasing bond mutual funds. Because the best prices on bonds are usually in very large increments (think $1,000,000 per purchase), individuals benefit from participating in a pool of professionally managed funds invested in the bond market. (For information on individual bonds, refer to Tip #24.) How you diversify your bond portfolio depends upon whether you're in the accumulation phase or the retirement phase of your life.

 Bond fund returns are especially sensitive to the fees of mutual funds because they typically don't see the high returns of stock funds. Keep an eye out for expense ratios of less than 0.30 percent.

Advice for Early- and Mid-Life Accumulators

Early- and mid-life accumulators can benefit from exposure to all parts of the bond market. Because of their long time horizon, these people don't have to be as defensive against hard times in the investment cycle. An early accumulator should invest bond money as follows:

- ✔ **Short-term bond fund:** 35 percent
- ✔ **Intermediate-term bond fund:** 35 percent
- ✔ **Inflation-protected securities:** 20 percent
- ✔ **High-yield bonds:** 10 percent

Different sources define short-, intermediate-, and long-term differently. But generally, *short-term* bonds have maturity dates of five years or less, *intermediate-term* bonds have maturities of five to ten years, and *long-term* bonds have stated maturities that are longer than ten years. *Inflation-protected securities* are a relatively new type of security and are called Real Return Bonds (RRBs — refer to

Tips #15 and #24). *High-yield bonds* are usually less creditworthy, which means they have to pay a higher rate to attract investors. These investments are riskier, but they can be appropriate for accumulators because the long-term horizons can temper the risk.

In this section, you discover how to allocate your bond investment if you have ten or more years until retirement.

Let returns and volatility direct allocation

Standard deviation is a way of measuring the volatility of bonds. A standard deviation of 4 percent means that historically, the returns of a given security class have ranged from 4 percent below the category average to 4 percent higher. The lower the standard deviation, the lower the volatility and market risk.

Table 3-7 shows that shorter-term bonds have lower volatility and that long-term, mortgage, and high-yield bonds have greater volatility. For a long time horizon, an ideal allocation is a blend of short-term bonds, intermediate-term bonds, and in some cases, mortgage bonds. The table uses the longer historical data available for the United States.

Table 3-7	Average Bond Returns and Volatility	
Bond Category	*Historical Average Return*	*Standard Deviation*
Short term	7.34%	4.14%
Intermediate term	8.24%	6.83%
Long term	8.63%	10.94%
Mortgage	9.49%	10.64%
High yield	8.86%	10.60%

Source: MoneyGuide Pro

As an individual investor, you don't get enough additional return from purchasing long-term over intermediate-term bonds, given the dramatic rise in volatility for long-term bonds. Long-term bonds are generally better for businesses such as insurance companies that need to match the maturities of their assets with their liabilities. High-yield bonds can sometimes be appropriate in an individual portfolio, but their risk and return profile fits more into a stock allocation than bond allocation.

Set up an ideal allocation among bonds

For most investors, an appropriate bond allocation puts equal amounts of money in short-term and intermediate-term bonds, as Table 3-8 shows.

Table 3-8	Bond Allocation for Early to Mid Life	
Allocation	Historical Return	Historical Standard Deviation
50% short term	7.34%	4.14%
50% intermediate term	8.24%	6.83%
Total bond allocation	7.79%	5.48%

Source: MoneyGuide Pro

You short- and intermediate-term bond funds should be invested in treasury bills (T-bills), agencies, corporate bonds, and mortgages. You want exposure to all parts of the bond market with these funds. (For information on government bonds and T-bills, refer to Tip #15.)

Table 3-9 shows a slightly more aggressive bond allocation that includes mortgage bonds. If mortgage bonds are appropriate for your portfolio given your risk profile, you can buy mortgage-backed securities (MBSs) through your bank. MBSs are usually backed by the Canada Mortgage and Housing Corporation (CMHC), a government agency that guarantees repayment of the principal at the bond's maturity. Sometimes MBSs are referred to as *Cannie Maes* — a play on the Government National Mortgage Association bonds, or *Ginnie Maes,* sold in the United States.

Table 3-9	Short-Term, Intermediate-Term, and Mortgage Bond Allocation	
Allocation	Historical Return	Historical Standard Deviation
35% short term	7.34%	4.14%
35% intermediate term	8.24%	6.83%
30% mortgage	9.49%	10.64%
Total bond allocation	8.28%	7.03%

Source: MoneyGuide Pro

If you go aggressive and invest in high-yield bonds, remember that they tend to be the most volatile. When times get rough, hold off allocating more money to these bonds until the storm begins to blow over. Knowing when things may turn around is impossible, so don't abandon your high-yield funds completely — just don't add new funds until the crisis of the day is no longer on the front page.

Bond quality

The quality of the bond also affects bond volatility. The higher the bond is rated, the less sensitive it'll be to uncertain economic times. Table 3-10 explains the ratings of two of Canada's largest rating agencies, Dominion Bond Rating Service and Canadian Bond Rating Service.

If you're an accumulator with a higher risk tolerance and a number of years before retirement, some lower-quality bonds may be appropriate. The higher yield and growth opportunities of lower-rated bonds come with more risk. If you're an investor with a shorter time frame, this risk may be unacceptable, so your mixture of bonds should tend toward the higher-quality side.

Table 3-10		Bond Ratings
Dominion Bond Rating Service	**Canadian Bond Rating Service**	**Meaning**
AAA	A++	Lowest risk
AA	A+	Slight long-term risk
A	A	Possibly vulnerable to changing economic conditions
BBB	B++	Currently safe but possibly unreliable over the long term
BB	B+	Somewhat speculative issue that offers moderate security
B	B	At risk of default in the future
CCC	C++	Clear danger of default
CC	C+	Highly speculative or may be in default
C	C	Poor prospects for repayment even if currently paying
N/A	D	In default

Source: Forefield Advisor

Advice for Almost-Retirees and Retirees

If you plan to retire in one to three years, your time horizon is a bit shorter, but by no means short! Inflation may be your biggest enemy, because the cost of living will most likely out-run your income after a few years of retirement. Stocks and stock funds can help take care of the dreaded effects of inflation, but you can use your bond portfolio to hold down your portfolio's overall volatility. You need a more conservative bond portfolio, like this:

- ✔ **Short-term bond fund:** 45 percent
- ✔ **Intermediate-term bond fund:** 35 percent
- ✔ **Inflation-protected securities:** 20 percent

This bond mix should work through most of your retirement years. When you know your current assets will last for the rest of your life, opt for a 100 percent short-term bond allocation.

Short-term bond funds suffer the least in turbulent times. So if in doubt, go short! But remember that you may be giving up growth or yield if you put too much in or stay in the short-term arena too long.

Diversify Your Portfolio with Alternative Vehicles

By Kevin O'Reilly

In unpredictable times, knowing that your portfolio is well diversified is comforting. So besides diversifying among different flavours of traditional investments such as stocks, bonds, and mutual funds, why not consider different investments altogether? So-called *alternative investments* can perform very differently from stocks and bonds. This tip discusses some of these alternative investments, which span a broad set of choices: Common vehicles include private equity, hedge funds, and real estate.

Private Equity: Some Privacy, Please

Most people understand that public companies raise money by issuing stock that's bought and sold on exchanges. Less well known are the various ways that owners of private companies secure capital to grow their businesses. They do this through *private equity*. You have to have significant assets and/or income to participate in this arena.

Private equity vehicles are generally required by law to accept money only from individuals who are accredited investors. An *accredited investor* is a person who is permitted by applicable Canadian securities law to invest in unregistered securities, mainly because he or she understands and can afford to take the financial risk. To be an accredited investor, you must meet one of the following conditions:

✔ You have individual net worth, or joint net worth with your spouse, that exceeds $1 million at the time of the purchase.

✔ You have an income exceeding $200,000 in each of the two most recent years, or a joint income with your spouse that is more than $300,000 for those years, and you have a reasonable expectation of maintaining the same income level.

✔ You can make a minimum investment, which varies depending on the province or territory where you live. Minimum investments tend to range from $97,000 to $150,000, and each provincial or territorial jurisdiction has specific restrictions as well.

Investing in private equity can be very lucrative. For example, Table 3-11 shows historical returns for Thomson Financial's U.S. Private Equity Performance Index (PEPI). However, the range of private equity investments is broad, and the return can vary significantly. Investing in this manner can be complex and frustrating. A financial advisor can help with the how-to as well as suitability issues.

Table 3-11	Private Equity Performance				
	1 Year	*3 Year*	*5 Year*	*10 Year*	*20 Year*
Private equity	22.5%	13.4%	3.6%	11.4%	14.2%
NASDAQ	5.6%	10.2%	0.0%	6.2%	11.7%
S&P 500	6.6%	9.2%	0.7%	6.6%	9.79%

Source: Thomson Financial/National Venture Capital Association

Hedge Your Bets with Hedge Funds

Hedge funds — which are designed to maximize gains while minimizing risks — pursue higher returns using many different strategies. For instance, they may be made up of assets that don't move in the same direction as traditional investments, or they may be short-selling those assets.

You can't look at hedge funds as a homogenous asset class, because they're lightly regulated and invest in a broad spectrum of vehicles to meet a wide range of goals. Nonetheless, looking at the overall performance of hedge funds over time, they clearly stack up well against more traditional investments. As Table 3-12 indicates, hedge funds can provide a solid alternative during periods of poor stock market performance.

Table 3-12	Hedge Fund Performance in a Down Market	
Year	*S&P 500*	*All Hedge Funds*
2000	−9%	9%
2001	−12%	7%
2002	−22%	6%

Like private equity (see the preceding section), hedge funds come with steep requirements, and you have to be an accredited investor to participate.

One approach, however, brings hedge funds within reach of a broader group of investor: the *fund of funds* (FoF). The managers of these FoFs wade through the sea of hedge fund information to identify a handful of hedge funds that, together, may best meet your objective. They then bundle these various hedge funds into a single investment vehicle, which they offer to the public.

Investing in an FoF can be very expensive. The underlying hedge funds themselves may charge around 1 percent plus 20 percent of the profits of the fund. If you're investing through an FoF, the manager of *that* fund will charge up to 1.5 percent of assets plus 10 percent of their profits. Note, however, that despite the high fees, investors who can afford to invest in a hedge fund may benefit from the diversification an FoF provides. In fact, about 30 percent of investments in the Canadian hedge fund industry are allocated to FoFs.

Seek Diversification with Real Estate

Don't let recent housing market slides scare you away from real estate investing. Depending on where you invest, long-term returns can be attractive. If you have much of your retirement savings in the stock market through a group or individual RRSP, real estate investing can offer a way to ensure all your eggs aren't jammed into one basket.

Get in it for the long haul

Single-family rental housing can be a solid hedge against an uncertain future — just make sure you view the investment as a long-term proposition. If you buy a rental house tomorrow and the economy experiences a period of significant inflation, your investment will likely appreciate at a rate at least close to inflation. The rent you collect will also grow with inflation while your mortgage payments remain static.

The idea that all real estate is local is a cliché in the industry — and it's true! Even though the market has softened overall in Canada, some housing markets rose or at least held their value.

Proceed with caution with residential real estate

You may have several reasons to think twice about investing in residential real estate:

- ✔ Housing isn't liquid.

- ✔ This is a hands-on investment. You need to maintain the home and collect rent. You need to perform upkeep to prepare the home for new renters. You can hire a management company to perform these services for you, but this expense comes out of your profits.

- ✔ Renters are short-term visitors. You can protect yourself through security deposits and lease provisions, but your renters most likely won't treat your investment as if it were their own.

- ✔ Rent cheques don't always arrive as stipulated by the rental contract. Sometimes, rent cheques bounce. People rent for many different reasons, but the fact is that renters are sometimes renters simply because they're unable to buy a home for cash flow and/or credit score reasons. You can mitigate these problems by carefully screening renters, but that reduces your market for potential renters.

If you still think residential real estate investing is for you, check out *Real Estate Investing For Canadians For Dummies* (Wiley) or *House Flipping For Canadians For Dummies* (Wiley).

Commercialize with corporate buildings

Commercial real estate is an option for real estate investors. Although far from certain, rent cheques tend to be a bit more reliable coming from established corporate entities rather than individuals. Typically, a third party manages the property, making the investment easier to deal with on a day-to-day basis. But you have to pay for that property management, which eats into your returns.

The commercial real estate market is more efficient than the residential market. Investments are typically valued based on the *capitalization rate* (cap rate), which is simply the net cash flow divided by the investment cost. Prevailing cap rates change over time, but finding bargain prices in commercial real estate is less common than it is in residential properties. In short, people buy and sell houses for many different reasons, only some of which are profit-oriented; however, profit motive is generally the biggest driver for commercial real estate transactions.

Look to REITs

Perhaps the easiest way to diversify your portfolio with real estate is through real estate investment trusts (REITs). Think of REITs as mutual funds that invest in real estate. Numerous specialty REITs invest in apartment buildings, strip malls, and office buildings.

Historically, REITs haven't correlated to the stock market. They've moved in the same direction as equity markets less than 50 percent of the time. Refer to Tip #21 for a more thorough review of investing in REITs and how they may fit into your portfolio.

#45

Employ a Conservative Portfolio

By Peggy Creveling, CFA

What is a conservative portfolio? Is it what you need? This tip delves into the building blocks used in designing a conservative portfolio, highlights the historical returns and risk profile of each component, and guides you through developing a conservative portfolio to serve you through all economic climates.

Determine Whether a Conservative Portfolio Is Right for You

Consider a conservative portfolio if the following applies:

- ✔ **You need the money in the next five to ten years.** For goals less than five years away, you want to avoid exposure to the markets. The risk of a loss is too high. Instead, use a money market account, GIC, or ultra-short-term bond fund to finance short-term goals.

- ✔ **You're unable to bear much risk.** If you can't accept the consequences of your investments' not producing results in the time period needed, you can't bear much risk. For example, if you're retired and dependent on investments for essential living expenses, you can't accept much risk. If you've got those living expenses covered with pensions, CPP, OAS, and/or annuities, you can afford to take more risk.

- ✔ **You're an inexperienced investor.** Almost all people overestimate their ability to handle market volatility. If you don't have much investment experience, start conservatively. You'll be less likely to sell your portfolio in a panic when the market drops.

- ✔ **You're averse to risk (market volatility).** If dips in your portfolio keep you up at night, stick with a more conservative portfolio. You'll sleep better and be better off than if you were outside your comfort zone.

Although less volatile than a more-aggressive portfolio, a conservative portfolio can still produce negative returns in any given year, or in rarer instances, for more than one year in a row. And of course, the trade-off for lower volatility is lower returns.

Decide Which Asset Classes to Use

An enormous number of asset classes are available. Many, however, don't belong in a conservative portfolio. Table 3-13 gives examples of the more traditional asset classes for a variety of increasingly complex portfolios. If you're just starting out, stay with the simple portfolio; as your nest egg grows, add additional asset classes as illustrated in the more-complex and complex portfolios.

Table 3-13	Asset Classes for Model Portfolios	
Simple Portfolio	*More-Complex Portfolio*	*Complex Portfolio*
Cash	Cash	Cash
Bonds	Short-term bonds	Short-term bonds
Canadian and U.S. total stock market	Intermediate-term bonds	Intermediate-term bonds
International equity	Canadian and U.S. large cap	High-yield bonds
	Canadian and U.S. small cap	Global bonds
	International developed	Canadian and U.S. large cap value
	Emerging markets	Canadian and U.S. large cap growth
		Canadian and U.S. small cap
		International developed
		Emerging markets
		Real estate
		Commodities

Increasing the number of asset classes potentially increases your long-term return while decreasing volatility. After 8 to 12 asset classes, the value of piling on additional asset classes actually diminishes. Weigh the added benefit against the time and effort you'd expend managing all those investments.

Know How Much to Allocate to Each Asset Class

The split between fixed income (bonds) and equity (stocks) has the biggest impact on the likely long-term returns and volatility. No one right answer exists, but because the goal is a less volatile portfolio, the range for cash and fixed income should be about 55 to 80 percent. Equity and alternative investments should fill in the remaining 20 to 45 percent.

To further lower volatility, consider swapping riskier asset classes (which have a higher standard deviation) for less-risky asset classes under the broad bond/equity split. For example, use intermediate-term bonds instead of long-term bonds, large-cap stocks instead of small-cap, and so on.

Table 3-14 provides data on various asset classes. Use this information to decide how conservative you need or want to be.

Table 3-14	Asset Classes in a Conservative Portfolio		
Asset Class	Holding Ranges (%)	Long-Term Historic Returns*	Standard Deviation**
		Nominal (%)	Real (%)
Fixed Income	55–80		
Cash	0–10	6.0	1.4	±2.9
Short-term bonds	20–40	7.3	2.7	±4.1
Intermediate-term bonds	20–40	8.0	3.3	±6.5
High-yield bonds	0–5	9.2	4.8	±9.1
Global bonds (unhedged)	0–5	8.4	3.7	±6.7
Equity	20–45		

Asset Class	Holding Ranges (%)	Long-Term Historic Returns*	Standard Deviation**	
		Nominal (%)	Real (%)	
Large cap	10–25			
Value		10.7	6.1	±15.4
Growth		10.2	5.6	±18.1
Small cap	0–10	14.3	9.7	±22.2
International developed	5–15	11.7	7.1	±21.4
Emerging mar-kets	0–3	11.6	7.0	28.0
Alternative	0–6			
REITs	0–3	13.0	8.4	17.1
Commodities	0–3	11.7	5.6	24.2

Source: Long-term historic returns and standard deviation figures from MoneyGuidePro/ PIE Technologies for time period 1972–2007.

*Nominal returns are returns before inflation. Real returns exclude inflation (average 4.63 percent per year for the period 1972–2007).

**One standard deviation describes the range that returns will likely fall within two-thirds of the time.

Consider breaking your investments into a number of mini-portfolios, each with an allocation suited for that particular time frame and objective. You'll remove much of the stress of trying to fund a number of diverse goals from the same portfolio.

Finally, Figure 3-1 displays sample portfolios along with historical performance. The information on historical returns uses the longer-term data available for the United States.

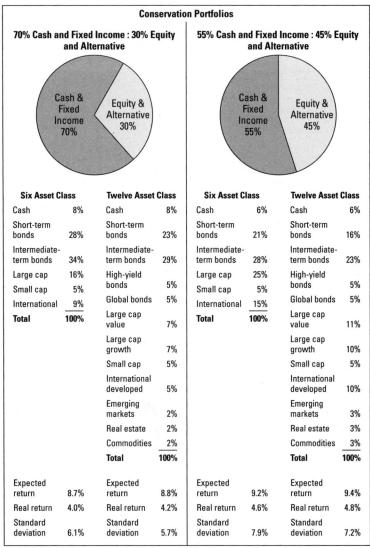

Conservation Portfolios

70% Cash and Fixed Income : 30% Equity and Alternative

Cash & Fixed Income 70%

Equity & Alternative 30%

55% Cash and Fixed Income : 45% Equity and Alternative

Cash & Fixed Income 55%

Equity & Alternative 45%

Six Asset Class		Twelve Asset Class		Six Asset Class		Twelve Asset Class	
Cash	8%	Cash	8%	Cash	6%	Cash	6%
Short-term bonds	28%	Short-term bonds	23%	Short-term bonds	21%	Short-term bonds	16%
Intermediate-term bonds	34%	Intermediate-term bonds	29%	Intermediate-term bonds	28%	Intermediate-term bonds	23%
Large cap	16%	High-yield bonds	5%	Large cap	25%	High-yield bonds	5%
Small cap	5%			Small cap	5%		
International	9%	Global bonds	5%	International	15%	Global bonds	5%
Total	**100%**	Large cap value	7%	**Total**	**100%**	Large cap value	11%
		Large cap growth	7%			Large cap growth	10%
		Small cap	5%			Small cap	5%
		International developed	5%			International developed	10%
		Emerging markets	2%			Emerging markets	3%
		Real estate	2%			Real estate	3%
		Commodities	2%			Commodities	3%
		Total	**100%**			**Total**	**100%**
Expected return	8.7%	Expected return	8.8%	Expected return	9.2%	Expected return	9.4%
Real return	4.0%	Real return	4.2%	Real return	4.6%	Real return	4.8%
Standard deviation	6.1%	Standard deviation	5.7%	Standard deviation	7.9%	Standard deviation	7.2%

Source: Portfolio expected returns and standard deviation figures from Moneyguide Pro/PIE Technologies based on historic performance during the period 1972–2007

Figure 3-1: Sample conservative portfolios.

Employ a Moderate Portfolio

By Peggy Creveling, CFA

The moderate portfolio shifts up the risk, volatility, and return scale when compared with the conservative portfolio, including perhaps more years of loss and an increased chance of multi-year losses. The reward for bearing more risk is the opportunity for a higher long-term return when compared with the conservative portfolio (refer to Tip #45). The difference between an expected return of 9.94 percent for a moderate portfolio and 8.96 percent for a more conservative one may not look like much, but it can really add up. In the next section, Figure 3-2 shows the range of possible values that $100,000 invested in a moderate and conservative portfolio may earn over time. (The figure's statistics come from the United States, where longer-term historical returns are available.) In the long term, the moderate portfolio's expected or *mid value* is higher than that of the more conservative portfolio, and the potential range of values is wider.

Choose to Create a Moderate Portfolio

A moderate portfolio is appropriate if you meet the following criteria:

- ✔ **You won't need the money for about ten years.** In general, the longer time horizon allows you to add more equity and other risky assets, which should increase your long-term return. With a longer time frame, extreme up and down years tend to cancel each other out, and your return will trend much closer to the expected long-run return.

- ✔ **You have increased ability to bear risk.** Someone in his 20s or 30s with decades of earnings ahead of him — and not dependent on income from the portfolio — can afford more risk in search of a higher return than a retiree with her working years behind her. Similarly, a retiree with adequate health and long-term care insurance and a hefty retirement pension can bear more risk than a retiree who is dependent on his portfolio to fund essential expenses.

✔ **You can tolerate a moderate amount of market volatility.**
You already have some experience in the market and are
comfortable with some volatility, but you're unwilling to
accept the more extreme movements that come with a more
aggressive portfolio. For example, a moderate portfolio with
an expected annual long-term return of 9.6 percent may be
expected to return between 1.8 and 17.4 percent two-thirds of
the time.

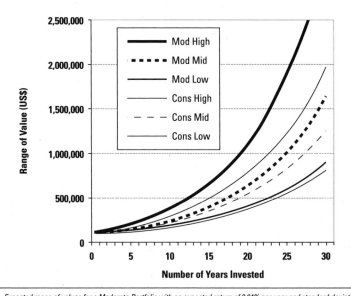

Expected range of values for a Moderate Portfolio with an expected return of 9.94% per year and standard deviation
of 10.10% and a Conservative Portfolio with expected return of 8.96% per year and standard deviation of 7.02%,
assuming returns are normally distributed. Portfolios are expected to earn above the lower boundary 90% of
the time and below the upper boundary 90% of the time.

Figure 3-2: Range of possible ending-portfolio values, moderate versus
conservative.

Construct a Moderate Portfolio

Building a moderate portfolio follows the same process as
constructing the conservative portfolio. You use the same asset
classes for the level of portfolio complexity you prefer (refer to
Tip #45); only the weightings change.

Keeping equity and alternative investments in the 45 to 65 percent
range, and cash and fixed-income investments in the 35 to
55 percent range, is a good idea.

The same steps apply as with the conservative portfolio:

1. **Keep the overall split between equity and fixed income within the ranges for a moderate portfolio, as specified in Table 3-15.**

2. **Balance the number of asset classes with the size of your portfolio and your ability to manage it.**

   Having more than 8 to 12 asset classes isn't necessary.

3. **Allocate funds to the various asset classes within the ranges indicated in the table, depending on how much risk you're willing to take in the attempt to earn a higher return.**

   Focus on overall portfolio performance. By design, you'll always have some asset classes in your portfolio doing better than others. The impact of having some investments zigging while others are zagging lowers overall portfolio volatility and potentially increases portfolio return. (Refer to Tip #39 for more on diversification.)

4. **Choose one or two mutual funds for each asset class, depending on the size of your portfolio.**

   If most active fund managers have trouble beating the market or their respective benchmarks in a one-year period, what chance do they have of beating their benchmark over longer periods? And what chance do you have of choosing that manager ahead of time? By choosing passively managed funds (index funds and exchange-traded funds) over actively managed ones, you may improve your chances of earning the market return over the long run. Refer to Tips #18 and #20 for details.

5. **Rebalance periodically back to your target allocation.**

   In volatile markets in particular, ensure you don't stray too far from your target weightings. This may mean you have to sell assets that are doing well and buy those that are doing poorly. But you'll be well positioned when the market recovers because you've bought low and sold high along the way.

Table 3-15 gives suggested asset class percentages. The material uses the longer-term data available for the U.S. market.

Table 3-15	Asset Classes in a Moderate Portfolio		
Asset Class	Holding Ranges (%)	L/T Historic Returns		Standard Dev (%)
		Nominal (%)	Real (%)	
Fixed Income	**33–55**			
Cash^	0–10	6.0	1.4	±2.9
Short-Term Bonds	15–25	7.3	2.7	±4.1
Intermediate-Term Bonds	15–25	8.0	3.3	±6.5
High-Yield Bonds	0–5	9.2	4.8	±9.1
Global Bonds (unhedged)	0–5	8.4	3.7	±6.7
Equity and Alternative	**46–65**			
Large cap	20–40			
Value		10.7	6.1	±15.4
Growth		10.2	5.6	±18.1
Small cap	5–10	14.3	9.7	±22.2
International developed	5–20	11.7	7.1	±21.4
Emerging markets	0–5	11.6	7.0	±28.0
Real estate	0–5	13.0	8.4	±17.1
Commodities	0–3	11.7	5.6	±24.2

^ Cash allocation is needed for portfolios where you'll be making withdrawals. L/T historic returns and standard deviation figures from MoneyGuide Pro/PIE Technologies, 1972–2007. Real returns based on long-term U.S. inflation of 4.63%.

Note the Historical Performance of Moderate Portfolios

Figure 3-3 provides two examples of moderate portfolios, using the longer-term data on historical returns available for the United States. The first portfolio shows a moderately conservative allocation using both 6 and 12 asset classes. The second example shows the same historical results for a portfolio that has more opportunity for growth. The key statistics are shown on the bottom line — you want the highest return with the lowest amount of volatility (as measured by standard deviation) for your personal comfort level.

Note that the additional asset classes in the more complex portfolio result in a higher expected return and lower standard deviation in both cases, although the simple portfolio captures most of the benefits of diversification.

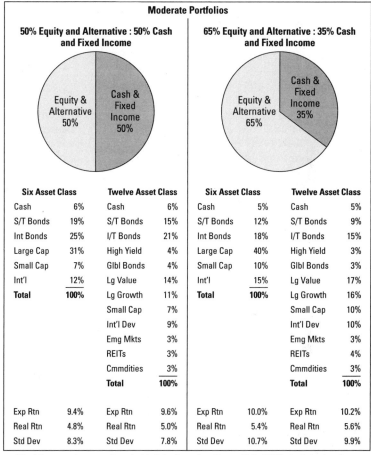

Moderate Portfolios

50% Equity and Alternative : 50% Cash and Fixed Income

Six Asset Class		Twelve Asset Class	
Cash	6%	Cash	6%
S/T Bonds	19%	S/T Bonds	15%
Int Bonds	25%	I/T Bonds	21%
Large Cap	31%	High Yield	4%
Small Cap	7%	Glbl Bonds	4%
Int'l	12%	Lg Value	14%
Total	**100%**	Lg Growth	11%
		Small Cap	7%
		Int'l Dev	9%
		Emg Mkts	3%
		REITs	3%
		Cmmdities	3%
		Total	**100%**
Exp Rtn	9.4%	Exp Rtn	9.6%
Real Rtn	4.8%	Real Rtn	5.0%
Std Dev	8.3%	Std Dev	7.8%

65% Equity and Alternative : 35% Cash and Fixed Income

Six Asset Class		Twelve Asset Class	
Cash	5%	Cash	5%
S/T Bonds	12%	S/T Bonds	9%
Int Bonds	18%	I/T Bonds	15%
Large Cap	40%	High Yield	3%
Small Cap	10%	Glbl Bonds	3%
Int'l	15%	Lg Value	17%
Total	**100%**	Lg Growth	16%
		Small Cap	10%
		Int'l Dev	10%
		Emg Mkts	3%
		REITs	4%
		Cmmdities	3%
		Total	**100%**
Exp Rtn	10.0%	Exp Rtn	10.2%
Real Rtn	5.4%	Real Rtn	5.6%
Std Dev	10.7%	Std Dev	9.9%

^ Portfolio expected returns and standard deviation figures from MoneyguidePro/PIE -Technologies, based on historic returns from 1972-2007

Figure 3-3: Two sample moderate portfolios.

#47

Employ an Aggressive Portfolio

By Peggy Creveling, CFA

An aggressive portfolio bears nearly the full brunt of market volatility in an attempt to achieve higher long-term returns. More years of losses and more periods of multi-year losses will occur, countered by some extremely good years of positive returns. You'll need to stomach large swings in the value of your portfolio, sometimes on a daily basis, without losing your nerve and bailing out. Your returns in any one year can vary widely, but the longer you hold the portfolio, the closer your return will be to the long-run expected return.

Is a portfolio that's earning only 1 to 2 percent more than a less volatile one worth the stress and anxiety? Over the long haul, yes. That additional 1 to 2 percent doesn't seem like much on its own, but compounded over a 20- to 30-year time period, the impact can be huge, as Figure 3-4 shows. (The chart uses the longer-term data on historical returns available in the United States.) For longer time periods, an aggressive portfolio is likely to do better than more conservative ones. The trick is staying invested for long periods despite the turmoil you'll most likely experience. In this tip, you explore aggressive portfolios.

Know Whether an Aggressive Portfolio Is Right for You

Consider an aggressive portfolio only if you meet the following conditions:

✔ **You have a long time horizon.** You need the extremely bad and good years to cancel each other out and settle around the longer-run expected return.

With an aggressive portfolio, the long run should be 15 to 20 years or more. Anything shorter and your returns may be significantly lower than your expected return.

✔ **You have a high capacity to bear risk.** In other words, you can weather the storm financially if your investments don't work out within the time period expected. This may be because your goal is flexible or because you have a way to make up the shortfall by adding savings, extending the time period, or funding the goal from another source.

✔ **You're an experienced investor and know that you can stomach a lot of volatility.** The returns of an aggressive portfolio in any one year may vary widely. If you've invested during a prolonged period of market uncertainty before, you have a good idea of how you'll react when the financial media starts churning out stories of impending financial Armageddon. If you stuck it out through past periods without panicking and selling out, an aggressive portfolio allocation may be for you.

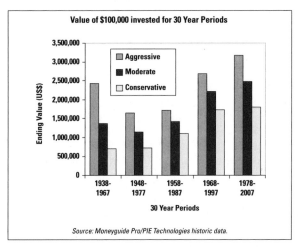

Figure 3-4: Comparing ending values of aggressive, moderate, and conservative portfolios.

An aggressive portfolio isn't appropriate for all goals — the risk of shortfall is too high. Using an aggressive portfolio to fund university costs for your 13-year-old isn't a good idea, but it may be appropriate for a younger person saving for retirement or even a retiree whose living expenses are covered by a pension or other income and who is growing the portfolio to pass on to heirs.

If you're dependent on income from your portfolio, the risks of an aggressive portfolio may be unbearable. Making regular withdrawals, especially in years of bad returns, can devastate your portfolio and your life (see Tip #62 for details). On the other hand, if you have an emergency fund in place, and your essential living expenses are covered by CPP/QPP, OAS, company pensions, or other sources of income (not part-time work), then you may be able to stomach some additional risk. If you're primarily dependent on your portfolio to cover your basic living expenses, an aggressive approach is not appropriate for you.

In a household where more than one person is affected by the investment decisions, both need to be comfortable with the portfolio's level of volatility. Go with the risk tolerance level of the more conservative person.

Constructing an Aggressive Portfolio

Building an aggressive portfolio follows the same process as building moderate and conservative portfolios. You use the same asset classes for the level of portfolio complexity you prefer (refer to Tip #45); only the weightings change.

An aggressive portfolio has a greater percentage invested in equity and alternative holdings and a lower percentage in fixed income. Experts suggest keeping equity and alternative investments in the 70 to 90 percent range and fixed-income investments in the 10 to 30 percent range.

The same steps apply as with the conservative and moderate portfolios:

1. **Keep the overall split between the broad fixed income, equity, and alternative asset classes within the ranges shown in Table 3-16.**

2. **Balance the number of asset classes with the size of your portfolio and your ability to manage it.**

   Use no more than 8 to 12 asset classes.

3. **Allocate funds to each selected asset within the suggested ranges, ensuring that the total doesn't exceed the recommended range for the broader asset classes (fixed income, equity, or alternative).**

   Consider index funds and exchange-traded funds (ETFs) for each asset class to keep fees low. (Refer to Tips #18 and #20 for more on these funds.)

Table 3-16 gives you an idea of how to split the asset classes. It uses the longer-term data on historical returns available in the United States.

Table 3-16		Asset Classes in an Aggressive Portfolio		
Asset Class	**Holding Ranges (%)**	**Long-Term Historic Returns***		**Standard Deviation** (%)
		Nominal (%)	**Real (%)**	
Fixed Income	**10–30%**			
Cash*	0–5%	6.0	1.4	±2.9
Short-term bonds	0–15%	7.3	2.7	±4.1
Intermediate-term bonds	0–15%	8.0	3.3	±6.5
High-yield bonds	0–5%	9.2	4.8	±9.1
Global bonds (unhedged)	0–5%	8.4	3.7	±6.7
Equity	**60–90%**			
Large cap	25–50%			
Value		10.7	6.1	±15.4
Growth		10.2	5.6	±18.1
Small cap	10–20%	14.3	9.7	±22.2
International developed	10–20%	11.7	7.1	±21.4
Emerging markets	0–10%	11.6	7.0	±28.0
Alternative	**0–20%**			
Real estate investment trusts	0–20%	13.0	8.4	±17.1
Commodities	0–5%	11.7	5.6	±24.2

*Cash allocation is needed for portfolios where you'll be making withdrawals. L/T historic returns and standard deviation figures from MoneyGuide Pro/PIE Technologies, 1972–2007. Real returns based on the historical U.S. inflation rate of 4.63% per year during the same period.

Examples of Aggressive Portfolios

Figure 3-5 shows some sample portfolios of differing complexity along with their historical performance. (The data comes from the United States, where such long-term performance results are available.) Find the portfolio that's most comfortable and appropriate for your needs by focusing on the bottom line — the most return with the lowest volatility or standard deviation.

Structure different portfolios to fund different goals. Your goals vary in terms of time horizon and importance, so they affect your ability to handle a shortfall and market volatility.

Aggressive Portfolios							
75% Equity and Alternative : 25% Cash and Fixed Income				**90% Equity and Alternative : 10% Cash and Fixed Income**			
Six Asset Class		**Twelve Asset Class**		**Six Asset Class**		**Twelve Asset Class**	
Cash	2%	Cash	2%	Cash	2%	Cash	2%
I/T Bonds	23%	S/T Bonds	7%	I/T Bonds	8%	I/T Bonds	5%
Large Cap	35%	I/T Bonds	10%	Large Cap	45%	Glbl Bonds	3%
Small Cap	15%	High Yield	3%	Small Cap	15%	Lg Value	19%
Int'l	15%	Glbl Bonds	3%	Int'l	20%	Lg Growth	15%
REIT	10%	Lg Value	18%	REIT	10%	Small Cap	15%
Total	**100%**	Lg Growth	14%	**Total**	**100%**	Europe	10%
		Small Cap	15%			Asia Pacific	10%
		Int'l Dev	10%			Emg Mkts	8%
		Emg Mkts	5%			REITs	10%
		REITs	10%			Cmmdities	3%
		Cmmdities	3%			**Total**	**100%**
		Total	**100%**				
Exp Rtn	10.8%	Exp Rtn	10.9%	Exp Rtn	11.3%	Exp Rtn	11.4%
Real Rtn	6.2%	Real Rtn	6.2%	Real Rtn	6.6%	Real Rtn	6.8%
Std Dev	11.8%	Std Dev	11.2%	Std Dev	13.9%	Std Dev	13.4%

Source: Portfolio expected returns and standard deviation figures from Moneyguide Pro/PIE -Technologies, based on historic returns from 1972-2007

Figure 3-5: Two aggressive portfolios.

Part IV
Investing for Accumulators

"It's surprising considering his portfolio is so conservative."

In this part...

This part covers everything from what you need to save to be prepared for a major life event, such as raising children and paying for their education, to making sure you're saving enough so you can retire someday if you choose. You also discover investment vehicles and tips that are appropriate whether you're just beginning to invest or you have a good-sized nest egg and want to make sure you don't lose all you've accumulated.

Save for Emergencies

By Dylan Ross, CFP

*E*ven if you've never had to quickly drum up money for something totally unexpected, you always face the possibility of needing money in an emergency. Emergencies are unplanned expenses that require more money than you can cover with your paycheque, even if you cut some expenses until next payday. When you don't have enough savings, emergencies can put you in debt or deeper in debt. An emergency fund helps protect your finances.

Unexpected expenses may be one-time or recurring. Potential uses for emergency funds include car repairs, paying bills if you're out of work, insurance deductibles, critical home repairs, legal fees, travel to attend a funeral, natural disasters, and so on.

Figure How Much to Set Aside

At an absolute minimum, set aside enough money in your emergency fund to pay for at least three to six months of *basic living expenses* (the regular and essential expenses you must pay to live). These expenses don't include discretionary items like entertainment, dining out, spa treatments, or DVDs. Keep at least six months of basic living expenses in your emergency fund if you're single or living on one income, or if one income in your two-income household varies a lot from month to month or isn't secure.

Your emergency fund does more than just cover expenses in case you lose your job. So resist the temptation to keep a smaller emergency fund if your job is iron-clad, or if you think you could find work quickly if you got laid off. Basing the size of your emergency fund on monthly expenses establishes a guideline, but the fund covers other emergencies, even while you're employed.

If you anticipate more frequent or more severe emergencies than three to six months of basic living expenses can cover, increase the size of your fund. For example, you may need a larger emergency fund if

✔ Your job security is questionable.

✔ You're about to have a baby or purchase a new home.

✔ You have numerous, aging household appliances.

✔ You drive an older car.

✔ You live in an area prone to severe weather, earthquakes, or other disasters.

✔ You're without a dental plan, and you're tortured by a niggling toothache.

Your emergency fund is handy when you need to make insurance payments or pay for charges that your provincial health, dental, or vision plans don't cover. You may need cash until your insurance company reimburses you. Consider any unreimbursed health-care expenses from the past few years when deciding whether to increase your emergency fund.

If you're feeling especially uncertain, add to the size of your emergency fund. You can always reduce it after you've made it through the rough patch.

When purchasing household appliances, decline the offers for extended warrantees and add that money to your emergency fund instead. If you self-warranty several appliances, you spread out the risk of needing to repair any one of them. If you don't need to make repairs, you keep the money!

Handle Your Emergency Fund with Care

The tricky thing about financial emergencies is that you don't know what they'll be, when they'll happen, or how much you'll need to cope until you recover. All these unknowns make your emergency fund an important part of your financial profile and one that you should treat with special attention and care.

Make your fund a high priority

The harder you think it is to dredge up money for an emergency fund, the more you need one. If coming up with money to start an emergency fund now will be a sacrifice, imagine how tough it will be when you have to pay out cash in an emergency situation.

If you're trying to pay off credit cards or high-interest loans, start with an emergency fund that could cover one month of basic living expenses. When you've accumulated that, put extra money toward your debt payments. When your debt is paid off, build your emergency fund as quickly as possible. Otherwise, a sudden emergency could send you right back into the red.

Keep your fund liquid

Keep your emergency fund in cash-types of investments (refer to Tip #14 for more on cash investments). This money should be quickly available with no risk of decreasing in value at any time. An emergency fund is self-insurance, not an investment. You want your money to be accessible, but you also want to earn some interest on it so that you offset inflation at least partially, if not completely. The next section offers advice on where to invest your emergency fund money.

Invest your fund

Some places to keep your emergency fund savings include the following:

- **High-yielding direct savings accounts:** Online savings accounts often pay a higher than average interest rate. You can, and should, establish an electronic transfer link to your chequing account.

- **Savings and money market accounts:** These are interest-bearing accounts at banks or credit unions. Being able to electronically transfer money to your chequing account is best.

- **Money market funds:** Not to be confused with money market accounts, these are funds offered by mutual fund companies and investment dealers. You redeem fund shares to get cash out. Some accounts allow you to write cheques to access the cash.

- **Interest-bearing chequing accounts:** These accounts may pay less interest than savings accounts.

- **Guaranteed Investment Certificates (GICs):** These banking deposits guarantee a specific interest rate if you hold them for a specified period of time. They aren't an ideal place to keep emergency fund money because you usually have to pay a penalty to get your money out early.

When deciding where to keep your emergency funds, make sure you know how and when you can access your cash. Can you get to your money after business hours? What about on weekends and holidays? Can you use cheques, a bank machine, or a debit card? Also, make sure you're comfortable with whether or not the account is insured.

Don't use available credit as an emergency fund! Credit cards and home equity lines of credit could serve as a backup to your emergency funds in the event of a catastrophe, but the whole idea of an emergency fund is to prevent you from adding debt. Some emergencies could affect your ability to make minimum debt payments, and missed payments, late penalties, and finance charges can easily snowball out of control.

Keep a small amount of cash (enough for some groceries or to get out of town in an evacuation) stashed away at home for emergencies. During local emergencies like storms and blackouts, nearby merchants may not accept cheques or be able to process credit and debit cards.

Use your fund wisely when the time comes

Come up with a plan for dealing with emergencies. Prioritize which expenses you could cut or reduce in an emergency. Know what you have to do, whom you have to call, and how long it will take to cancel unnecessary services. Write it all down and keep it somewhere you can find it when you need it.

Sooner or later you'll have a large, unexpected expense you can't cover with your paycheque. First, decide whether it's a real emergency. Do you need to spend the money right now? Can you make do until you can save up to meet the expense? Other events may influence your answer. For example, if your dishwasher bites the dust, you may decide to hand wash dishes while you save for a new one because of layoff rumours at work.

When you face a real emergency, use only the minimum amount of money necessary to get you through. Cut any unnecessary expenses and direct the extra income toward your emergency before accessing the emergency fund. When the emergency is over, rebuild your emergency fund as quickly as possible, before reinstating nonessential expenses.

Provide for Large Expenses

• •

By Eileen Freiburger, CFP

• •

In a perfect world, you'd have cash in the bank long before you needed it for a large outlay. But the world isn't perfect. National or local economic uncertainty can put a spanner in the works when it comes to making purchase decisions. Having a plan or a set of guidelines for funding large purchases can help you make better decisions when the time comes. An obvious decision with large expenses is to just say "no" until the economy turns around. But, with careful planning, you may be able to manage the expense and still keep your head above water financially.

Buying a Car

Whether you buy a car every three years or drive the one you have until it's ready for the junkyard, you generally know well ahead of time that a purchase is pending. Because ego and emotions often influence your choice of vehicle, having guidelines for yourself can prevent you from forking over too much money for a hot little sports car that you really can't afford — a purchase that could launch your own personal debt crisis when the economy gets tough.

Buying most cars using a bank loan or dealer financing is about the same as renting the car. Most of your monthly payment is just interest expense; you're not building any ownership of the vehicle, which itself will depreciate quickly. During uncertain times, paying cash for a two- to three-year-old used car with a service warranty will be the best deal.

Do your prep work

Start by reviewing your current assets. Do you have enough cash in a car fund to pay for the new vehicle? If not, review current spending. If you take out a loan to buy the car, what monthly payment can you afford to add to your current expenses? Choose an amount that you can afford even if your finances get tight.

If you know today that you'll be replacing a car in the future, start saving now. (Refer to Tip #14 for more on investing the savings.) You'll use this money within a short time and won't have time to recover from a stock market dip, so invest the funds in a way that protects your cash and provides modest growth. Keeping the funds in a Tax-Free Savings Account (refer to Tip #32) is a great way to shelter any interest you earn from taxes.

Next, comparison shop. Here are some useful Web sites:

- ✔ **www.canadianredbook.com:** Review the retail price of used cars ($19.95 for single issue to $195 for online subscription).
- ✔ **www.carcostcanada.com:** For $39.95, get reviews, feedback from car buyers, prices negotiated in your area, and a list of rebates and incentives.
- ✔ **www.carquotes.ca:** For a one-time fee of $21, find out the dealer cost of your car of choice, including factory installed options, rebates, and incentives.

Knowing the retail price of a new or used vehicle, what others have paid for it, and the dealer cost can boost your negotiating position. That should help reduce your total cost and your loan payment.

Car values depreciate quickly, so buying a two- to three-year-old used car with a service warranty may be the best deal.

Pay for your car

You have three options for buying a car:

- ✔ Save and pay outright.
- ✔ Prearrange a loan.
- ✔ Use dealer financing.

Having a hefty down payment may help you get better terms on a loan. Check your credit score too — it affects the loan terms offered and hence the monthly payment you'll make (refer to Tip #10).

Visit www.money.canoe.ca to check out car loan rates. Shop local lending institutions for their rates, check the interest rate each dealer offers, and compare all rates to find the lowest. Table 4-1 shows how different loan rates affect your monthly payment.

Table 4-1	Monthly Payments on a $25,000 Loan		
Rate of Loan	*3-Year Loan*	*4-Year Loan*	*5-Year Loan*
0%	$694	$520	$416
3%	$723	$553	$449

Rate of Loan	3-Year Loan	4-Year Loan	5-Year Loan
5%	$749	$575	$471
5.5%	$754	$581	$477
6%	$760	$587	$483

Buying a Home

Whether to buy or rent is a major financial decision. You need to have both feet on the ground when you figure out what kind of monthly mortgage payments you can manage. Read on for a few things to take into account.

For a more detailed guide to the process of buying and selling a home, check out *Buying and Selling a Home For Canadians For Dummies,* by Tony Ioannou and Heather Ball (Wiley). If you're considering investment property, pick up *Flipping Houses For Canadians For Dummies,* by Ralph R. Roberts, Joe Kraynak, and Camilla Cornell (Wiley).

Don't buy a home you can't afford just because the initial monthly payments look to be within your reach. And *don't* rely on a lender to tell you what's affordable.

Make sure you understand the terms and conditions of the mortgage you're committing to, especially whether the interest rate will be level for the length of the loan or if it'll vary and under what conditions. Variable interest rate loans, as well as those that are interest-only for a limited time period, can create financial problems in an uncertain economy.

Note how long you'll stay in the home and whether you can afford this loan into retirement. If you plan to stay for the long term, you might consider a fixed-rate mortgage payable over 15, 20, or 30 years. Table 4-2 gives you an idea of what your monthly payment could be on a 30-year fixed-rate mortgage.

Table 4-2   Payments on a 30-Year Fixed-Rate Mortgage

Loan After the Down Payment	Interest Rate	Monthly Payment
$300,000	6.5%	$1,896
$300,000	6.0%	$1,799
$250,000	6.5%	$1,580

(continued)

Table 4-2 (continued)

Loan After the Down Payment	Interest Rate	Monthly Payment
$250,000	6.0%	$1,499
$150,000	6.5%	$948
$150,000	6.0%	$899

Taking on higher monthly expenses than you should can quickly put you in debt and expose you to the risk of losing everything during bad times. Ask yourself these tough questions:

- ✔ How much down payment do you need to make? And do you have the cash to do so? If your credit is average or below average, you may need a down payment of at least 10 percent. Before you go shopping for a home, obtain a pre-approval letter from your lender.

- ✔ Do you have an RRSP, which can help you with your down payment through the Home Buyer's Plan (see Tip #30)?

- ✔ What mortgage payment, property taxes, and insurance premiums fit into your current budget?

- ✔ Would you be able to make these payments if you were laid off, lost your job, or had an extended illness and couldn't work?

- ✔ Does the home need any repairs or remodelling, and if so, how soon? Will those costs be included in your mortgage?

- ✔ With these new expenses, could you still afford to contribute to your retirement accounts? Would you still have sufficient emergency cash reserves? Would you be able to put a reasonable monthly savings amount toward your children's university or college educations?

For help with mortgage decisions, a step-by-step home-buying guide, and a mortgage calculator, the Canada Mortgage and Housing Corporation (www.cmhc-schl.gc.ca) is a wonderful resource.

Doing Home Repairs and Remodelling

Your options for financing home repairs, updates, and additions can present a challenge. You may choose to borrow the money you need by using a fixed- or variable-rate home equity line of credit or a second mortgage. Or you may consider refinancing your current loan for a larger amount and take cash out. Or you may decide to use money you've set aside for taking advantage of opportunities that may come up. First consider the following:

- ✔ **A home equity line of credit** gives you ongoing access to money. But after you tap into a line of credit, the payments add up. Also, keep in mind these are interest-only loans. Ask your lender to confirm what payment you'd make and how long it would take you to pay it off. Don't kid yourself; $40,000 at 5 percent interest and a $166.66 payment per month sounds reasonable, right? But this payment means the loan is *never* going away during your lifetime. By adding another $100 for a $266.66 payment, you still have more than 19 years before you pay the loan in full. Know the payoff schedule before you commit!

- ✔ **Home equity loans** are also home loans, but with a fixed loan amount and a monthly payment plan. The amount of the loan is generally based on a percentage of the amount of equity you have in your home. If your home has appreciated in value, this loan can be a way to access that appreciation and use it to improve the value of your home even more. However, pay attention to what's happening with the values of homes in your area, and whether they're currently moving up or down, as well as what's been happening over the last several years. Putting a tonne of money into a home in a nasty neighbourhood isn't likely to pay off in a higher sale later on.

- ✔ **Refinancing your mortgage** for a larger amount and using the extra cash for home updates works for many consumers. Are you planning to stay in your home? Can you absorb the higher fixed costs? Look at this financing option with an eye toward the future. But note that when home prices are depreciating, many homeowners won't qualify for refinancing due to tightened credit and income requirements. This option may not be viable during tough times.

  Before refinancing, determine the new loan amount you owe and the repayment schedule. Could you buy a new house for less that has all the features you want to add? Fees to refinance are usually around 1 percent of the new loan amount. Is it worth it? Can your budget, livelihood, and future retirement handle the new payments? Don't make this decision lightly; you could have a loan well past retirement on a significantly higher balance than you anticipated. Don't rush into anything without reviewing the financial merits first.

Plan to Provide for the Kids

By Eileen Freiburger, CFP

Most of the considerable costs of raising children are blended in with your everyday living expenses, such as housing, food, clothing, transportation, and child care. However, you can plan for several large expenses. This tip tells you how to be ready.

The Mat-Leave Money Crunch

Many families are completely unprepared for the money crunch that goes along with the birth of a child. In order to qualify for maternity benefits, you can't be self-employed and you must have accumulated 600 insured hours in the last 52 weeks or since your last claim. Even if you do qualify for mat leave, you'll be receiving only 55 percent of your insured earnings to a maximum of $435 weekly.

If you're lucky enough to work for a company that tops up your maternity leave benefits, you'll still likely be living on 80 percent of your usual salary or less. So your income is reduced, just as you face the additional expenses associated with a baby — a double-whammy! Read on for suggestions for how to enjoy your new baby *and* keep your finances on track.

✔ **Build up a nest egg.** Bank overtime pay; save your tax refund; if you're in a couple, try living on one salary and saving the other; or have funds automatically withdrawn from your account to build up a cash cushion that will see you through baby's first months.

✔ **Track your expenses.** Having trouble stretching your income to cover the monthly expenses? First, you must figure out exactly how much you have coming in and where your money goes. Keep a log of expenses for a month (or even a few weeks) by throwing every receipt into an envelope and then tallying them.

✔ **Separate wants from needs.** Needs include housing, food, and commuting costs. Wants cover vacations, dining out, and recreational expenses. Then hash out your priorities.

✔ **Cut costs.** Starting with the items on your want list, look for opportunities to economize. You might start by giving up movies and dinners out. Then find ways to shave the cost of necessities, such as grocery bills and baby supplies.

✔ **Delay expenditures.** Avoid building up debt if you possibly can. Even Baby Einstein's college fund can wait.

Saving for Post-Secondary Education

Start saving for your kids' university educations as soon as possible with regular contributions. How much to save is the first question to answer. An education costs calculator on ww.globalemc.com came up with the estimates in Table 4-3. The example is based on projected costs for a four-year degree, taking into account 3 percent inflation and a portfolio with an after-tax return of 6 percent.

Table 4-3	Sample Estimates of How Much to Save for University		
	Age 1	*Age 5*	*Age 10*
Future cost of school	$67,718 (home)	$58,414 (home)	$50,388 (home)
	$117,286 (away)	$101,172 (away)	$87,272 (away)
Years until the child starts	17	13	8
Monthly amount of savings	$192 (home)	$250 (home)	$415 (home)
	$335 (away)	$435 (away)	$712 (away)

Many parents are comfortable funding part of their children's university educations and letting the kids pay the rest.

Mother's (And Father's) Little Helper: The RESP

Most financial advisors regard Registered Education Savings Programs (RESPs) as a great way to save for education costs. These are the main benefits:

✓ **You can get a government grant of up to $500 a year — or 20 percent of your contribution — toward your child's education.** To get the full grant, you'd have to contribute $2,500 a year (per child) for 18 years and you'd end up with an additional $9,000.

✓ **You don't have to pay tax on the investment earnings accumulating in the plan.** When you turn the money over to your university-aged sons or daughters to cover school expenses, they'll be students (and hence broke), so they're not likely to pay any tax at all.

Comparing pooled and open RESPs

Two basic kinds of RESPs are available:

✓ **Pooled plans:** These plans are often referred to as scholarship trusts. You pay a set amount monthly and the plan administrator invests it, usually conservatively, and doles it out to the beneficiaries according to its own rules. If you drop out of the plan, you forfeit your earnings to the plan, so others benefit.

✓ **Self-directed plans:** These plans are available through investment dealers, banks, and mutual fund companies. You contribute what and when you wish, choose the investments yourself, and dole out cash as you will so long as it's within 25 years of opening the account. If your child doesn't go to university, you can roll the earnings over into your RRSP if you have the contribution room.

Most financial advisors favour self-directed plans because of their flexibility.

Considering the disadvantage of RESPs

The main disadvantage of any kind of RESP is that you can name one or more beneficiaries, but if none of them enroll full-time in a university, college, CEGEP, or designated post-secondary school by the time they're 21, then you have to give the government grant money back to the government.

Transferring RESP funds into an RRSP

You can get your original contributions back, and you can transfer as much as $50,000 of the earnings on those contributions to your own RRSP, providing that

✔ Your plan allows for that option.

✔ You've been paying into the plan for at least ten years.

✔ You have enough unused contribution room. Whatever you can't transfer becomes taxable income, and you get charged a 20 percent penalty tax on top of that (30 percent in Quebec).

Looking at Other Alternatives

Although an RESP is your best bet for saving for your child's post-secondary education, it's not your only option. Here are a couple of other alternatives, along with the reasons you might want to consider them:

✔ **Open a Tax-Free Savings Account (TFSA).** If you're not certain that your kids will opt for post-secondary education, but you want to set aside some cash anyway to get them launched in life, consider making use of the new TFSA (refer to Tip #32). You can put away up to $5,000 per year and the earnings accumulate tax free. That's money your children can use to put a down payment on a house, travel the world, or launch a business.

✔ **Save your child tax benefit (but no other money) in a special account for the kids.** You'll need to get Social Insurance Numbers (SINs) for the children and set up the account in their names. Any interest or earnings from that money will be attributed to them rather than you, and taxed at their lower tax rate.

Money-saving tips

By implementing a few cost-saving measures, you can stay on budget and spend your time bonding with your baby, rather than stressing about finances.

✔ Opt for "previously loved," whether clothing, furniture, or toys. Check out garage sales, second-hand stores, consignment shops, and flea markets.

✔ Cut back on grocery bills. Plan your menu, make your list accordingly, and stick to the list to eliminate impulse purchases. Cut down on expensive prepared foods and dispense with expensive last-minute visits to the corner store.

✔ Trade babysitting services with other parents.

✔ Defer RRSP contributions until you're back to work. The contribution room carries forward, so you won't lose it.

✔ Start your own gourmet club. Each couple can make a course, bring their babies along, and have a wonderful night out for a pittance.

#51

Save for Retirement Regardless of the Shape of the Economy

By Christine Falvello, MS, CFP

What could be more gratifying than faithfully making your retirement contributions month after month and year after year while the value of your plan increases? Each good day in the market brings you closer to your retirement dreams. Making those contributions is easy when you're watching your account grow.

But what about when the economy's not so strong? In an uncertain economy, the financial markets can appear to be going nowhere, and your retirement plan can seem to be sleeping. You keep pumping in your money and your plan repays you with a value that stays the same. Or even more nerve-wracking, it sinks like a stone. You ask yourself, "Why should I keep giving my hard-earned money to this ungrateful retirement plan that doesn't reward me by growing?" This tip explains why.

Buy Low: A Sale's the Best Time to Shop

Imagine that instead of an uncertain economy, the reverse is true. The economy is humming along as you continue to save; with few bad days in the market, your account grows nicely. How gratifying! The markets may even be doing so well that your family, friends, and colleagues talk about how they're investing and freely share that advice with you.

Now look at how investors behave in an uncertain economy. You know uncertain markets can be volatile and cause assets to decrease in value, sometimes by a lot. Those same people talk about putting an end to retirement savings. Some may even change their investments to cash, figuring they'll wait for the market to bottom out and then jump back in. They assume they'll know the right time to start investing again. You may have even thought about doing this yourself.

This isn't a smart move. Here's why:

✔ Even the experts don't know when the market will hit rock bottom and start to move back up. If the experts don't know, how will you?

✔ On certain days throughout the history of the stock market, the market rallied quickly and dramatically. Those who were in cash and missed a key day had portfolio returns lowered, sometimes significantly. They got back into the market, often at higher prices.

Those who simply stopped making retirement plan contributions missed a great sale. And Canadians love a good sale.

By continuing to save when the market is down, you purchase more shares for your money. When things improve, the additional shares you bought on sale increase the value of your account even more.

Take Five Steps to Retirement Accumulation

Here are five simple steps you can follow in any market to make your retirement dreams come true:

1. Save and invest regularly.

Set up automatic payroll deductions for retirement contributions. If you don't have a retirement plan where you work, or you're self-employed, open a Registered Retirement Savings Plan (RRSP). Use a discount brokerage firm to save fees, and set up a monthly fund transfer from your chequing account into your RRSP account. (Learn more about RRSPs in Tip #30.)

2. Start saving early.

The sooner you save, the more you'll enjoy the power of compounding. For example, a 30-year-old who invests $200 a month for four years at an 8 percent return will have $62,000 at age 55. A 40-year-old who saves $800 a month at the same return for four years will have $57,000 at age 55. The 40-year-old saved twice as much and had less money at 55. Remember, starting sooner means saving smarter.

3. **Maximize contributions to qualified retirement accounts.**

   Always max out your retirement plan contributions. Doing so gives you more flexibility about when you can retire, and your retirement income will be higher. If your employer matches contributions through a workplace pension plan, contribute at least as much as needed to get the entire employer match. If you've got additional cash available, maximize RRSP contributions.

   Don't forget about the tax advantage to RRSP contributions. Your taxable income for the year is reduced by the amount you contribute to your plan, so you'll pay less income tax. Think of it as having the Canadian government subsidize part of your retirement savings plan!

4. **Make sure your portfolio is diversified.**

   The old saying about not putting all your eggs in one basket is true of investing. Own a mix of different assets, including stocks, bonds, and to a lesser extent, cash. Your stocks should include growth and value, as well as shares of large, medium, and small companies. For bonds, think about using a laddered bond strategy — short-, intermediate-, and long-term.

5. **Make savvy investment choices.**

   Make sure your investments are financially sound and perform well compared to other investments of the same type. If returns are compared to an index, look for funds that perform at least as well as that index.

If your retirement plan offers company stock, limit it to 5 percent of your overall retirement plan. If your company does poorly, your job *and* the value of your retirement plan are at risk.

Seek More Information

To determine how much you'll need to save, pick up Vancouver-based financial planner Diane McCurdy's book *How Much Is Enough?* (Wiley). Also, check out these other good resources:

✔ Fiscal Agents provides free online retirement savings calculators (www.fiscalagents.com). Just click on "Financial Tools" to find it.

✔ *MoneySense* magazine offers an RRIF planning tool that allows you to calculate how long your money will last in retirement (www.canadianbusiness.com).

✔ Service Canada offers a guide to government benefits available in retirement, as well as online application forms (www.servicecanada.gc.ca).

Determine How Much Money Is Enough for the Rest of Your Life

By Garry Good, MBA

Think of your retirement as the most expensive purchase decision you'll ever make. Even more daunting: You have only one chance to get it right. A bad decision has implications for the rest of your life. Before pulling the plug on a career and current income stream, develop a clear image of what you're buying and how much it's going to cost.

So what's a good retirement worth these days? How much do you need for the rest of your life? To solve this dilemma, the following formula should be useful:

> "Rest of life" cost = (Annual expenses – Retirement income) × (Life expectancy – Retirement age)

In this formula, retirement income includes Canada/Quebec Pension Plan (CPP/QPP), Old Age Security (OAS), the Guaranteed Income Supplement (GIS) — whichever apply at your income level — as well as private pensions and Registered Retirement Income Fund (RRIF) payouts. Adjust your annual expenses for inflation.

The following sections look at these variables and discuss ways to take advantage of the factors you do control and to manage the risks you can't control. *Note:* This simplified equation identifies the key factors involved and illustrates the basic concept of retirement planning; but you need to crunch some real numbers to figure out just how much is enough for you.

Create a Fact-Based Retirement Budget

How can you really predict your expenses over the remainder of your lifetime? Believe it or not, this is one area where you have considerable control. The following process can help you allocate enough funds to face the ups and downs of your retirement years:

1. **Establish a current budget based on actual expense data.**

   Five or six months' worth of data should be enough, but be sure the period you choose represents your average spending patterns.

2. **Develop a reliable post-retirement budget.**

   Don't factor in inflation. While focusing on the future, simply conduct a line-by-line review of your expenses:

   - Look for expenses that'll be reduced or eliminated at retirement (work clothes, commuting expenses, and so on).

   - Identify spending categories that are likely to increase, perhaps travel.

   - Add a budget line for unforeseen expenses. You don't know exactly what or when, but count on unforeseen expenses occurring — car repairs, appliance repairs or replacement, general home maintenance, root canals, and so on.

   - Envision your retirement on a day-to-day basis. What have you been looking forward to? How do you see yourself spending all that free time?

 When you make budget cuts during the planning process, you leave no room to compensate later for events that are beyond your control. People tend to adopt optimistic assumptions to trick their plans into telling them what they want to believe. To make an early retirement look viable, you may rationalize that you can easily get by on less. Making a deliberate choice to reduce your lifestyle can be a legitimate component of retirement planning — but only if you'll remain committed. Ideally, your budget should include expenses that you can trim to stay on track even in the face of change.

Imagine that you're retired and the economy isn't cooperating with your well-crafted plans. Inflation is heating up. The stock market (and your portfolio) is taking a nosedive. These events are all beyond your control. The good news? With appropriate planning, you can limit the damage. You can tighten your belt by choosing to eliminate or delay expenditures — as long as these expenses were in your original plan.

Nail Down the Numbers

After estimating your retirement expenses, deduct retirement income that you'll receive from government and private pensions to determine your actual (net) cash flow needs. Read on for some suggestions for nailing down those pension income numbers:

- ✔ Every year, you're provided a current estimate of your future monthly CPP/QPP benefit. In spite of what fearmongers tell you, CPP/QPP (which is funded by contributions from you and me) and OAS (which is funded by government revenues) are both in good shape. But they're meant to provide just a subsistence level of retirement income.

- ✔ If you're lucky enough have a defined benefit pension plan (refer to Tip #31), just call up your company's human resources department to find out what kind of monthly cheque you can expect in retirement.

- ✔ If you have a defined contribution plan or RRSP (Tip #31), your calculations will involve some uncertainty, depending on how the cash is invested.

 Want your money to last for 30 years? A good rule is to withdraw no more than 4 percent of its initial value per year (adjusted for inflation). So for each $100,000 you begin with, given a 3 percent rate of inflation, withdraw $4,120 the first year, $4,243 the next year, and so forth.

 If your income is below a set low income threshold (which differs depending on whether you're a single person, the spouse of a pensioner, the spouse of a non-pensioner, or the spouse of an allowance recipient), you may be eligible for the Government of Canada's Guaranteed Income Supplement, which is worth a maximum of $562 monthly for a single person.

Estimate Your Life Expectancy — Then Plan to Live Longer

Fortunately, most people aren't born with an expiration date tattooed on their bottoms. Count your blessings and embrace this uncertainty! At the same time, the risk of longevity is one of the challenges you face in retirement planning.

Plan to live longer than you expect to live. Consider this: The average person has a 50 percent chance of exceeding life expectancy. In other words, planning for your expected life results in a fifty-fifty chance of running out of money too soon.

What type of longevity should you plan for? This depends largely on how much risk you're willing to assume. The current life expectancy for Canadians is about 80 years. The following chart shows an individual's likelihood of surpassing additional milestones:

Age Reached	Likelihood (Percent)
Age 80	50%
Age 85	42%
Age 90	24%
Age 95	10%
Age 100	3%

Making financial provisions for your life expectancy plus 17 years doesn't even guarantee success! On the other hand, you may be reluctant to fund this contingency, fearing your financial sacrifice could be wasted if you live a normal life or happen to die prematurely. Think of longevity planning as buying insurance with an interesting twist: Insurance compensates you for a loss, but longevity planning pays off when you win!

Make the Final Call: When to Retire

Whereas life expectancy is the great unknown, the timing of your retirement (health permitting) is your decision. This call has the potential to stabilize your plan or jeopardize your financial life. Make an active decision considering all options and implications. Don't retire simply by default.

When contemplating retirement, ask yourself the following questions:

- ✔ Are you really prepared financially for a secure retirement?
- ✔ Would you still want to retire if you were very happy with your job? Your boss? Your employer? Your career?

Sometimes a retirement goal is no more than an escape from a bad situation. If you still enjoy working (though not necessarily at your current job), consider a job or career change instead — or simply focus on doing your current job better. To expand your options and retire on your terms, invest in yourself through continuous education, network to tune in to new opportunities, and embrace change throughout your working life.

#53

Tips for Beginning Investors

By Robert Oliver, CFA, CFP

If you're just getting started investing, you may wonder whether you should put any of your hard-earned money at risk during a period of economic uncertainty. You're not alone. Even the most experienced investors become uneasy when the economy stumbles and their portfolios hiccup.

However, some fundamental truths of investing will serve you well no matter the state of the economy. So don't be daunted by the thought of getting started in a period of economic uncertainty. Some of the best buying opportunities come during economic turmoil.

Pay No Attention to Timing Predictions

Before investing, the first and perhaps most important concept to understand is that no one can consistently or regularly predict peaks and troughs of economic or market trends. Yet many investment managers and information services claim they can, and they ramp up their marketing during periods of bearish economies. But if someone could regularly time markets or economic cycles, there'd be no need to sell the knowledge.

Focus on low-cost, buy-and-hold investment strategies and disregard market timing services that claim to predict market trends.

Instead of trying to decide the best time to move your money in and out of the market, spend your time and energy researching and understanding the cost of investments.

Consider Costs and Index Funds

For any investment you own or consider owning, understand these two key elements of cost:

✔ **Transaction costs:** How much it costs to buy and sell an investment; brokerage and sales commissions fall into this category

✔ **Holding costs:** How much you're charged annually for holding the investment; mutual fund management expense ratios (MERs) and trailer fees are the most common examples

Small costs can have big effects on your portfolio. Even a 1 percent increase in fees or charges can reduce your capital by about 20 percent over 25 years. That could make the difference between being comfortable in your golden years and struggling to make ends meet.

For most people, mutual funds and exchange-traded funds (ETFs) are the best ways to invest in securities. You can find fund expense data and other fund details at www.morningstar.ca or www.finance.yahoo.ca.

One way to easily reduce the cost of your investments is by using passively managed funds, also known as *index funds*. Instead of trying to beat the return of a specific benchmark, such as the S&P/TSX Composite Index, an index fund's goal is to mirror the return of its benchmark. An index fund can charge a low expense ratio because its managers don't spend time and money trying to suss out the best companies within its benchmark. Actively managed funds, which do try to beat their respective benchmarks, pass along the cost of research to you — the investor — in the form of higher expense ratios.

You may wonder whether you'd be better off paying more for an actively managed fund that more than makes up for the higher fee with a higher return. If your name is Nostradamus, this may be a good plan. You could look into the future and see which funds are going to have superior returns and invest in them. But in the real world, the only information you have is the past performance of funds, and research shows that past performance is a poor predictor of future returns. In other words, you have no way to know which actively managed funds are worth the additional price of admission. But you do know that you pay more to invest in an actively managed fund than you do an index fund. According to Morningstar, 58 percent of all actively managed funds lost more in value than the benchmark they measure themselves against.

Keep most of your mutual fund expense ratios below 2 percent, and use no-load index funds whenever possible to keep costs low. Low expenses are especially important when markets are struggling.

Determine Your Asset Allocation

The cost of your investments is important, but research shows that over 90 percent of your portfolio's return is determined by *asset allocation* — the process of determining how much you invest in each type of investment or asset class, such as stocks, bonds, and cash. To determine which asset classes are appropriate for you, consider the following:

- ✔ **Your risk tolerance:** Quantify the loss you can sustain in your portfolio's value before you change investments. Because most investors don't have a good sense of their tolerance for loss until they actually experience it, uncertain and volatile markets generally provide a clearer picture of risk tolerance than consistently increasing markets. Ask yourself what you would do if your portfolio lost 10 percent, 20 percent, or 30 percent, and choose your asset allocation accordingly.

- ✔ **Your goals and time horizon:** Why are you investing? When do you need your money? You may be building a nest egg for retirement or saving for your next vacation. The time between today and when you need your investment is your *time horizon.* If you're just starting your career and retirement nest egg, you won't need the money for decades. Therefore, you can wade through periods of volatility and take on more risk. However, if you're saving for a vacation six months from now, you may not want to jeopardize your vacation by investing your savings in risky stocks. Generally, you should invest less of your portfolio in stocks or equity mutual funds as your time horizon shortens.

Allocate assets for short-term goals

If you want to invest some money that you plan to use in ten years or less, be careful how much you invest in volatile asset classes like stocks. If you plan to use the money in one year or less, such as for next summer's vacation, avoid investing in stocks altogether.

 Use cash-like investment vehicles — such as savings accounts, money market accounts and funds, Guaranteed Investment Certificates (GICs), treasury bills, and short-term bonds — for money you need within a year. For more on cash vehicles, refer to Tip #14.

As your time horizon lengthens, you can begin to invest a portion of your portfolio in stocks. In *The Intelligent Asset Allocator* (McGraw-Hill), financial theorist William Bernstein recommends investing no more than ten times the number of years you'll be invested in stocks. For example, if you need the money in three years, you should invest no more than 30 percent of your portfolio in stocks with the remainder invested in bonds and cash. This is a good rule, but you probably shouldn't invest more than 80 percent of your portfolio in stocks, even if you don't need the money for ten years.

Unless you're taking advantage of the federal government's Home Buyers' Plan or Lifelong Learning Plan, avoid using tax-deferred accounts such as Registered Retirement Savings Plans (RRSPs) for short-term goals. The tax you'll pay will likely outweigh the benefit.

Allocate assets for long-term goals

Although many people want to be saving for short-term goals such as a trip to the Bahamas, the reality is that whatever savings you can afford should go toward retirement savings, especially in periods of economic uncertainty. For most beginning investors, retirement is at least ten years away.

With those factors in mind, Table 4-4 provides sample portfolios for retirement savings for investors with moderate risk tolerance. The chart uses the longer-term data on historical returns available in the United States.

Table 4-4	Sample Portfolios for Moderate-Risk Investors		
Years to Long-Term Goal	**10 Years**	**25 Years**	**40 Years**
Stocks	**35%**	**35%**	**40%**
Large cap	30%	27%	30%
Small cap	5%	8%	10%
International stocks	**10%**	**15%**	**20%**
Developed markets	7%	10%	15%
Emerging markets	3%	5%	5%
Real estate (via a REIT)	**5%**	**10%**	**10%**
Bonds	**50%**	**40%**	**30%**
Investment-grade	30%	20%	15%
Inflation-protected	15%	10%	5%
High-yield	5%	10%	10%

Investors with a higher tolerance for risk may increase their over-all exposure to stocks and riskier asset classes, such as high-yield bonds and real estate, but more-conservative investors would reduce their exposure to them.

Generally, you should invest in tax-advantaged accounts for long-term savings. If you have limited dollars to invest, find out whether your employer-sponsored plan, such as a group RRSP, provides a match on the dollars that you invest. If so, contribute at least enough to maximize the match.

After you determine your target portfolio and invest accordingly, rebalance your portfolio back to its target percentages annually. This discipline forces you to stay invested during the year and then to sell the asset classes that have done well (sell high) and buy those that have underperformed (buy low) at year-end. It also helps you remove emotions from your investment decisions. For ideas on asset allocation and rebalancing, refer to Tips #37 and #38.

Investments for Beginning Investors

By William Keffer, ChFC, CFP

Investing when you're just getting started can be intimidating, especially in an uncertain economy. You face a tough balancing act. You can't ignore important long-term goals such as retirement or a post-secondary education for your kids. Maybe you're trying to bulk up reserves while paying off a credit card, too. But relax — you can build an investment plan that gets you up and running with confidence.

Getting Started

To begin building an investment plan, you need the following:

✓ A budget with cash earmarked to invest

✓ Specific goals, with costs, due dates, and savings requirements for each (Tip #11 can help with this)

Your projected timeline helps determine how much risk you can take so you can choose the right investments. A goal chart, such as the one in Table 4-5, helps you focus on the key element of the time horizon for each objective.

Table 4-5	Sample Goal Chart		
Goal	*How Much*	*Monthly Allocation*	*Goal Date*
House down payment	$40,000	$450	4 years
Retirement savings	$2,750,000	$1,000	35 years
Education fund for child	$120,000	$340	16 years

Matching Investment Types to Your Time Table

With the investment industry so anxious to sell stuff, people have come up with a dazzling number of products — so many that even the experts have trouble sorting through all the options. So what'll it be? RRSPs? RESPs? TFSAs? Stocks? Bonds? Mattresses?

For most purposes, investments can be broken down into three categories:

- ✔ **Stocks:** *Stocks* are shares of ownership in a company that entitle you to part of the profits, and they produce the biggest returns. But they also carry the most risk. They go up and down in value more frequently. The swings, called *volatility,* are greater than in bonds, too.

- ✔ **Bonds:** *Bonds* represent a debt that a company or government owes you, the investor. They give you more modest returns but a smoother ride than stocks. The company or government that issues the bonds agrees to pay interest and to return the principal.

- ✔ **Cash:** In investment terms, cash is a short-term store of value that's accessible, safe, and can pay interest. Cash doesn't change in value very much. The amount of risk to your principal is little or none, but the downside is that cash offers low returns. (Refer to Tip #14 for details on the types of cash accounts available.)

Risk is the amount of volatility in returns over a given period — in other words, how drastically the value of your investment goes up and down. High risk generally leads to a higher return, but lower risk ensures the funds you need in the short term don't disappear just when you need them. So for your emergency fund (refer to Tip #8), a low-risk fund such as cash is the best bet. For a retirement that may be 30 or more years off but will require a substantial pile of money, more stocks are a good choice. Bonds are a great fit for a goal coming due in an intermediate period of time.

Risk is a normal and even healthy part of the market cycle, and avoiding all risk isn't an option. Investments that are too conservative may mean you're just trading the risk of gut-wrenching market gyrations for the equally scary prospect of having to move in with your adult children. For long-term goals, get comfortable with investment risk and stay the course (but review your portfolio annually to make sure you're still on track).

In any economy, you should tie your investment decisions to when the money must be available. Check out Table 4-6, which matches time tables with acceptable levels of risk.

Table 4-6	Investments for Short-, Intermediate-, and Long-Term Goals		
	Short-Term Goals	*Intermediate-Term Goals*	*Long-Term Goals*
Years until	0–3 years	4–10 years	11+ years
Acceptable risk	Low	Low to moderate	Higher
Type of assets	Mostly or all cash	Cash and bonds	Stocks and bonds
Investments you may pick	Savings accounts Money market funds GICs Short-term bond funds	GICs Short-term bond funds Intermediate-term bond funds Conservative allocation funds	Mostly stock and bond funds Growth and income funds Target-date funds Target-allocation funds
Accounts you may use	Bank, credit union, or trust company TFSAs Investment accounts	Bank, credit union, or trust company TFSAs Investment accounts	RRSPs RESPs TFSAs Investment accounts

Here's a guideline for the maximum percentage of a portfolio that should be invested in stocks, based on when you'll need the funds:

Time Horizon	*Maximum Invested in Stocks (Percent)*
0–3 years	0%
4–5 years	20%
6 years	30%
7 years	40%
8 years	50%
9 years	60%
10 years	70%
11+ years	80%

Building a Beginner's Portfolio

No one can reliably predict the markets. But because investment requires being *in* the markets, controlling what you can is important so you limit potential losses. The things within your control include the following:

- ✔ **Allocation:** Allocation is the portion of your treasure in each of the big three: stocks, bonds, and cash.

- ✔ **Diversification:** Diversification means owning enough different investment positions in each asset category.

- ✔ **Costs:** High investment expenses can eat away at your earnings.

As a beginning investor, you need just a few investment vehicles — or maybe even just one —to hit all your asset classes and to be diversified. And you don't want to pay big expenses and commissions. *Mutual funds* — investment companies that sell shares to the public, pool their money, and buy a large number of various stocks or bonds — are the best choice for beginning investors because they offer automatic diversification.

 Mutual funds can be either actively or passively managed. *Actively managed funds* have managers who try to beat the market by stock picking and market timing. *Index funds* own shares of an entire sector, hoping to passively match the market. Fans of indexing believe that markets move randomly, so active managers can't accurately and consistently predict the direction or timing of markets. And because active management has higher costs, index funds may have a leg up. (For more on mutual funds, see Tip #18.)

Following are a couple of ideas for beginners' portfolios:

- ✔ **One-stop shopping:** A number of fund companies now offer life cycle, target date, or asset allocation funds that include large and small Canadian stocks, U.S. and international stocks, bonds, and cash in one bucket. Some are geared for a particular objective, such as retirement, ratcheting back the riskier assets as the goal approaches. Others cater to specific asset mixes, from conservative to aggressive. These plug-and-play funds are good options if your funds are limited or if you just like the convenience. Look for one using index funds to keep costs low.

✔ **Simple index fund portfolio:** For beginning investors who want more leeway on allocations, *MoneySense* magazine offers what it calls the Classic Couch Potato Portfolio:

- Total Canadian stock market index

- Total U.S. stock market index

- Total Canadian bond

Plunking 33.3 percent of your cash into each category can provide a moderate investor with broad diversification and a great start toward building long-term wealth. See Part III for tips on getting the asset mix that's right for you. Do a search for "couch potato portfolio" at www.canadianbusiness.com for more details on the *MoneySense* approach.

#55

Strategies for Intermediate Investors

By James Taylor, CFP, and Buz Livingston, CFP

Maybe you just got invited to your 30-year high school reunion. Or perhaps the grey is showing around your temples. Whether you like it or not, you're getting older, and just as you (hopefully) mature, your investment strategy should, too.

Parts I and II of this book address building a secure foundation and employing different investment tactics, and Tip #54 demonstrates the use of three basic portfolio building blocks: stocks, bonds, and cash. This tip addresses additional investments to help further diversify and maximize your returns.

You don't have to be a CARP (Canada's Association for the 50-plus) member to be an intermediate investor, but here are some asset classes you may want to include as your portfolio grows:

- Small company stock mutual funds
- Emerging market stock mutual funds
- International small company stock mutual funds
- Real estate investment trusts (REITs)
- High-yield bond funds
- Canada Real Return Bonds (RRBs)
- International bond mutual funds

This tip also discusses a couple of other options — micro-cap stocks and commodities — and gives you some general investment tips.

Own It: Equity Asset Classes

Equity asset classes are groups of stocks that have similar characteristics and perform the same in the marketplace. Here are the next four asset classes to add to your portfolio:

- ✔ **Canadian small company stocks:** Consider an actively managed small-cap fund. Knowledge of the market helps at this level. In fact, in a 2004 study by Standard & Poor, 82.5 percent of Canadian small-cap equity funds beat the S&P/TSX small-cap index.

- ✔ **U.S. small company stocks:** U.S. small caps make up the second asset class you may want to add to your mix. Over the last 80 years, the U.S. Small Cap Index has outperformed the S&P 500, earning 12.2 percent annually versus the S&P's 10.4 percent. The trade-off is volatility, because the prices of small companies can swing dramatically compared to their larger counterparts.

- ✔ **Emerging markets:** These assets may make sense for a small portion of your portfolio, but their volatility is even more dramatic than small company North American stocks. For instance, the MSCI Emerging Market Index was up over 66 percent in 1999 and down over 30 percent the very next year. Last year emerging market stocks were down some 47.2 percent overall.

- ✔ **International small company stocks:** Like their North American cousins, international small-cap stocks are more unpredictable than stocks of larger companies.

- ✔ **Real estate investment trusts (REITs):** In 2005 the iShares Canadian REIT Sector Index Fund, which tracks the S&P/TSX Capped REIT Index, returned 35.5 percent. But as of December 2008, its one-year return was –38.5 percent and its three-year return was –8.8 percent.

Emerging market stocks, international small company stocks, and REITs can add a little punch to your portfolio, but they're also extremely volatile. Never let them reach a double-digit allocation in your portfolio. Experts recommend a higher allocation to large company stocks versus small company stocks.

Why include these additional investments? The answer is simple: diversification. In 2001, the S&P 500 was down almost 12 percent while the NAREIT Index was up almost 14 percent.

Successful investors don't chase the highest performing asset class from one year to the next. Instead, they use investments that perform differently under the same economic conditions. In doing so, they diversify their portfolios and lower their risks.

Lend It: Bond Asset Classes

As with stocks, investors benefit by including different types of bonds or fixed income in their portfolios. Dissimilar asset classes of bonds perform in distinct ways:

- ✔ **High-yield bonds (junk bonds):** These pay higher yields and sometimes pay capital gains.

- ✔ **Canada Real Return Bonds:** RRBs provide stability during periods of high inflation.

- ✔ **International bond funds:** These funds allow an investor to profit from changes in the value of the dollar and fluctuations in U.S. and overseas interest rates.

 The best way to add these asset classes is through low-cost index funds or exchange-traded funds (ETFs — refer to Tip #20). Unfortunately, none exist for high-yield bonds.

Risk It: Other Asset Classes for the Intermediate Investor

Intermediate investors with a high risk tolerance may want to consider two additional asset classes: micro-cap stocks and commodities. *Micro-cap stocks,* also called penny stocks, are the smallest stocks trading in the Canadian stock market. They provide diversification but are also extremely volatile. Only the most aggressive and sophisticated investor should own this asset class.

You may face uncertain times, but one thing is certain: Commodities frequently perform very well in periods of uncertainty. One example is the Criterion Diversified Commodities Currency Hedged Fund, offered by the mutual fund family Criterion Investments. The fund is noteworthy in that it offers currency hedging, so returns aren't affected by changes in the Canada–U.S. exchange rate. Several other choices are available in the form of U.S.-listed exchange-traded funds and exchange-traded notes, which are a cousin of the better-known ETF. In the United States, PIMCO and Oppenheimer have long-established mutual funds that track specific indexes. Investors also can use an ETF from iShares that tracks the GSCI Commodity Trust. This index and the two mutual funds invest in a basket of diverse commodities such as oil, agricultural products, and precious metals. Avoid investing in only one type of commodity.

Micro-cap stocks and commodities are among the most volatile of asset classes. Make sure your risk tolerance is suitable for either of them.

Follow It: Advice for Intermediate Investors

Investment decisions aren't easy for intermediate investors. You have plenty of opportunities but also a fair amount of risk. These tips may help:

- ✔ **Don't limit your investments to your company's retirement plan.** Many people begin investing via their employer's group RRSP plan. But if that's all you have, it's not enough. Intermediate stage investors should have investments in Tax-Free Savings Accounts (refer to Tip #32) and taxable accounts (Tip #29) to take advantage of long-term capital gains rates. You should also invest in individual RRSPs (Tip #30), which come with a tax deduction.

- ✔ **Use Registered Education Savings Plans (RESPs) for children or grandchildren.** The government gives you a grant of 20 percent on your contributions (up to $2,500 per child), and earnings grow tax free. Also, payouts for qualified higher education expenses are taxed in the hands of the student, so they're effectively tax free. (Tip #50 tells you more about saving for university and college.)

- ✔ **Make sure your insurance is appropriate.** You've worked hard to build a nest egg — don't lose it! Your life, disability, and liability coverage should be adequate. Not everyone needs or can afford long-term care insurance, but you should probably plan for the possibility of needing long-term care.

- ✔ **Avoid mutual funds and ETFs that are country-specific (such as Brazil or China) or sector-specific (such as health care or technology).** In 2008, almost every mutual fund that invested in China and related markets such as Taiwan and Hong Kong went down more than 50 percent. Diversifying reduces risk, so don't concentrate your investments.

#56

Investments for Intermediate-Stage Investors

By Thomas Arconti, CFP

You've been investing for a while. You have your asset allocation in place and have rebalanced your portfolio a few times. You know the ups and downs of the stock market and even feel comfortable with the swings in your portfolio's value. Now, like that basic food recipe you've cooked countless times, you're ready to kick it up a notch and experiment with the ingredients.

Supplement Your Core Portfolio: The Satellite Approach

As you look to add additional investments to your portfolio, the first thing to remember is not to dismantle your well-balanced, diversified portfolio. Instead, consider this your core portfolio — the one to hold for the long term that will continue to stand the test of time. Supplement your core portfolio with one or more satellite portfolios, made up of more narrowly focused holdings that you believe will enhance your overall risk/return profile.

The satellite portfolios can be constructed with mutual funds or exchange-traded funds (ETFs). Some examples of satellite funds include the following:

- Commodity funds
- Emerging market bond funds
- Foreign currency funds
- High-yield bond funds
- Long/short funds
- Mega- or micro-cap funds
- Preferred stocks
- Real estate investment trusts (REITs) of varying kinds
- Sector funds

Uncertain economic times generate anxiety about overall market performance, but they also provide opportunities. The challenge is to assess what's happening, predict what's likely to happen, and choose investments that may profit from the upcoming changes — no easy task and not something to make large bets on. Use only a small percentage of your investable funds in your satellites — an amount that you can comfortably risk.

Invest in the next hot sector

Sector funds are mutual funds or ETFs that invest only in companies belonging to the same industry. You can choose from hundreds of sectors; some can be narrowly focused on a subsector of a particular industry (for example, Fidelity Select Medical Equipment [FSMEX] is a subsector of health care, investing mainly in companies that develop, manufacture, and sell medical equipment and devices).

Here's a small sampling of some of the sectors you can invest in:

- Biotechnology
- Consumer discretionary
- Consumer staples
- Defense and aerospace
- Financials
- Gaming
- Health care
- Information technology

- Nanotechnology
- Oil and gas exploration
- Real estate
- Solar energy
- Transportation
- Utilities
- Water resources

When investing in sector funds, keep the following in mind:

- If the sector is already hot, you're probably too late.
- Know the sector weighting in your core portfolio; choose something that may be missing or underrepresented in your core. (Refer to Tips #45 through #47 for more on sector weighting.)
- Be aware of the typically higher management fees and any short-term redemption fees.
- Be prepared to pay closer attention to the sector funds on an ongoing basis; know when to get out.

Not sure you can predict which sectors may come into favour? Consider a *sector rotation fund* and leave it to professional money managers. They may not choose any better than you would, but at least you're transferring the research to others. Of course, you'll pay higher fund management fees. One example is Manulife Sector Rotation Fund.

Invest in long/short funds

In an uncertain economy, stocks go up and down. Sophisticated investors have long employed strategies to take advantage of both movements, through short selling, options, and hedge funds. (Tips #25 through #27 give more information.) As an intermediate investor, you can tiptoe into this arena with long/short mutual funds or ETFs (sometimes also referred to as *market neutral* or *130/30* funds). Basically, the fund manager buys some stocks she anticipates will go up (long positions) and sells (actually borrows and sells) other stocks she anticipates will go down (short positions). Long/short funds may be a good diversifier in a down economy.

When investing in long/short funds, keep the following in mind:

- ✔ Minimum purchase requirements may be high.
- ✔ Returns may be mediocre at best when the overall market is good.
- ✔ Typically higher management fees and any short-term redemption fees may apply.
- ✔ These funds will have higher turnovers and subsequently higher tax consequences.
- ✔ These funds are relatively new and don't have long track records.

Some examples of long/short funds include BluMont Hirsch Long/ Short Fund and the Barometer Long Short Equity Pool.

Bet on the value of currencies

As the overall Canadian economy rises and declines, the value of the loonie rises and declines in relation to other currencies. You can purchase mutual funds or ETFs that track a single currency, such as the Swiss franc, or that track several currencies. If you think the Canadian dollar is strengthening relative to the U.S. dollar, you could profit by purchasing an ETF like the CurrencyShares Canadian Dollar Trust (FXC) or a mutual fund like the Merck Hard Currency Fund (MERKX), which invests in multiple currencies. If you think the strength of the U.S. dollar is on the rise, you could consider the Powershares DB U.S. Dollar Bullish (UUP).

When investing in currency funds, keep these points in mind:

- ✔ You need to be concerned with economies and market factors in two or more countries (the United States and all the foreign currency countries involved).

- ✔ You may be introducing new types of risk into your portfolio. Examples include political issues, trade deficits, interest rates, and national debts — both at home and abroad.

- ✔ Current events may drastically affect currency rates in a matter of days.

Currency funds are usually a zero sum game, meaning one side wins at the expense of the other. Accurately predicting whether the value of the Canadian or U.S. dollar will rise or fall, and investing accordingly, is important.

Add an income-producing satellite

Perhaps you're content with your core portfolio and merely want additional income. Accomplish this goal with investments beyond the traditional fixed-income holdings in your core. Intermediate-level, income-producing investments may include the following:

- ✔ **Municipal and provincial bonds:** These bonds usually pay a lower interest rate than corporate or agency bonds, but they're generally safe (check the credit ratings).

- ✔ **High-yield bonds (a nice way of saying *junk bonds*):** These bonds typically pay more interest than investment-grade bonds, but they also carry a high degree of default risk.

- ✔ **Preferred stocks:** These securities are somewhat of a cross between a stock and a bond. They generally pay a relatively high yield in the form of quarterly dividends.

- ✔ **High-grade corporate or government agency bonds:** The quality and interest rates paid by these bonds vary by their credit ratings, length of their term, and the general interest-rate market.

When investing in bonds or preferred stock, you should

✔ Become familiar with the credit ratings issued by Dominion Bond Rating Service (DBRS) and Canadian Bond Rating Services (AAA/A++ = the best, C/D = the worst).

✔ Understand the effect that buying a bond at a discount, at par, or at a premium has on your expected yield to maturity (YTM).

✔ Be aware of call features associated with your bond.

✔ Diversify your investments among several income-producing holdings to reduce risk.

Increase Your Tolerance for Risk

New investments in your portfolio bring new risks. Continue to analyze the risk/reward profile of any new investment and fully understand its place in your portfolio. Follow this advice:

✔ **Knowledge is power, so go beyond the basics and commit to learning as much as you can about the interactions between your investments.** Develop a good understanding of risk and performance measurements, such as standard deviation, beta, correlation, alpha, and the Sharpe index. Know where your aggregate portfolio falls on the Efficient Frontier.

✔ **Don't go it alone.** Get a buddy or mentor with the same interests in investing. Bounce ideas, concerns, and new knowledge off one another. Having a sounding board helps you to better understand the issues, and two heads are often better than one. Consider joining or starting an investment club.

✔ **History often repeats itself, so take some time to gain historical perspective of the Canadian economy and the stock market.** Look specifically at difficult periods in Canadian history (refer to Tip #2) and find out how the market performed leading into it, during it, and afterward.

✔ **Seek a professional opinion.** Find an hourly, fee-only financial advisor in your area to provide a second opinion. The fee may well be worth having your assumptions validated or discovering hidden issues.

Part V
Heading into Retirement

The 5th Wave   By Rich Tennant

"I've been working over 80 hours a week for the past two years preparing for retirement, and it hasn't bothered me OR my wife, what's-her-name."

In this part...

*J*ust as retirement draws nearer, you may be faced with unforeseen expenses, such as assisting aging parents or adult children. In this part, you find out how to prepare for these possibilities and how to position your investment portfolio to give you the flexibility you need. You also discover how to maximize your employer-provided retirement plans, understand your Canada/Quebec Pension Plan benefits, and explore other assets you may not have considered.

Be Prepared to Fund Large Expenses

- -

By Corry Sheffler, MBA, CFP, CFE

- -

*Y*our retirement looms on the horizon. Are you dreaming of that little cabin on the lake? Maybe you're planning to buy a boat and cruise the Caribbean? Are your golf clubs going to get a workout on the nation's best courses?

If you're thinking about how to fund such large expenses, you're taking an excellent first step! Now — during your peak earning years — is the time to look ahead and prepare for those big pre- and post-retirement expenditures.

This tip tells you how to determine how much you'll need, how much to put away to reach your goal, and where you can put it to grow along the way. Because of the appearance of the first large *sandwich generation* — those who face caring for both aging parents and their own children — you also see some specific planning information on those topics.

Figure Out How Much You May Need and How to Get It

Many large expenses come with a known price tag: what they cost today. However, inflation will likely increase that cost when the time comes to buy. Use an inflation calculator such as the one from Bankrate.ca to determine the future cost of a large expense. Go to www.bankrate.ca and type "inflation calculator" into the "Bankrate Search" box to try it out.

The costs of some large expenses, such as long-term care or in-home help for the aged, are more difficult to estimate. But again, your first step is to find out what something costs today. This may involve making a number of assumptions, but you have to start somewhere. For example, to plan for in-home care for elderly parents, you can check with local service providers to determine current costs. Account for inflation based on when you estimate care may begin, and you have your target amount.

This section explains how to figure out what you need to reach your goal and helps you decide whether to save that money or invest it.

Calculate periodic savings

To figure out how much you need to save, you need to know at least three of the following four items:

- ✔ How much money you'll need (remember to account for inflation)
- ✔ When you'll need it
- ✔ How much you'll (likely) earn on the money you save
- ✔ How much you can save, either today and/or each month until you reach your goal

With this information in hand, you can use one of the following online calculators to help you reach your goal:

- ✔ The W Network offers a savings goal calculator to help you create a savings plan. To find the Savings Calculator and other helpful tools, go to their Web site (www.wnetwork.com) and click on "Expert Tips" and then "Your Money."
- ✔ MyTelus Money offers a Spend or Save Calculator to show you just how much cutting back on your spending can help. Visit the "Tools" section of their Web site (http://money.mytelus.com) and click on "Calculators" to try it out.

Money you don't spend now is money saved, but money you do spend now is lost savings.

Decide whether to invest or save

When you know how much you need to sock away, the next step is deciding where to put that money to make it grow. If your time horizon is short, say six years or less, consider a CDIC-insured high-yield savings account, money market account, or Guaranteed Investment Certificate (GIC — refer to Tip #14). Visit www.money.canoe.ca/rates to comparison shop for rates. Online banks typically offer the best rates, and most are CDIC-insured.

If you have a longer time horizon before you need the money, the higher expected returns of balanced or growth-and-income no-load mutual funds may make more sense. (Check out Tip #18 for more on mutual funds.)

 As you approach the time when you'll need this money, shift your invested money into savings. Otherwise, if the market drops shortly before you need your stash, you may not have enough for your goal.

Prepare to Help Family

You may face large expenses if your parents or children need financial help. If you plan and save well, and if your finances are secure, you may be in a position to offer that help. Extra money gives you the option of helping your parents, kids, or both if they need it. Consider the following:

- ✔ **Adult children:** As you approach retirement, you may want to help out your adult children. Their issues may include job loss, house foreclosure, divorce, or health problems. Some people give money to their kids with no strings attached. Others loan their children money.

- ✔ **Elderly parents:** Besides offering financial support, you may eventually need to run all of your parents' financial affairs. If that happens, consider the services of a financial planner or investment advisor. A financial planner can help you understand the complete financial picture as well as estate matters.

 Keep the lines of communication open, so you're not gobsmacked by pending financial issues with your adult children or your parents. If you think they'll need your help, you can estimate an amount as a savings goal. Communicating with your kids and parents about money can give you a true picture of their situations and may allow you to help them avoid bad financial decisions.

#58

Consider Working in Retirement

By Cynthia Freedman

Some people discover retirement isn't all it's cracked up to be, leaving them bored and constantly underfoot around the house. Returning to work has concrete benefits, especially in uncertain economic times. They include the following:

✔ **Income:** Maybe you were downsized unexpectedly or your portfolio's value has dropped. Working in retirement can help make up the shortfall. Working part-time during retirement means you can reduce or delay withdrawals from your retirement nest egg. Earning $20,000 a year in retirement is the equivalent of withdrawing a safe 4 percent per year from a $500,000 nest egg. And if income isn't a pressing issue, working can boost your standard of living and provide a little more money to live the life of leisure you've always wanted.

✔ **Personal fulfillment:** Studies show that older people who stay physically and mentally active have longer, happier, and healthier lives. Your emotional well-being can also improve as you engage with other people, make new friends, and become a part of your workplace community.

You're generally not eligible for provincial drug care coverage until you're age 65. Although you may be able to continue your existing drug plan if you negotiate it through work, you'll lose any employer subsidy. Your only option may be an expensive individual policy. Getting a job with an employer who offers a group drug plan benefit can cover that gap in your health care.

Note the Drawbacks

Even if you want to go back to work, getting back on payroll may not be your best option. Here's why:

- ✓ **Current pension benefits:** If you're receiving an ongoing pension benefit, receiving employment income from another source may affect your benefit. Check with the pension benefit administrator to see what the impact will be. (This isn't an issue if you received a single lump-sum pension benefit.)

- ✓ **Leisure time:** If you're still working, you can't take off on a trip whenever you feel like it; you have to comply with the schedule constraints of your workplace. And when the holidays arrive, you may be the one who has to tend the store while your boss is home with his family.

- ✓ **Taxes:** If your job provides you with a high enough salary, you may be pushed into a higher income tax bracket. Contact an accountant or other qualified tax professional to see how working in retirement will affect your taxes.

As soon as you hit age 70, you have to start taking the minimum distributions required by your Registered Retirement Income Fund (RRIF), whether you're working or not. (Read more about RRIFs in Tip #60.) These distributions are taxed as ordinary income and are added to your other income to calculate your total taxable income. And if you're receiving Old Age Security benefits, the government claws back 15 cents on the dollar on earnings over $66,012.

If returning to the workforce isn't essential for your budget, consider volunteering. You'll feel great knowing that you've made an impact on someone's life by coaching a sports team, tutoring, or helping out at a women's shelter, for example.

Make the Transition

So you still want to work, but you don't want to go back to the same old grind you retired from, and you don't want to become a greeter at the local big box store. What should you do?

- ✓ **Consider your likes and dislikes.** Do you enjoy being with people, or do you like to work alone? Are you more productive when you focus on a single task, or do you need variety throughout your day? What social or charitable causes excite you? What hobbies are you passionate about?

✓ **Assess your skills and strengths.** Think about your job skills in general terms to help you see how the skills can transfer to other industries. For example, a good teacher may become a corporate trainer. Also consider personal skills. Are you organized? Do you speak well in front of groups?

✓ **Realistically consider your physical limitations.** Certain jobs may not be physically appropriate. Some older people start to lose their mental acuity and find it more difficult to learn new procedures, use a computer, or remember where specific items are located. (And your boss may not appreciate it if you need to take a nap every afternoon!)

For info about possible careers, see Human Resource Development Canada's Job Futures Web site (www.jobfutures.ca), which lists training and education needed for various jobs, as well as average earnings, average unemployment levels, expected job prospects, what workers do, and working conditions.

After you decide what you want to do, you can gear up to re-enter the workforce:

✓ **Network.** Join a professional organization. E-mail friends and family, telling them about your plans and asking them whether they know of any openings or if they can introduce you to someone who works in your target field.

✓ **Gain any needed training or experience before you start the job.** Check course offerings at local colleges or an online university. Can you justify the amount of time you have to put in for training by the amount of time you expect to spend working in your chosen field? Volunteering, interning, and working through a temp agency are all great ways to get experience.

✓ **Polish your resumé.** Many books and articles discuss how to write a resumé, what to expect in job interviews, and other job search issues.

After you find that dream job, enjoy. And remember that at some point, you'll be able to walk away from this job, too, and resume your date with leisure time.

Use Your Home as a Source of Income

By James Taylor, CFP, and Robert Friedland, PhD

Your home is more than just the place where you hang your hat and raise your family. It's one of your biggest investments and an important part of the foundation of your financial security. For most people, paying for a home takes decades. But when you've accumulated a lot of equity or have paid off the mortgage, your home could start paying you back. This tip tells you how.

Have the Lender Pay You with a Reverse Mortgage

If you have a home, you probably had a mortgage. In a forward mortgage, you pay the lender every month. With a *reverse mortgage,* the lender pays you! The money you receive is tax free and you have a choice of a lump sum, a monthly payment, or a line of credit with which you can take out funds when you need to. Any combination of these choices is also an option.

You don't have to meet any medical, income, or credit requirements, and no income tax liability exists. But you must be at least 60 years old to qualify for a reverse mortgage (although your spouse can be as young as 55). The amount of the loan increases each month because interest accrues on the loan balance. In addition, you have to keep the home maintained and insured, and all property taxes and condo or maintenance fees must be paid. (***Note:*** In many municipalities, seniors can defer property taxes to be paid by their estate.) The home remains in your name, and no repayment is required until the loan matures. Maturity occurs

> ✔ When the last borrower no longer resides in the home due to death or sale of the home, or when the term of the reverse mortgage is up (say five or ten years)

✔ When the last surviving borrower fails to live in the home for 12 consecutive months

Any financial planner or mortgage broker can set up a reverse mortgage, but some companies, such as Toronto-based Canadian Home Income Plan (CHIP) (www.chip.ca) and Mississauga, Ontario–based Seniors Money Ltd. (www.seniorsmoney.ca), focus on reverse mortgages.

Weigh the Benefits and the Costs

Reverse mortgages may work for you under some circumstances, but look before you leap.

Here are the positives:

✔ Because the money you receive from a reverse mortgage isn't considered taxable income, it doesn't affect payments from Old Age Security or the Guaranteed Income Supplement.

✔ You can use the cash any way you like — for making home repairs, taking that trip to Florida, paying off debts, or simply having extra spending money.

✔ A reverse mortgage is an alternative for raising money during retirement without using a line of credit or a standard consumer loan (which might not be easy for a non-working retiree to get).

✔ Your home equity gradually decreases as your debt load goes up. But you can never owe more than the value of the home.

✔ Generally the amount borrowed through a reverse mortgage doesn't exceed 35 to 40 percent of the value of your home.

Read up on reverse mortgages

Good sources of information on reverse mortgages include the following:

✔ **Financial Consumer Agency of Canada:** www.acfc.gc.ca (Search for "reverse mortgages".)

✔ **CARP:** www.50plus.com (Search under "Money" for "reverse mortgages".)

What does a reverse mortgage cost? It ain't cheap! Here's an example cost estimate:

- ✔ **Appraisal fee:** $175 to $400
- ✔ **Closing fees and administration charges:** $1,900
- ✔ **Lawyer's fees:** $500-plus
- ✔ **Higher borrowing rate:** Usually 1.5 to 2 points above the prime lending rate
- ✔ **Repayment penalty:** Usually applicable if you sell or move out of your home within three years of obtaining a reverse mortgage

The total cost to set up a reverse mortgage begins at around $3,500, and interest on the loan compounds quickly. In fact, borrowers often owe more than double the amount they received within ten years. These high costs should make a reverse mortgage an option of last resort.

Some advisors encourage eligible seniors to get a reverse mortgage and put all the proceeds into an annuity. Doing so offers the advantage of a guaranteed income for life, whereas monthly income from the reverse mortgage can run out before the borrower dies. In addition, the reverse mortgage lender can charge up to $35 per payment to the home owner. However, the annuity can have income tax consequences. Furthermore, the costs of the fees and commissions of the combined reverse mortgage and annuity can be extremely high.

Keeping it in the family: A couple of reverse mortgage options

You may consider arranging your own reverse mortgage with a family member who has the resources to provide you with the stream of income you need. That family member would place a lien against your home — just as any other lender would — to protect his or her "investment" when you eventually pass away or the home is sold.

Here's a similar alternative: If a family member is willing and able to purchase your home, he or she can make mortgage payments to you and let you live in your home as long as you want.

#60

Understand Retirement Resources

By Janice Swenor, MBA, CFP

When people retired in the 1970s, their sources of retirement income were few. They may have had a nice pension from their employer and Canada Pension Plan. Boy, have things changed! Employer pension plans are being replaced by retirement plans to which both employers and employees contribute. Generally these plans expose retirees to a higher level of risk. When the stock market tanks, wealth can evaporate. But pension plan members are still in a better position than the approximately 62 percent of all Canadians who don't have access to a company pension plan at all. So what are your retirement resources, and how do you plan for them so you don't sink in retirement? This tip has you covered.

Assess Your Government Income Sources

No one wants to be stuck sitting on the corner with a tin cup during retirement. But to ensure that you're financially able to survive the economy's ups and downs, you need to have a clear idea of where your retirement income will come from. This section covers the government sources of retirement income.

Canada/Quebec Pension Plan

If you've worked, you've probably paid into Canada/Quebec Pension Plan (CPP/QPP). This government retirement plan requires you and your employer to contribute a specific amount, based on your income. If you're self-employed, you contribute double the amount (your share and the employer's share). You get monthly payments after you reach a minimum age of 60.

How much you get in CPP/QPP payments when you retire depends on the dollar amount of earnings credited to your account and the age at which you retire. Basically, you're required to pay 4.95 percent of what you earn in CPP/QPP payments, as is your employer. Self-employed people pay 9.9 percent. The maximum CPP/QPP payout for 2009 was $908.75 per month.

 A study by the Retirement Planning Institute (RPI) revealed that one in every six CPP audits showed calculation errors. The average under-payment received because of these errors was $2,800. And in seven cases, the under-payments were more than $20,000. Can you afford to miss out? Investigate the following to make sure you're not leaving money on the table:

> ✔ **Check the records or request a pension audit.** For CPP go to www.servicecanada.gc.ca to check your records or call 1-877-454-4051 to request a pension audit; for QPP try www.rrq.gouv.qc.ca to check your records or 1-800-463-5185.
>
> ✔ **Remember that parenting is a job.** If you stay home with the kids, you're entitled to a pension, too. The most common error the RPI found came from miscalculating the child-rearing dropout provision. CPP/QPP rules allow parents to drop out of the workforce to raise a child for as long as seven years. During that time period, CPP/QPP rates are supposed to accumulate as normal.
>
> ✔ **Apply for credit splitting.** Separated or divorced spouses are allowed to apply for CPP/QPP credit splitting. That way the lower-income spouse can receive part of the pension benefits earned by the higher-earning spouse during the period they lived together.

Old Age Security (OAS)

OAS is available to everyone, regardless of work history, as long as you apply. The basic OAS payment for 2009 was $516.96 per month. The only problem: Pensioners with an income of more than $66,012 (as of 2009) will begin to have benefits clawed back.

Guaranteed Income Supplement (GIS)

This benefit goes to Canadians who are already receiving a full or partial OAS pension, but have little or no other income. The maximum monthly benefit is $652.51.

Spouses or common-law partners of GIS and OAS recipients can apply for a spousal allowance as long as they're between the ages of 60 and 64 and have lived in Canada for ten years or longer after the age of 18.

You don't receive the GIS automatically; you must re-apply every year. Bear in mind that even if you didn't qualify this year, you can always try again next year. Call 1-800-277-9914 for an application or go to www.servicecanada.gc.ca.

Defined benefit pensions sometimes take into account the pension you receive from CPP/QPP. If so, they're called *integrated* plans. If you retire early, the pension your plan provides will likely be reduced once you're 65 and are receiving CPP/QPP benefits. Find out now if your pension plan is integrated and how that'll affect your monthly pension income throughout retirement.

Wade through Your Provincial Health-Care Plan

Medicare is the blanket name for Canada's public health insurance program covering doctors' services and hospital stays. In reality, though, no single national plan exists — every province has its own (such as the Ontario Health Insurance Program and Manitoba Health). The plans share some common features and basic standards of coverage; for example, physician visits, hospital stays, and the drugs you use in hospital are always covered. However, some services and treatments may be provided in one province, but not in another. For example, massage therapy is covered in Alberta but not in Newfoundland and Labrador.

Knowing what's covered

Find more information on medicare through Health Canada at www.hc-sc.gc.ca/hcs-sss/medi-assur. Available resources include information on the Canada Health Act that governs the provincial and territorial plans, as well as on each province's individual plan. You can find more information on your province's plan at your local health insurance office or on your province's Web site.

Provincial health-care plans don't cover a number of items and services, such as prescription drugs, hearing aids, dental care, eyeglasses, physiotherapy, and so on. To help pay out-of-pocket costs, most people rely on employer-sponsored health-care plans, privately purchased plans, and government programs. Provincial drug plans mostly cover seniors aged 65 and older, but if you retire early, you have to pay for prescriptions out of your own pocket. You can claim these medical expenses as a deduction when tax time rolls around, but if you're on a limited income, they can take a hefty bite out of your budget.

Looking at provincial drug plans

Provincial drug plans cover the cost of prescription drugs for vulnerable Canadians, such as welfare recipients and seniors, and also provide immunizations. Some provinces cover people who require very costly drugs to treat an illness. Keep in mind, though, that provincial and territorial plans cover only what is on the list or *formulary* of drugs approved by the province.

 Some provinces allow doctors to request to have a medication covered for a patient even if it isn't on the formulary. If you have a reaction to a listed drug or can't take it for whatever reason and you'd like to substitute an unlisted drug, ask your doctor if getting special consideration is possible.

Know Your Employer Pension Plans

Employer pension plans are becoming rare as employers change to other types of retirement plans. If your employer still offers one, understanding your payout options is important. Your income benefit is generally based on a formula that includes the number of years of employment, a final average salary, and a percentage-of-income replacement factor.

As a rule, your spouse will receive about two-thirds of your pension if you die, but alternative payout options include the following:

- ✓ **A single life benefit:** This option pays the largest amount over your single lifetime. Upon your death, the benefit stops and your surviving spouse receives nothing.

- ✓ **An enhanced spousal benefit:** Upon your death, your spouse receives more than two-thirds of the pension benefit.

- ✓ **A reduced spousal benefit:** The benefit paid to your spouse on your death is reduced below two-thirds.

At retirement, you and your spouse have to agree and then sign a waiver if the option you choose will result in your spouse's receiving reduced income that may significantly affect his or her standard of living.

Before retirement, you may consider a life insurance policy to replace any loss of income to your spouse, depending on the payout option you choose. Evaluate whether the insurance premium makes sense compared to the additional income you may receive. Make sure the insurance is in place prior to signing the release.

Also ask the following questions about your pension:

- ✔ Is your pension plan integrated with CPP/QPP?

- ✔ How financially sound is your pension plan? Can it meet its promised benefits, and if so, how far into the future?

- ✔ Will you receive a yearly cost-of-living adjustment (COLA) during retirement?

Use Personal Retirement Accounts

Depending on your current age, Registered Retirement Savings Plans (RRSPs), Tax-Free Savings Accounts, and taxable accounts may be your only retirement income sources. If you've been contributing to these accounts regularly, you hope to have enough by the time you retire. How much you can plan to withdraw after you retire depends on when you retire and your asset allocation before and during retirement.

When you turn 71, you must roll your RRSP over into a Registered Retirement Income Fund (RRIF) or an annuity and begin taking minimum withdrawals. If you choose to withdraw all the funds, you have to declare them as income, and you'll be taxed on the entire amount.

For more information on retirement plans, see Tips #30, and #31. For more on investment strategies before and after retirement, see Tips #53 through #56.

Collect Income from Continued Employment

The definition of retirement has changed over the last 20 years. Retirement is often about having the financial freedom to do what you want. This may mean working part time, opening a small business, or working full time at a job you love.

If you're planning to work past your full retirement age, remember that health issues may derail your plan. Make sure that by a specific age, such as 65 or 67, you're set financially regardless of whether you decide to work. This target age varies depending on your current health and family history.

#61

Make Sure You're Accumulating Enough

By Ben Jennings, CPA/PFS, CFP

Naval aviators (think *Top Gun*) have a tough job: landing a jet that's moving at 240 kilometres per hour and buffeted by wind and turbulence in a space 6 metres wide and 41 metres long on a carrier deck that's possibly heaving in stormy seas and always moving away at an angle. One tool they depend on is a lens reflecting a coloured light *(the ball)* up the target *glide slope* to the ship's flight deck.

Preparing for retirement during an uncertain economy can make you feel like one of those pilots. Experiencing market volatility is stressful. The critical questions to ask are "Am I still on track to have enough?" and "How much will be enough?"

Determine How Much Is Enough

The answer to how much is enough depends, of course, on the answer to another question: "Enough for what?"

Estimate retirement spending needs

You can estimate your retirement spending needs by using a couple of approaches: top-down or bottom-up.

Top-down

Common rules assume some *replacement ratio,* a percentage of your pre-retirement income that'll cover your spending needs in retirement. Think of this as the *top-down approach.* The replacement ratio is easy to calculate, but you need to think carefully about adjusting it to your situation.

Replacement ratios often use 70 to 80 percent of pre-retirement gross income. This lower amount reflects that during retirement, you won't have to allocate money for retirement savings, a mortgage you paid off before retirement, payroll taxes, and so on.

Bottom-up

A more refined method for estimating retirement needs is the *bottom-up approach:* Start with your expenses now and consider how they may change in retirement.

Some expenses will, of course, go down:

- ✔ Your mortgage will hopefully be paid off before retirement, but costs such as property taxes will continue.

- ✔ If you have kids, you know how much money they required.

- ✔ You don't typically need life and disability insurance in retirement.

On the other hand, consider these additional costs:

- ✔ You may spend more on travel, entertainment, or hobbies.

- ✔ You may have to pay for dental care and prescription drugs, as well as other health-care costs that your employer may have previously paid.

- ✔ At some point, you may need to outsource household services and maintenance that you do or did yourself.

- ✔ Whether or not you use insurance to help, you may need to save for potential long-term care expenses.

Finally, make sure you consider costs you'll incur only periodically:

- ✔ You need to maintain your home for the long term. Think about roof replacement, painting, major appliance replacement, and so on. A common guideline for annual costs is 1 percent or more of the home's value.

- ✔ You may need to replace your car from time to time.

- ✔ You may have to pay for special family events, such as weddings, that fall during your retirement years.

Convert current spending targets to future dollars

Whatever your estimated expenses may be, they're likely to cost more in ten years than they do now. So far, you've probably thought of your future expenses in today's dollars. Now you need to adjust for inflation.

Try one of the following two approaches. First, you may use an average rate of increase over time.

Alternatively, you can look at the specific mix of expenses you anticipate in retirement and consider how these may change over time to create your personal inflation rate:

- ✔ A few may stay about the same (any mortgage repayments remaining in retirement).
- ✔ Most will increase about with general inflation.
- ✔ Others will go up much faster than inflation.

Table 5-1 lists multipliers for various periods of time until retirement, assuming average inflation rates of 3 or 4 percent.

Table 5-1	Calculating Inflation for Your Retirement	
Years Until Retirement	**3% Average Inflation: Multiply Spending By**	**4% Average Inflation: Multiply Spending By**
5	1.16	1.22
10	1.34	1.48
15	1.56	1.80
20	1.81	2.19
25	2.09	2.67
30	2.43	3.24

For example, suppose you're 15 years from retirement, anticipate a 3 percent average annual inflation, and determine you'll need $30,000 in today's dollars. Multiply $30,000 by 1.56, and you see that at 3 percent inflation, your expenses will be $46,800 by the time you reach retirement.

Calculate the assets required

After you determine your total expenses to be covered each year, subtract the portion that future income sources — such as a pension or Canada/Quebec Pension Plan (CPP/QPP) and Old Age Security (OAS) — will provide during retirement.

A good tool for determining future CPP/QPP income is your annual Statement of Contributions. The benefit amounts on these statements are in today's dollars, so just subtract the estimated benefit from your spending target before multiplying by the inflation factor in Table 5-1.

To estimate your OAS and Guaranteed Income Supplement (GIS) income, check out the average payments at www.service canada.gc.ca. Remember that these federal programs are designed to favour lower-income earners. If you have an individual net income above $66,012, you have to repay part or all of the maximum OAS pension amount. (The repayment amounts are normally deducted from monthly payments before they're issued.) The full OAS pension is eliminated when your net income is $107,692 or above. To qualify for GIS, you must be entitled to OAS.

Now you're ready to determine the number:

1. **Determine either a certain percentage of your pre-retirement income or calculate the specific expenses that add up to your desired amount in dollars.**

   For example, perhaps you need 50 percent of your pre-retirement income of $60,000, which would be $30,000. (Refer to the "Estimate retirement spending needs" section.)

2. **Convert that dollar amount to a likely equivalent in future dollars.**

   For example, maybe you expect your $30,000 needs to grow to $46,800 by the time you retire. (Refer to the "Convert current spending targets to future dollars" section.)

3. **Reduce your retirement need by the amount to be provided by CPP/QPP, OAS, and the GIS.**

   For example, if CPP/QPP and OAS will cover $11,700, or 25 percent of your $46,800, you have to fund $35,100 from your savings.

4. **Multiply that number by 20 and write it down; then multiply it by 25 and write that down.**

   This step calculates the upper and lower ends of the target range for your investment accumulation for retirement. The 20 and 25 factors come from several historical studies that found that initial withdrawal rates between approximately 4 and 5 percent can sustain withdrawals over at least 30 years.

   For example, suppose you determine you need $35,100 in the first year of your retirement. Multiply that by 20 for a result of about $700,000. Multiply by 25, and the result is $875,000. This means $700,000 to $875,000 is a good range for total savings. You can withdraw $35,100 from your investments in the first year of retirement, adjust that amount annually for inflation, and be confident that you won't run out of money during a 30-year retirement.

Figure Out Whether You're On Track

After you know how much is enough, you have to figure out whether you're saving enough to get you there. You need to know the following:

- ✔ **Your current savings:** Include Registered Retirement Savings Plans (RRSPs), Tax-Free Savings Accounts, and taxable and other investment assets. You probably shouldn't include your home equity or other assets that you can't convert to cash in retirement.

- ✔ **How much your investments should earn:** Keep in mind that many market observers may be anticipating investment returns below the long-term historical average in the next few years.

- ✔ **How much you're saving each year:** This includes not only salary deductions for RRSPs and after-tax savings, but also any employer contributions to your retirement account.

Also consider whether your savings are increasing each year. This tends to be automatic if you're saving a percentage of your income, but you may need to evaluate this number if you target a specific dollar amount each year. If your savings aren't increasing annually, do you anticipate saving more later (for example, when the kids are out of university)?

If you find you need to save more, increase savings by directing at least a portion of any pay increases to savings. This can be a more comfortable way of gradually adjusting your lifestyle to a sustainable level.

Using one of the many Web-based investment calculators is the easiest way to evaluate how much you need to save. The investment goal calculators at www.mackenziefinancial.com are excellent. *Note:* Because you express your investment goal in future dollars in this book, you don't need to account for inflation again.

Compare the result from the online calculator to the target you previously determined, and you'll have some idea whether you're on the right track amid the market turbulence.

Allocate Assets at the Current Stage of Your Life

By Garry Good, MBA

Your investment mix should always reflect your financial objectives, time horizon, and risk tolerance. A well-designed portfolio has to be aggressive enough to achieve your financial goals while minimizing the risk of scrambling to sell assets during a bear market.

An aggressive asset allocation is unpredictable in the short term but will deliver maximum output given enough time. Time serves as the buffer against uncertainty. Lose this buffer, and you've got no choice but to downshift into a slower, more reliable gear: a more conservative investment allocation. This tip tells you how and when to make the switch as you approach retirement.

Decide When to Switch to a More Conservative Asset Allocation

How do you know when to start downshifting your portfolio? And how much change is required? Before answering, consider your tolerance for short-term risk. The next three sections cover aggressive, moderate, and conservative investors.

Aggressive investor

For an aggressive investor (with a high risk tolerance), a transition path for your portfolio may look something like Figure 5-1.

Upon retirement, you need a reliable income stream — something an aggressive portfolio isn't optimally designed to provide. This calls for a less volatile asset mix, but you can't wait until retirement to flip the switch. Converting an aggressive portfolio into income-distribution mode takes a more extensive change. Start the transition early — ten years prior to retirement — to avoid forced selling of equities during a bear market. Keep in mind that market cycles sometimes last several years.

As you make this transition, note that your personal risk tolerance hasn't changed. You may be tempted to keep the throttle wide open with higher-risk investments; however, you have to let your time horizon trump your attitude about risk.

In the final stage of the process, you need to convert enough funds into cash-like instruments to cover retirement expenses over a one- or two-year period. You may think this reserve is excessive, but it provides a buffer, giving you more control over when to liquidate assets for income.

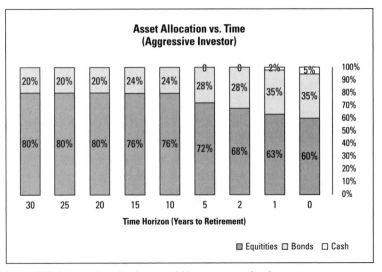

Figure 5-1: A more-drastic change within ten years of retirement.

Moderate investor

As a moderate investor, you can stomach a loss — within limits — but a more balanced portfolio helps you sleep better at night. After you've developed a moderate portfolio, your transition path to retirement should be a breeze. Compared to the aggressive investor, the required changes are less severe and can begin later. Remember — your risk tolerance has already reduced the volatility in your portfolio. Start the process five years before retiring, as Figure 5-2 illustrates.

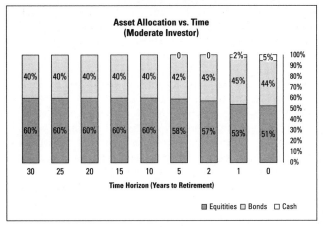

Figure 5-2: A fairly mild change within five years of retirement.

Conservative investor

As a conservative investor, you enjoy watching the money flow while the market goes strong. Then the money stops coming in — and you go a while without. You begin to think, what if the money flow never starts up again? Do you need a different investment? Does this sound familiar? If so, you can't handle high gear! And your portfolio should look like Figure 5-3.

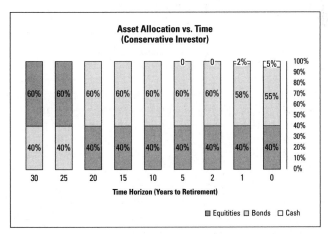

Figure 5-3: Conservative portfolios receive minimal adjustment.

In this case, your risk tolerance takes precedence over time horizon as a controlling factor in your portfolio design. You may not even need to change the pace — you're already in first gear. That's okay! A portfolio that exceeds your risk tolerance is like an accident waiting to happen. During a bear market, you'll be pressured to sabotage your plan by selling off assets at precisely the wrong time.

Having a highly conservative asset allocation 30 years before retirement may make accumulating enough wealth for a cushy retirement impossible. Make sure you have realistic expectations and that your investment returns will be adequate to achieve your goals. If not, you may be tempted to play catch-up and assume too much risk later on.

Transition to a More Conservative Asset Allocation

As soon as you have an appropriate transition path for your portfolio, you need a plan to manage the process. Here are some suggestions.

Use new contributions to revise the asset mix

If you're making significant contributions to your retirement savings, you can change your portfolio's asset allocation by simply applying a more conservative mix to all new investments.

Consider the following example: You're 50 years old, and you plan to retire in 15 years. You have $800,000 in current savings, 80 percent of which is equities ($640,000) and 20 percent of which is fixed income ($160,000). Your goal is to steadily transition your asset allocation to a 76-24 split in five years. Your annual contributions, including employer match, total $24,000 per year. The solution? Designate a 50-50 allocation to all new savings. In five years, your overall portfolio (ignoring growth) will stand at $700,000 equities (76 percent) and $220,000 fixed income (24 percent).

Modify your rebalancing plan

One way to change your asset allocation is to incorporate a shift in your asset mix while carrying out a typical portfolio rebalancing program. Normally, *rebalancing* involves swapping funds to restore a portfolio to your original asset allocation targets. Some investors may choose to rebalance on a regular basis — annually is usually sufficient.

Alternatively, you can establish a predetermined deviation trigger, which signals the need to rebalance. For example, if your target mix is 60-40, you can rebalance whenever your allocation in equities either exceeds 65 percent or falls below 55 percent.

Sometimes during a market decline, your portfolio may even self-adjust to a more conservative allocation. In this event, you may not need to rebalance and you can avoid selling equities during a down cycle. Conversely, you may see equity allocation increase during a period of market growth. This provides a win-win opportunity to benefit from market timing — you'll be selling appreciated stock to reduce your asset allocation below its prior level.

Tip #71 names a rebalancing plan that can take you through retirement.

#63

Minimize Your Portfolio Risk

By William Keffer, ChFC, CFP

You may be bearing down on retirement with a full head of steam. You're planning a fast-paced life of skydiving, casino jaunts, and adventure travel, right? When building your retirement nest egg, however, you may want to check some of that adventurous mentality at the door. Without the right amount of risk in your portfolio and a clear idea of your needs, you may find yourself having to ratchet back your recreation plans — not because you're physically unable, but because you can't afford them. In this tip, you discover how to handle investment risks.

Assess Your Need for Income

You can't assess the risks to your portfolio if you don't know for sure what you need to live on. Therefore, your first step is to assess how much income you'll need in retirement.

Identify your basic needs foundation

If you were building a house, would you start by shopping for door-knobs and lighting? Hopefully, your first concerns would be a solid foundation and structural design. The foundation of a solid retirement plan involves having a detailed knowledge of basic ongoing costs, especially in uncertain times. The old rule of needing 70 to 80 percent of current income in retirement may or may not apply to you. Although job-related expenses like commuting costs, clothing, or professional fees will probably go down in retirement, travel and leisure costs may go up.

Accept the importance of a (yawn) budget

Fact is, everyone's needs are different, and needs differ from wants and luxuries. Thinking about what you could live without isn't fun, but take the time to calculate precisely what you need to live on so you can get a secure income stream or safe assets to support it.

This is where a budget comes in. Look through recent credit card and bank statements. Enter your must-have monthly expenses on a worksheet. Budget tools are available in most personal finance software, or you can do an online search for "budgeting tools". After you enter your current numbers, do a retirement version. Think through it item by item. If your monthly need is greater than your monthly income, the difference must come from your portfolio.

Assess Your Need for Liquidity

Having enough liquid assets on hand when major needs arise is critical, not only to your peace of mind but also to protecting your portfolio in uncertain markets. The last thing you want to do is to sell assets in a down market to cover living expenses or a vacation.

Retirement budgeting starts with knowing what you need and when you'll need it. Basic expenses come first. Make sure you plan for other major expenditures outside your regular budget, such as car replacements, home maintenance projects, or maybe leisure travel. A goal tree that identifies these major liquidity events can help.

Make Sure the Funds Are There

When you know your needs, work on protecting the nest egg you've accumulated. This section explains how to limit investment risks and make sure the money will be available when you need it.

Increase returns while decreasing risk

In an uncertain market, the key to managing risk is diversification. By combining different types of investments, you can get the major benefit of diversification: a relatively high rate of growth, with smaller fluctuations in total value from year to year.

The most common measure of investment risk is called *standard deviation.* Standard deviation measures *volatility,* or how much annual returns deviate from average returns. High volatility means the security's value goes drastically up or down from one year to the next. Consider two baseball players: They have the same number of total bases, but one hits singles every time, while the other swings for the fences, striking out a lot, but also hitting more home runs. Same average, different standard deviation.

Standard deviation — and growth potential — differs for different types of securities:

- ✔ Stocks, which produce the highest long-term returns, have higher standard deviations than bonds.

- ✔ Small company stocks are more volatile but generally grow more than large company stocks.

- ✔ International company stocks, especially those from emerging markets like India and China, have even higher returns and standard deviations.

The neat thing for investors is that the returns produced by different types of investments don't move in tandem. So when stocks are down, bonds may be up. When Canadian markets are in the doghouse, Asian stocks may be booming.

Investing in non-correlated securities produces less volatility (or risk) *and* higher returns. Say you have half your money in a Canadian stock fund and the other half in a bond fund. Although the return on the portfolio is simply the average returns of the two funds, the standard deviation, or risk, of the two combined is *less* than the average of the two funds' individual standard deviations.

Manage other risks to your portfolio

In addition to volatility of individual securities, you face risks related to your life span, market changes, and more. Table 5-2 explains how to minimize risks.

Table 5-2	Risk Management	
Risk	**Definition**	**Management Techniques**
Longevity risk	The risk that you'll outlive your money	Make sure you have a sensible withdrawal rate. Know what you need for big purchases and for basic expenses. Consider a no-load, low-cost immediate annuity to guarantee an inflation-adjusted lifetime stream of income, at least sufficient to cover basic needs that CPP/QPP, OAS, and any pension benefits don't cover.

Risk	Definition	Management Techniques
Liquidity risk	The risk that you won't have cash on hand when needed, forcing you to sell assets in a down market	Assign chunks of cash to major goals. Plan to have more accessible liquid assets, such as short-term bonds and cash, in those accounts as the time approaches.
Inflation risk	The risk that inflation will outpace the return on your investments, reducing your purchasing power	Long-term inflation is near 4%; underestimating the effect of price increases can put your portfolio and income stream at risk. Use a realistic inflation factor in planning. Include enough equity in your mix to grow long-term money faster than inflation.
Market risk	The risk that stock and bond markets as a whole will fall	Get a mix of stocks, bonds, and cash that makes sense for your risk toler-ance and time horizon.
Manager risk	The risk that your actively managed mutual fund will do worse than the market on a risk-adjusted basis	Consider using index mutual funds or exchange-traded funds (ETFs) that try to match the performance of a given market sector. Accept what the markets give you and enjoy the lower costs.

Follow an investment strategy

When you know the amount for basic living expenses and major goals, use the technique in Table 5-3 to minimize the risk and ensure liquidity for the retirement-funds part of your portfolio.

Table 5-3	Balancing Risk and Liquidity			
Account	*Amount*	*Invested In*		*Refill*
Your local bank or credit union	One year's living needs + any goals due this year	50% savings	50% GICs tied to goal dates	From cash reserve account annually
Cash reserve account	Two years' living needs + goals due in two and three years	25% money market	75% high-quality short-term bond fund	From investment portfolio when rebalancing
Investment portfolio	Remainder	Your targeted cash allocation*	Your targeted bond allocation*	From your targeted stock allocation*

*Allocations would be adjusted for bonds and cash held in bank and cash reserve accounts.

Manage Your Registered Retirement Plan Investments

By Kathy Hankard

Traditionally, retirement was a pension plan courtesy of your employer. These days, that's rarely the case. Most folks are responsible for funding their own retirement (with some assistance from Canada/Quebec Pension Plan and Old Age Security) — and that's just what Registered Retirement Savings Plans (RRSPs) and, most recently, Tax-Free Savings Accounts (TFSAs) were designed to do.

Maybe you've been putting money away in your retirement plan for years. And maybe you've paid attention to how the money was invested — or maybe not. Now's the time to take stock of what you have, determine what you need, and make a plan to get there.

Figure Out What You Have

To determine whether you have enough saved (or whether you're on track to save enough), you first need to know how much you have. Add up the following (and refer to Tip #60 for more on retirement income):

- ✔ The vested balance in your current employer plan (If you're not 100 percent vested, you're not entitled to the full balance — if you quit tomorrow, how much would you get?)

- ✔ Money still lingering in an old employer plan

- ✔ Money in RRSPs

- ✔ Money in TFSAs

- ✔ Money in regular, taxable accounts earmarked for retirement

For example, perhaps you have $400,000 in your employer plan, $50,000 in an old plan, $25,000 in an RRSP, $10,000 in a TFSA, and $15,000 in other accounts. That gives you a total of $500,000.

Calculate What You Need

Determining how much you have is a lot easier than figuring out how much you'll need. A gazillion variables exist, but follow these steps to get a rough idea:

1. **Determine current living expenses.**

   How much money do you spend each year? If you have no idea, take a look at your tax return. Subtract your actual taxes paid (federal and provincial) from your income. Then subtract any money saved. The remainder is what you're spending. Here's an example:

   > $100,000 income – $30,000 taxes – $10,000 savings = $60,000

2. **Figure out retirement living expenses.**

   Do you think you'll spend more or less in retirement? Adjust the answer from Step 1 accordingly. (You can say *less* only if you really plan to change your lifestyle.) A paid-off mortgage is a legitimate reason for reduced expenses.

   > $60,000 current living expenses – $12,000 paid off mortgage = $48,000

3. **Determine what you need to provide annually from savings.**

   Subtract your projected CPP/QPP and OAS benefit (per your most recent statement) from the answer to Step 2. Also subtract any pensions or other income that'll continue in retirement. That's how much money you'll need to provide each year to fund your retirement.

   > $48,000 retirement living expenses – $16,000 CPP/QPP and OAS = $32,000

4. **Take 4 percent of the total you've saved.**

   Use the calculation from the preceding section. The answer is how much your savings could probably provide for you annually.

   > 4% × $500,000 = $20,000

5. **Determine your savings shortage.**

   Take the difference between Step 3 and Step 4, and multiply it by 25. That's about how much *more* you need to save to fund your retirement.

   > ($32,000 – $20,000) × 25 = $300,000

The Guaranteed Income Supplement provides additional money, on top of the Old Age Security pension, to low-income seniors living in Canada. To be eligible, you must be receiving the Old Age Security pension and meet the income requirements.

Consolidate Old Plan Assets

If you have money in an old employer plan, you want to roll it into a Locked-In Retirement Account (LIRA) or a Locked-In Retirement Savings Plan (LRSP) in most cases. Why? The employer plan probably has a limited set of investment options, and it may have additional fees that you wouldn't have to pay in a LIRA or LRSP. LIRAs and LRSPs have the same tax-deferral benefit.

You can open a LIRA or a LRSP at an investment dealer or a no-load mutual fund provider, such as the big banks, Mackenzie Financial and Fidelity. Note that you can't roll over your current qualified employer plan until you actually quit working for that employer.

Here are some precautions to take when doing a rollover:

✔ Be sure you do a direct rollover from your employer plan to your new LIRA/LRSP, or you'll risk owing income tax on the entire amount. Just triple-check with the employer and the new LIRA/LRSP custodian to ensure your rollover is direct. Ideally the employer and the new custodian will cooperate to do the transfer — so you never actually have access to the money and therefore can't be taxed or penalized. You never want a rollover cheque paid directly to you.

✔ Don't invest your LIRA or LRSP in an annuity. The major reason to own an annuity is for tax-deferral. Your retirement accounts are already tax-deferred, so don't pay the extra costs associated with an annuity.

✔ At age 50 you can convert your LIRA or LRSP into a Locked-In Retirement Income Fund (LRIF), a Life Income Fund (LIF), or an annuity and start receiving a pension.

#65

Invest to Supplement Income Needs

By Kevin Brosious, MBA, CPA, CFP

One of the best ways to save for retirement is through automatic payroll deductions into group or individual Registered Retirement Savings Plans (RRSPs) or Tax-Free Savings Accounts (TFSAs). Because of the special tax status of these accounts, you're limited as to how much you can contribute. Consequently, many people have assets outside tax-advantaged investment vehicles.

For these savings, the goal is to invest tax-efficiently while maximizing portfolio growth. Accumulating funds is one thing; keeping them out of the hands of the tax collector is quite another. This tip explains how to do both.

Invest with an Eye on the Tax Man

Ignoring the tax impact of investing can cost you between 1 percent and 5 percent per year in returns. Because you're going to pay up to 48 percent on investment earnings depending on your income, your province, and the type of investment, always consider taxation when making investment decisions. But don't hold an investment solely for tax reasons; it has to make good investment sense as well. By following a few basic guidelines, you can minimize the tax bite on your investments.

Know what to hold in tax-advantaged accounts

Probably the first principle of tax-smart investing is to shelter the investments yielding the highest amount of taxable earnings in your RRSP or TFSA, including:

✔ Interest-bearing investments such as bonds, bond funds, cash, and Guaranteed Investment Certificates (GICs), because earnings are taxed at the same level as income (up to 48 percent).

✔ Foreign stocks that regularly pay dividends, income, or other distributions. If you're in the top marginal income bracket, you'll pay from 27 to 37 percent on dividend income from foreign stocks, even if you just reinvest the earnings.

✔ Stocks or equity funds that you don't intend to hold for the long-term, or mutual funds that are heavy traders, because you're forced to pay tax on earnings when a sale is made.

. . . And what to hold in taxable accounts

If you're lucky enough to have additional cash to invest once you've maximized your RRSP, RESP, and TFSA contributions, your regular account is the place for truly tax-smart investments such as the following:

✔ Buy-and-hold stocks or mutual funds. Why? Because you're not taxed on capital gains until you sell your investment or the money manager sells and distributes the gains to unit holders. The easiest way to avoid tax in the short term is to avoid selling any assets with accrued capital gains. After all, a tax deferral is the next best thing to a tax deduction!

✔ Canadian stocks or equity mutual funds that pay out dividends. In the top marginal tax bracket, you pay a maximum 14 to 33 percent tax (depending on your province) on dividend income from Canadian stocks. That beats the 48 percent tax you pay on interest income.

✔ Any potential money-loser, including risky stocks or specialized mutual funds that you're taking a flyer on. If you're betting, for example, that a new manager can pull off a turnaround, a particular sector is due to rise from the ashes, or a startup business is destined for great things, make the investment in your taxable account. The reason? You can't write off losses inside your RRSP. Outside your RRSP, you can at least use capital losses to offset any capital gains made in the last three years. Or you can carry the loss forward indefinitely, lowering your tax bill.

Under Canada Revenue Agency (CRA) superficial loss rules, if you (or your spouse or your business) buy back into an investment 30 days before or after selling it at a loss, you won't be able to use the capital loss to offset current capital gains.

Exchange-traded funds (ETFs) trade like stocks; you don't pay a load when purchasing them. You do pay normal trading commissions. In addition, ETFs offer some of the lowest annual management expenses in the industry. Considering that more than 75 percent of mutual funds can't match the performance of their benchmark index, an ETF is a sensible choice for many investors.

Time Your Purchases and Sell-Offs Correctly

Don't buy mutual funds just prior to their fiscal year-end. Mutual funds generally pay out all of their income and net realized capital gains (basically the profits on stocks traded within the portfolio) every year. Although the payout date can vary, many funds allow the income to accumulate all year long and then shell out in December to unit holders of record on that date. You, in turn, have to declare any gains distributed by your funds to the CRA, even if you simply reinvest them.

What this means in real life is that if you buy into a fund on December 10, you may pay an inflated price. Why? Because you fork out for the short-term income and capital gains that were accumulating all year. And here's the clincher: You still have to pay tax on that distribution, even though you didn't really earn it and you're getting no benefit from it at all.

 Wait until January to invest in mutual funds. By that time, the fund will probably have already paid out its yearly distribution (depending on the fiscal year-end and normal distribution dates).

Aim to sell off money-losing mutual funds or stocks in taxable accounts before the end of the calendar year. Stock market or mutual fund sales have to take place no later than December 31 to count as a loss for the current tax year (which can then be applied against capital gains to reduce taxes). Most advisors recommend you have your redemption order in by December 24 to be certain it's processed in time.

Watch for Unrealized Capital Gains

Long-standing funds with a buy-and-hold strategy may be sitting on a hefty load of profits (unrealized capital gains). But if a new manager comes on board and cleans house or the fund gets caught in a downturn, it may have to sell off some of those stocks. Who ends up with part of the tax liability? *You* do, even if you just bought in and didn't actually earn all those gains. When choosing a fund, consider its potential tax liabilities when making the decision as to whether to buy in.

Part VI

Living on Your Investment Earnings and Drawing Down Your Assets

"I just don't know where the money's going."

In this part...

In this part, you discover how to maximize your Canada/Quebec Pension Plan and Old Age Security benefits and any pension benefits you have. You look at the best ways to position your nest egg to provide you with a steady stream of retirement income, whether you're a conservative, moderate, or more aggressive investor. You also discover how to reduce your risk of ever running out of money and how to hang on to assets you can transfer to your heirs.

Benefits Timing: Make CPP/QPP Work for You

By Tom Nowak, CFP

*U*nlike most investments, your contributions to the Canada/ Quebec Pension Plan (CPP/QPP) aren't exactly voluntary. That tiny issue aside, a great way to make CPP/QPP work for you is to look at it as an investment. Some of the considerations in analyzing investments are evaluating risk, looking at the tax angles, contemplating your time horizon, and controlling your emotions. But one of the most critical decisions in investing is when to buy and when to sell.

The good news is that your *buy* decision has already been made: You're in the program or you aren't. The bad news? The *sell* decision takes some serious thought. For CPP/QPP, the *sell* decision is choosing the date you begin to take benefits. Although the conventional age to begin receiving benefits is 65, you can begin as early as 60, as late as 70, or any time in between.

At age 65, you qualify for the normal retirement amount, which varies according to your contributions to a maximum of $908.75 per month in 2009. But take note that CPP/QPP payments don't begin automatically. You have to apply. Service Canada recommends applying six months before you want to start receiving your CPP/QPP benefits.

If you want to collect CPP/QPP before age 65, you have to meet another requirement. To get CPP/QPP payments between the ages of 60 and 64, you must have either stopped working or earned less than the current monthly maximum CPP/QPP benefit in the month your pension begins and the month prior.

Also know that you pay for the privilege of collecting early. For every month that you get payments before you turn 65, the government subtracts 0.5 percent from the monthly benefit you're entitled to get. That means that if you begin taking CPP/QPP at 60, your benefit would be reduced by 30 percent (60 months × 0.5 percent).

For every month *after* you turn 65 that you delay the start of CPP/QPP benefits, you can add 0.5 percent to the monthly benefit, up to age 70. That means your monthly benefit increases by 30 percent. Whether to take CPP/QPP early, at the typical age of 65, or later is a one-time decision.

In this tip, you discover the factors that go into deciding when to start collecting. *Note:* As with other investments, CPP/QPP decisions are not one-size-fits-all. The Service Canada Web site (`www.servicecanada.gc.ca`) is chock-full of information that you should become familiar with.

You don't have to apply for CPP/QPP benefits and retire at the same time. You *can* continue working. Look at your overall income plan to see what's in your long-term best interest. Tip #60 provides more information on how to make all your retirement income work together.

Look at All the Angles

As with other investments, one of the secrets of success to timing CPP/QPP benefits is to look at the big picture to develop a strategy that leaves you with the most money in your pocket at the end of the day. Here are a few considerations:

- ✔ Taking CPP/QPP payments early allows you to take advantage of income splitting earlier, which could save you money on taxes. Because you're allowed to direct up to 50 percent of your pension to your partner, the higher earner can transfer income to the lower earner (called *pension sharing*). This lowers the household's overall tax burden.

- ✔ You may actually *want* lower CPP/QPP payments overall to reduce taxable income as you age. By law, you have to transfer your Registered Retirement Savings Plans (RRSPs) to a Registered Retirement Income Fund (RRIF) or annuity at age 70, and you're required to cash in a set percentage of the fund yearly, which becomes part of your taxable income. Lower CPP/QPP benefits just might put you in a lower tax bracket, potentially preventing a clawback of your Old Age Security (OAS) payments.

- ✔ If you arrange to take CPP/QPP early and then go back to work, you could contribute the full amount to your RRSP. The transaction would be tax neutral, since CPP/QPP is taxable income.

✔ If you begin taking CPP/QPP at age 60, you no longer have to pay into the plan. That's a bonus, particularly if you're self-employed and have to fork out both the employer and employee share of the CPP/QPP contribution.

✔ You can view delaying CPP/QPP benefits as a deferred income strategy, with the goal of maximizing ultimate return and peace of mind.

The age of eligibility for OAS benefits is fixed at 65. In 2008, the average monthly OAS benefit was $476.05, while the maximum was $505.83. Like CPP/QPP, OAS benefits are fully taxable, but OAS is also subject to a *clawback* — a reduction in benefits for seniors with higher incomes. In 2009, OAS claws back for pensioners with a net income above $66,335 and eliminated completely for those with a net income of more than $107,750.

Sometimes things just don't seem to work out. If your nest egg has lost significant value, you may have to work longer to give it a chance to grow back. If you can't work full time, consider part-time work. If you can't work at all, you probably can't consider delaying your CPP/QPP benefits. See Tip #70 for ideas on how to allocate your remaining assets for this stage of your life.

Looking at the CRA tax tables might make your eyes glaze over. Just be sure to talk to your tax preparer and financial planner before filing for benefits.

Contemplate Your Time Horizon

The purpose of your CPP/QPP benefits is to provide income when you're older and in less of a position to earn wage income. With any luck, you're in good enough health to be more concerned about running out of money than breath. But consider your health when deciding when to begin taking CPP/QPP benefits:

✔ If your doctor is constantly giving you a hard time about a growing number of risk factors, maybe you're a good candidate for taking benefits as soon as possible (age 60).

✔ If you have a reasonable chance of living past 80 ("the new 60"), you should consider delaying benefits for what'll seem like a long time — age 66, 67, or even 70.

If you live to age 90, you might have been better off taking CPP/QPP at 65. If you die at 72, you'd have been better off starting payments at 60. The break-even point is about 78.

Control Your Emotions

Finding reasons to make an emotional decision is easy, especially concerning money. If you're facing a CPP/QPP payout decision in the next five to ten years, and you're already thinking of one of the following reasons for taking an early payout, investigate further:

- ✔ **You don't think you're likely to live past the break-even age or average life expectancy.** According to actuarial data, about half of all 65-year-olds today will live past age 85. About 8 percent of us will celebrate a 95th birthday. Consider the role your CPP/QPP cheque may play in your future.

- ✔ **You don't trust the government to continue paying benefits — maybe you'll buy an annuity instead.** If the government runs into trouble, how do you think company- or insurance-industry-guaranteed income promises will fare, keeping in mind that they'll likely be holding a lot of government bonds in their portfolios?

- ✔ **You'll take the payout early and invest it to get a better return.** Nifty idea, but not thrifty. If you can afford to take the investment risk that'd be necessary to beat the rate of return you get by waiting, you probably don't need to take CPP/QPP early and wouldn't want to for tax reasons. If you delay taking payments until you're 70, your monthly benefits increase by about 30 percent. What's more, that initial higher payment is indexed for inflation. No low- or no-risk investment strategy is likely to boast a similar return.

- ✔ **You don't want to take withdrawals from your RRSPs too soon — they need to grow.** Yes, taking CPP/QPP early may allow your RRSP to grow for a few years longer. But after that, the smaller government cheque will probably require even larger RRSP withdrawals.

All the preceding scenarios are well and good, but for many, many people, the argument for cashing in on CPP/QPP early is much simpler and more emotional: They really need the money now. And that's a great reason. However, consider one point: You'll probably really, really need the larger amount later, so try to postpone benefits as long as possible. Each month you delay between the ages of 60 and 70, the amount you receive for the rest of your life goes up.

Get the Most Out of Your Pension

By Liane Warcup, CFP

Most people who are nearing retirement and have an employer pension are looking forward to a monthly paycheque. Unfortunately, many of those people are fuzzy on the details. More than 5.7 million workers from a variety of industries (including teachers, provincial and federal employees, construction and manufacturing workers, financial services employees, and many more) belong to a Registered Pension Plan (RPP) provided through an employer or a union. Each person's benefits will be different depending on

- The employer's formula for determining benefits
- Whether cost of living adjustments are included
- Which distribution option is selected
- When benefits begin for the retiree

During times of economic uncertainty, understanding and protecting your pension income are doubly important, because during hard times, many companies lay off workers or force workers into early retirement. If you're prematurely forced out of your job along with many others, replacement jobs can be scarce. You may have to take your pension earlier than you want to or earlier than is optimal.

Take a Look at Your Pension

Answer *yes* or *no* to the following questions to see how much you know about your personal pension:

- I have a recent pension benefit statement and I understand what it says.
- I know whether my pension includes cost of living adjustments.
- I know what distribution (payment) options are available.

✔ I know how soon/late I can begin drawing my pension.

✔ I know whether my pension provides a disability payment.

✔ I know my pension's survivor benefits.

If you answered *no* to any of these questions, don't just sit there — talk to your employer to find out what your pension will do for you.

Meanwhile, read on for the basics to understand why knowing your options is so crucial, especially in difficult times.

Determine Your Benefits

Somewhere in all those documents you glanced at and then filed (or possibly threw away) when you were hired, is a formula for calculating your estimated pension benefit. If you can't find this paperwork (called a *summary plan description*), request a copy from your human resources department. One of the most common benefit formulas is based on the total number of years of service multiplied by a percentage of an average of your final years of earnings. Usually, the longer you work for the same company, the larger your current income and the larger your pension income during retirement.

Before you get too excited about this pension income, keep in mind that employers usually design pension benefits to replace about 40 to 60 percent of income, anticipating that Canada/Quebec Pension Plan (CPP/QPP) and Old Age Security (OAS) benefits and private savings will cover the difference.

Ask for a pension benefit statement from your employer if you haven't received one in the last year. You should receive this summary of your pension benefit annually.

Consider Cost of Living Adjustments (COLA)

Receiving a regular income for the rest of your life sounds like a good deal. But does the dollar amount increase each year to compensate for inflation? If it does, stand up and cheer. You have a pension that should keep up with the rising costs of goods and services. Table 6-1 shows the increasing value of a pension with a cost of living adjustment (COLA). As you can see, a little COLA in your pension makes a big difference over time.

Table 6-1	The Effects of COLA on Pension Benefits	
Age	**Pension (No COLA)**	**Pension (3% COLA)**
65	$3,000/month	$3,000/month
75	$3,000/month	$4,032/month
85	$3,000/month	$5,418/month

If you don't already know, find out whether your pension includes cost of living adjustments. This has grave implications on how much money you need to save outside of pension plans for your future retirement. If your expenses already outweigh the combined expected income from your pension and CPP/QPP plus OAS, and if your pension doesn't have a COLA, the disparity between income and expenses is going to grow rapidly over time. You have to make up for that gap with your savings and other assets.

Know Your Distribution Options (How Much Money and for How Long?)

When you're ready to retire, you may have several pension payment options to consider. Here are the most common:

- ✔ **Single life annuity:** You get monthly income payments for your life only. So if you're married and you die shortly after retiring, your dearly beloved has to deal with losing you *and* your pension unless you have a hefty life insurance policy to make up the difference. This is the highest payment option available, but your spouse has to sign off on it.

- ✔ **Single life period certain:** Payments continue at least for your life span or a set number of years (usually 10, 15, or 20 years). The amount of this payment is less than for the single life annuity because of the guaranteed payment stream for a set number of years.

- ✔ **Joint and survivor annuity:** You receive reduced monthly income payments for life. When you die, your spouse gets a survivor benefit for life (usually 50, 75, or 100 percent of your payment) or, in some provinces, a lump sum, if preferred.

- ✔ **Bridging benefits:** If you retire early, you get an additional benefit until age 65, aimed at replacing the CPP/QPP and OAS benefits you'd be entitled to at 65. Companies usually use this as a carrot when downsizing.

✔ **Lump sum payout:** Your employer converts your monthly retirement benefit into a single lump sum payout. The catch? You still have to use that money to provide for a retirement income. RPP money is *locked in,* so even though you may control how the funds are invested, the governing legislation controls how the funds are used. Here are some additional issues to ponder:

- Depending on your province, RPP money must be converted to a Life Income Fund (LIF) or a Locked-In Retirement Income Fund (LRIF) on retirement. The rules regarding such funds state that you have to withdraw a set minimum amount every year. Also, limits exist on how much you can withdraw annually to try to ensure that your money lasts throughout your life.

- Your lump sum rollover to a LIRA or LIF must be invested just like all your other financial assets.

- You can purchase your own low-cost annuity with all or part of this money, but make sure that any annuity you pick is at least as good as the pension annuity you've turned down, especially if your pension has a COLA.

So which distribution option should you take? That's a sticky decision that requires you to evaluate your entire retirement income picture. At least consider the following:

✔ How much CPP/QPP and OAS income you'll receive

✔ When to begin your CPP/QPP payments

✔ How much, if any, your pension will offset some of your CPP/QPP and OAS benefits

✔ How much you've accumulated in your personal savings and investment accounts

✔ Your estimate of your retirement living expenses

✔ If you die, how dependent your spouse will be on your pension

Your choice of payment options is permanent (no pressure!). If these choices make your head spin, consult a financial planner or two for some pension planning advice. Refer to Tips #51 and #52 for more information on accumulating money for retirement and making sure it lasts a lifetime (or two).

Other pieces of the pension puzzle

The following issues may crop up depending on your situation:

✔ **Incapacitation:** Find out what the rules are if you become disabled before retirement. Some pension plans, including CPP/QPP, provide a benefit usually up until age 65, when the regular pension benefit begins.

✔ **Survivorship:** What happens to your pension if you die just *before* you retire? Will your spouse have a pension benefit? How much? If your personal retirement plan is dependent on your pension income, the survivorship question is crucial! If your plan doesn't have decent pre-retirement survivor benefits, you may need to increase your life insurance to cover this risk.

Get Your Money at the Right Time

Although many pensions are designed to begin paying out when you're 65, some plans give you a range of choices. Pension benefits may be available as early as age 55 or any time after you retire. Early pension payments will be smaller than if you wait until your normal retirement age (much like early CPP/QPP benefits are reduced). Sometimes you may have great reasons to take advantage of an early payout, such as bridging benefits.

Some pensions allow you to delay taking payment until long after you retire. You may find this hard to believe, but some people actually decide to delay their pension payments. People who delay payments are usually still working and have earnings pushing them into a higher tax bracket than their future retirement tax bracket. They may wait until they're fully retired because they don't need the pension income while they're still working, and they don't want to pay the higher taxes. Plus, the monthly pension benefit increases with age.

 Find out when your pension is available to you. Check with your employer or read the summary plan document to see when you can start your pension payments.

Understand Your Employer Retirement Plan

• •

By Brooke Salvini, CPA/PFS, CCPS

• •

Did you save money in a favourite piggy bank when you were a child? Do you remember the exciting day you finally got to shake out the bank, count your savings, and decide how to spend your money? As a new retiree, you're turning your bank upside down. You still need to be diligent about rebalancing, making smart investment choices, and managing expenses. But you also need to know the ins and outs of shaking loose your retirement savings so you pay minimum taxes and no penalties. This tip explains how.

Read Up and Talk about It

First, get a copy of your plan summary document, either from your human resources department or benefits coordinator or your company Web site.

Next, schedule an appointment with your human resources department. Ask to have your withdrawal choices fully explained, including possible consequences — that is, taxes and penalties — based on your current age and employment status (retirement isn't necessarily the same as not working, especially if you're a baby boomer breaking all past retirement notions).

This is also the right time to meet with your financial advisor. Your advisor can help you sort through the various withdrawal options for your retirement savings based on your personal goals and needs.

Ask Yourself This

Especially in uncertain economic environments, you should answer these questions before tapping into your retirement savings:

✔ What's your current age?

✔ What are your hopes and dreams for retirement?

✔ What are your other sources of retirement income?

✔ How long do you need your savings to last?

✔ How much do you need to live comfortably every month?

Don't answer these questions in five minutes; really think about them. Everyone has a unique vision of the perfect retirement. A variety of online calculators, such as Service Canada's retirement income calculator at www.servicecanada.gc.ca (search for "retirement calculator"), can help you answer these questions.

Important ages to keep in mind include the following:

✔ **Age 55:** If you leave your job before age 55, many pension plans levy substantial benefit penalties. No wonder that an average of less than 1 percent of Canadian workers aged 50 to 54 begin collecting pension benefits in any one year.

✔ **Age 60:** This is the earliest age you can obtain Canada/Quebec Pension Plan (CPP/QPP) benefits.

✔ **Age 64½:** This is the earliest age you can apply for Old Age Security (OAS) and Guaranteed Income Supplement (GIS) benefits.

✔ **Age 71:** Here, you should roll over your Registered Retirement Savings Plan (RRSP) into a Registered Retirement Income Fund (RRIF) and begin prescribed minimum distributions.

Remember, you *must* apply for government pension benefits like CPP/QPP, OAS, and the GIS. You can apply online through the Service Canada Web site (www.servicecanada.gc.ca).

Know Your Options When Leaving a Job

You generally have to participate in an employer pension plan for at least two years before you have a right to receive benefits from it. At that time, your benefits are *vested,* meaning your contributions are locked in and you can only use them to provide retirement income. If you leave your employer before your benefits are vested, you can get a refund of your contributions, plus interest. If you leave after your pension is vested, you normally have three options:

✔ Take a pension when you reach retirement age.

✔ Transfer your pension funds to a new employer's pension plan if your new employer agrees.

✔ Transfer your pension funds to a registered retirement account. This could be a Locked-In Retirement Account (LIRA) or a Locked-In Retirement Savings Plan (LRSP), depending on your original pension plan. At retirement, you're required to transfer your funds to a Locked-In Retirement Income Fund (LRIF) or a Life Income Fund (LIF), or use the funds to purchase an annuity.

Most near retirees are bombarded with a laundry list of important decisions regarding the future. This can be overwhelming, but don't let it stop you from making smart choices about the savings you've accumulated in the company retirement plan. The next sections cover the options to consider for your savings when leaving employment for good.

Leave your money in your employer retirement savings plan

If the plan allows and you're very satisfied with the available investment choices and performance, leave your money right where it is. You can always roll your money into an LRIF or LIF later.

At one time, Registered Pension Plans (RPPs) carried the added benefit of being creditor-proof. But as of July 7, 2008, all registered plans including RPPs, RRSPs, LIRAs, LRSPs, LIFs, RRIFs, and Deferred Profit-Sharing Plans (DPSPs) are protected from creditors because of potential lawsuits, bankruptcy, or other situations. The only qualification is that you must have held the assets for at least one year.

Take a lump sum

You can't generally withdraw a lump sum from locked-in accounts like LRSPs or LIRAs. However, special circumstances such as a shortened life expectancy, serious financial hardship, or a very small balance in the fund may allow you to withdraw a lump sum. The exception is if your marriage breaks down, then your spouse, common-law partner, former spouse, or former common-law partner can receive benefits either periodically or as a lump sum.

Locked-in plans go by different names in different provinces. In British Columbia, locked-in accounts are generally referred to as Locked-In Registered Savings Plans (LRSPs). In Alberta, Saskatchewan, Manitoba, Quebec, New Brunswick, Ontario, Newfoundland, and Nova Scotia, they're usually called Locked-In Retirement Accounts (LIRAs).

Roll your money into an LRIF or a LIF

Most of the time, rolling your retirement plan savings into an LRIF or a LIF is best. LRIFs tend to be more flexible in terms of withdrawal options, mainly because in some provinces whatever is left in your LIF at age 80 must be converted to an annuity. (See Tip #69 for info on LRIF withdrawal options.)

The most important thing to remember about a rollover is to request a direct trustee-to-trustee transfer. A direct trustee-to-trustee rollover saves you from unexpected and potentially nasty tax consequences.

Cha-ching! Shaking the Bank

So you've decided to stash your retirement savings in an LRIF or a LIF, but how much and when should you withdraw? In an uncertain economy, that's the million-dollar question. The longer you can allow your retirement plan savings to grow tax-deferred, the better.

Many new retirees mistakenly overspend in the early years. Don't deprive yourself, but remember that your retirement could be 30 to 40 years.

Determining the optimal withdrawal rate for your situation requires a lot of thought, but a general rule is to withdraw no more than 4 percent of your total savings in any one year. If your investment returns are poor in a particular year, revise this percentage downward. Conversely, you can revise your withdrawal upward if you make great returns one year.

Timing withdrawals from one tax year to the next provides another opportunity to reduce income taxes. For example, if you have unusually high medical expenses (perhaps prescriptions not covered by your provincial plan or dental work) in a particular calendar year that qualify as deductions, you may want to take some of your retirement withdrawals in December instead of waiting until January as a way of balancing income and expenses.

#69

Take Stock of Your Registered Accounts

By Rick DeChaineau, CSA, CRPC, CFP

After all those years of biting the bullet to put money in your Registered Retirement Savings Plan (RRSP), you can finally begin taking money out. This tip tells you how RRSP withdrawals are taxed and gives you advice on how to best manage your RRSP accounts.

Know the Taxes on Withdrawals

Knowing the basics of how RRSP withdrawals are taxed can save you money as you deal with uncertainties during your retirement.

RRSP withdrawals

If you squirrel away money in an RRSP, the profits you earn on that money aren't taxed until you begin to make withdrawals. Although you can take money out whenever you wish, you pay for the privilege. The government will have its hand out to collect the taxes it had earlier foregone on your contributions in the form of withholding taxes. As of 2008, you'd pay

- ✔ 10 percent on withdrawals up to $5,000 (or 21 percent in Quebec)

- ✔ 20 percent on the next $10,000 (30 percent in Quebec)

- ✔ 30 percent on withdrawals of more than $15,000 (35 percent in Quebec)

The government treats RRSP withdrawals as income. You pay income tax on that lump sum at your top marginal tax rate, so even after you pay withholding taxes you may be stuck with a big tax bill. Most advisors don't advocate such an action except under special circumstances. For example, you can withdraw money from your RRSP without penalty to participate in the federal Home Buyers' Plan or the Lifelong Learning Plan, as long as you pay that money back over time.

Registered Retirement Income Funds

At no later than age 70 you must roll your RRSPs over into a Registered Retirement Income Fund (RRIF). Then you can begin withdrawing money to live — in fact, you *must* begin minimum withdrawals, which are calculated as a percentage of the market value of your RRIF at the end of the previous year. Although you pay income tax on your RRIF withdrawals, you'll likely be in a lower tax bracket than you were when you were working.

Take a look at Table 6-2. It gives you a good idea of how much you have to withdraw yearly from your RRIF. Note that you can withdraw a larger portion of your funds if you wish.

Table 6-2   RRIF Minimum Withdrawal Percentage Rates

Age (on January 1)	Minimum Withdrawal %	Age (on January 1)	Minimum Withdrawal %
71	7.38	83	9.58
72	7.48	84	9.93
73	7.59	85	10.33
74	7.71	86	10.79
75	7.85	87	11.33
76	7.99	88	11.96
77	8.15	89	12.71
78	8.33	90	13.62
79	8.53	91	14.73
80	8.75	92	16.12
81	8.99	93	17.92
82	9.27	94+	20.00

Note: During 2008, RRFIF holders were allowed to reduce compulsory withdrawals by 25 percent; this temporary offer might become permanent due to the current uncertain economy.

Canada Revenue Agency doesn't care whether you have one or a dozen RRIF accounts. It looks at all your RRIF money as one big RRIF to determine minimum payout requirements.

Locked-In Retirement Income Funds or Life Income Funds

A locked-in account such as a Locked-In Retirement Income Fund (LRIF) or Life Income Fund (LIF) stems from having been a member of a company or government pension plan and having your employment end before you retire. The value of your company pension plan can be transferred to a special kind of RRSP called a Locked-In Retirement Account (LIRA) or a Locked-In Retirement Savings Plan (LRSP).

On retirement, just as RRSPs must be rolled into RRIFs, so LIRAs and LRSPs must be converted to LRIFs or LIFs. Conversion rules vary by province. Some provinces let you convert at any time. Others specify 54 as the earliest age you can convert. All provinces require conversion by age 70.

Match Account Contents with Tax Treatment

During retirement, your registered accounts will likely hold only a portion of your retirement assets. Your first step in managing your taxable income is to ensure that the right assets are in the right accounts. This assumes you already have various types of other taxable investment accounts. Do *not* pull money that you don't need out of an RRSP.

Because withdrawals from your registered accounts will be taxed as ordinary income, you want to hold ordinary-income assets, such as bonds, GICs, and so on, in your RRIF, LRIF or LIF.

Your personal (taxable) accounts should hold investments that are eligible to be taxed at the (currently) lower long-term capital gain and qualified dividend rates. Examples of these investments include stocks and equity mutual funds.

If you want your children to inherit your RRSP, you can invest more aggressively in your RRSP account. Note that they can still expect your estate to pay a hefty tax bite when you die.

Use Your Taxable, Partially Taxable, and Non-Taxable Investments Wisely

By Jeff Alderfer, CFP, AIF

After you spend a lifetime accumulating a tidy nest egg, you get to figure out how to spend it. It's not as simple as just buying all you need and some of what you want. You need to pay attention to which investments you spend now, which you spend later, and which you're going to leave to your kids. What's more, uncertain times can affect taxes as well as investing, so you need a plan that considers both. Without one, you're probably going to give more money to the government than you need to. So in this tip, you discover how to spend the money you've invested while minimizing the taxes you have to pay.

Separate Your Money into Tax Buckets

Sometimes explaining finances is easier using a bucket brigade rather than a spreadsheet. If you're like most people, your investment buckets are scattered about: a Registered Retirement Income Fund (RRIF), a workplace pension plan, a Tax-Free Savings Account (TFSA), a taxable investment account, a money market account, and maybe an annuity. The bucket concept makes things easier: Don't think about all the different accounts you have — just think about which tax bucket your money is in. Following are the only three tax buckets:

> ✔ **Bucket #1, the tax-free bucket:** This bucket contains all the money that will never be taxed. Specifically, this bucket includes TFSAs. No matter how much money you take out of this bucket in retirement, you won't have to pay income taxes on it.

Because this bucket contains only tax-free money, you can take out as much or as little as you want in retirement, with no tax liability.

✔ **Bucket #2, the tax-deferred bucket:** The taxes have been deferred for the accounts in this bucket. Some specific accounts include Registered Retirement Savings Plans (RRSPs) and RRIFs, Registered Pensions Plans (RPPs), Locked-In Retirement Savings Plans (LRSPs) and Locked-In Retirement Income Funds (LRIFs), and tax-deferred annuities. Refer to Tips #30 and #31 for more information about retirement accounts.

In general, any money you withdraw from these accounts is taxed as income, so you're taxed in whatever federal/ provincial tax bracket you're part of (as determined by your income).

✔ **Bucket #3, the taxable bucket:** This bucket contains accounts that receive no special tax treatment, and it includes un-registered brokerage accounts, money market accounts, and savings accounts. Here you pay taxes as you go, on a yearly basis.

The rules for taxation are the same as they were during your working years — that is, only 50 percent of capital gains are taxable at your marginal tax rate and eligible dividends (from Canadian companies) are taxed at the more favourable rate of 14 to 30 percent in the marginal tax bracket, depending on your province. (Tip #29 gives a more thorough explanation of taxable investments.)

The growth in value of a small business or real estate isn't taxed until you sell, so these investments can be a good way to defer taxes. That said, income you earn from either a small business or real estate is taxable as income.

Spend the Money in Your Buckets

After you figure out which tax bucket holds each of your invest-ments, the fun part begins: How should you spend your money? Here's a good general guideline:

✔ **Bucket #1, the tax-free bucket:** Use the money in this bucket *last.* It'll never be taxed, and it won't trigger clawbacks on Old Age Security (OAS) benefits and the Guaranteed Income Supplement (GIS). If you have money left after taking your forced RRIF or LRIF payments, you can pay tax on it and then contribute it to your TFSA. You'll never have to pay tax on it again, and if you never get around to spending it, your spouse or common-law partner can spend it tax free as long as you name her or him *successor holder* on the original application.

✓ **Bucket #2, the tax-deferred bucket:** Okay, pay attention here. Years ago, financial advisors used to recommend leaving your tax-deferred accounts untouched as long as possible to let them compound free of taxes. However, given the very real prospect of higher tax rates in the future, drawing down these funds sooner rather than later may be beneficial — even though this advice goes against the conventional wisdom of deferring taxes as long as possible (the mantra of all Chartered Accountants). Drawing money from this bucket gives you the added benefit of reducing the amount of your nest egg that will be subject to required minimum payouts when you turn 70.

✓ **Bucket #3, the taxable bucket:** Although tax rates are likely to climb in the future, capital gains taxes (those taxes that are due when you sell an investment) are likely to remain lower than ordinary income taxes. The caveat: When you die, a *deemed disposition* of all assets occurs — meaning the government acts as if you'd sold everything and taxes your estate willed to your heirs (excepting your spouse or common-law partner) accordingly.

To hedge your bets (or "diversify your risk" in financial planner–speak) in uncertain times, plan to initially take money out of Bucket #2 each year of your retirement. One clever approach is to draw from your tax-deferred (Bucket #2) accounts first, until reaching the upper limit of your current tax bracket (remember to include Canada/Quebec Pension Plan [CPP/QPP], OAS, and GIS payments, which are taxable), and then draw the remainder of your spending from your non-taxable accounts in Bucket #1 to ensure that OAS and (if applicable) GIS aren't clawed back. After you've moved money out of Bucket #1, you can replace those contributions with cash or investments from Bucket #3.

Here's a brief example:

Total funds available in retirement:

Tax Bucket #1:	$50,000 in a TFSA
Tax Bucket #2:	$150,000 in an RRSP
Tax Bucket #3:	$100,000 in an investment account

Total funds needed: $12,000 per year

Assume your workplace and/or government pension income puts you just $7,000 below the top of the 15 to 20 percent combined federal/ provincial tax bracket. Using this strategy, you withdraw $7,000 from your RRIF, which fills up that tax bracket. Then, to provide the rest of the money you need, you withdraw $5,000 from your TFSA — money that you can collect without paying income tax. The following year, you can replenish the money in your TFSA with cash from your taxable accounts (because you don't lose the contribution room). If you were to instead withdraw the entire $12,000 from your RRSP, that extra $5,000 would be taxed at the rate of 19 to 23 percent.

Allocate Assets in the Active Stage of Retirement

By Kay Conheady, CFP

With good health, you'll be active and living independently for most of your retirement. You may plan to travel, spend time with family and friends, pursue your favourite hobbies, volunteer, or even start your own business. To fund those dreams, you need to structure your nest egg to provide regular income that meets the following criteria:

✔ It adequately supplements workplace and government pension income to fund your desired standard of living.

✔ It'll be there in both good and uncertain economic times throughout your retirement.

✔ It lasts as long as you need it to.

This tip explains how to get your portfolio management off to a good start as you begin tapping into your nest egg.

Understand Retirement Uncertainty

Knowing which uncertainties will impact the success of your retirement can help you better plan and manage your assets and your income. Here are several risks to consider:

✔ **Longevity risk:** The risk that you'll run out of dollars before you run out of breaths

✔ **Inflation risk:** The risk that the cost of everything will go up faster than your income

✔ **Market risk:** The risk that you'll have to sell investments when they're down in value to produce needed income

✔ **Timing risk:** The risk that you'll experience large investment losses in the first three to five years of retirement

Your best defence is to hold off on retiring until you have a comprehensive plan to protect against these four risks. Asset allocation is your primary tool to manage them. Monitoring your plan and making periodic adjustments is also part of the process.

Decide Whether to Use Annuities

Allocating some of your nest egg to a fixed annuity creates a stream of income you can't outlive. Such a strategy can help overcome longevity risk. (For info on annuities, refer to Tip #16.) If you're married, buy a joint and survivor benefit so your surviving spouse will continue to receive income.

Before putting all or a portion of you nest egg into an annuity, even one that'll keep pace with inflation and fully fund your desired standard of living, understand that with an annuity, you give your money to an insurance company in exchange for the promise of a lifetime income. Once initiated, or *annuitized,* you can't stop or change the annuity, even if you no longer need that income or need additional money for unexpected expenses. Be sure to read the annuity policy and ask questions about how the policy works.

Deciding how much of your nest egg to allocate to an annuity is a real challenge. You have to assess the following to make a wise decision:

- ✔ The probability that you'll burn through your assets prematurely
- ✔ Your tolerance for investment risk
- ✔ The long-term trend of the stock market

If you're in danger of exhausting your assets prematurely, your tolerance for investment risk is low, or the stock market appears to be peaking or in the early stages of a downswing, consider allocating 60 to 80 percent of your nest egg to an annuity.

Allocate Your Nest Egg to Stocks, Bonds, and Cash

Longevity and inflation risk mandate that you allocate at least some of your nest egg to risky assets — stocks and bonds. These assets can help you stay ahead of inflation, although their returns aren't guaranteed. At the same time, investing in stocks and bonds can increase the uncertainties that may cause your accounts to decrease in value. This section explains how to find — and keep — the right balance.

Decide on your target balance

The first asset allocation decision you have to make is how much to invest in stocks versus bonds and/or cash. As an early stage retiree, a reasonable cash-bond-stock allocation is to keep

✔ Three years' worth of annual income in cash

✔ Three to five years' worth in bonds

✔ The rest in stocks

Using this allocation provides you with income for seven years. You get the opportunity to sell stocks when they're up in order to replace cash and bond assets that are used up by income withdrawals. Meanwhile, the bonds and cash investments help protect you against the large losses the stock market occasionally delivers. Bonds often provide positive returns when stocks are performing negatively, which helps reduce the negative impact on your total investment portfolio.

In early retirement, an allocation of 45 to 60 percent of your portfolio in stocks is reasonable. Allocating more than 60 percent to stocks in the early stages of retirement increases the risk of experiencing large losses, and allocating less than 45 percent increases the risk of depleting your portfolio due to feeble growth.

Diversify your investments

After you choose your overall allocation, you have to actually choose your investments. Here are a few bond suggestions:

✔ Diversify and buy lots of different types of bonds, keeping your investment in high-yield bonds relatively low.

✔ The majority of your bonds should be medium term — between five and ten years. Avoid owning too many bonds or bond funds with maturity dates longer than ten years because these tend to fluctuate in value more dramatically than medium- and short-term bonds.

✔ Consider putting 15 to 40 percent of your bond allocation in bonds designed to provide inflation protection. (Refer to Tip #15 for more information.)

Your stocks should make up 60 percent or less of your total portfolio. As you choose stocks, make sure you adequately diversify into the different classes of stocks, including the following (refer to Tips #39 through #42 for more info on diversifying your stock portfolio):

- ✔ Domestic and foreign
- ✔ Small and large cap
- ✔ Growth and value

Generally, growth stocks tend to be riskier than value stocks and small company stocks tend to be riskier than large company stocks.

For the cash portion of this portfolio, pursue the highest interest rates available, short of tying up your money in long-maturity government bonds. Check out Tip #14 to help you decide which cash savings vehicles to use during retirement.

Rebalance your investment portfolio

Because you'll be regularly depleting the cash portion of your investment portfolio, you need to periodically adjust the amounts you have in bonds and stocks so that the percentage of each in your total portfolio equals your target asset allocation.

Rebalancing within a taxable account can have potentially expensive tax ramifications. For taxable accounts, you may want to seek the help of a financial advisor who's experienced in retirement investing and taxation.

However, rebalancing within a Registered Retirement Savings Plan (RRSP) has no immediate tax ramifications, so the decision to rebalance is much simpler. For early stage retirees who've allocated three years of nest-egg withdrawals to cash and another five years to bonds, the concern is when to replenish the cash reserve. Here are three principles to remember for rebalancing:

- ✔ **Cash:** Replenish your cash stash at least every two years back to the three-year amount. To increase your cash, liquidate bond assets when stocks have performed poorly or use stock assets if they've done well.

- ✔ **Bonds:** Replenish your allocation to bonds back up to three to five years' worth of living expenses when the amount falls below two years' worth. If your bond portfolio exceeds five years' worth of withdrawals, divert assets first to cash and then to stocks to rejig the target balance.

✔ **Stock:** Make sure your stock allocation stays between 45 and 60 percent of your total portfolio. If you need to keep your stock allocation in check, having more than five to seven years' worth of living expenses in bonds and cash is better.

If you find that you can no longer maintain at least 45 percent of your portfolio in stocks after restocking your cash and bond reserves, this is a red flag that you may be consuming your nest egg too quickly. Do a comprehensive review of your retirement income plan and make adjustments.

If you experience large losses in the first two to five years of retirement, you need to redesign your retirement income plan. You may want to reconsider the role of immediate annuities in your plan. Get help from an experienced financial planner if your confidence is shaken.

Allocate Your Assets for the Slow-Down Stage of Retirement

By Kay Conheady, CFP

If you've been drawing income from your nest egg for a while, it may no longer be growing at a rate that outpaces or even equals inflation. Your annual withdrawals have likely grown steadily to meet your inflating expenses, which may have doubled since the beginning of your retirement.

Re-evaluate and determine whether you need to change the asset allocation of your investment portfolio. To intelligently assess your asset allocation, first do the following:

- ✔ Review your health and prospects for longevity (and those of your spouse).
- ✔ Review how well your nest egg has been doing and whether you can expect it to last as long as you do.
- ✔ Re-estimate your future expenses for
  - Everyday living
  - Health-care costs your provincial plan doesn't cover and the potential need for long-term care
  - Unmet retirement dreams
- ✔ Revisit your goals for leaving an inheritance to your heirs.
- ✔ Ask yourself whether you can and want to continue managing your own investments.

Doing this review should give you all the insights you need to make good asset allocation decisions.

Revisit the Four Elements of Retirement Uncertainty

Tip #71 discusses four causes of retirement uncertainty. Three of them still play a role in the slow-down stage of retirement:

- ✔ **Longevity risk:** Your updated retirement income plan can tell you whether this challenge is still a major consideration for you. Evaluating whether you'll outlive your money is a bit easier at this stage because you're planning for inflation, investment returns, and living expenses for fewer years.

- ✔ **Inflation risk:** As you revise your retirement income plan, pay special attention to inflation trends for the goods and services you need going forward — especially health-care costs your provincial plan doesn't cover, long-term care or home care, major home maintenance or remodelling, and other large periodic expenses.

- ✔ **Market risk:** Your asset allocation strategy for your updated retirement income plan will continue to address the risk that you'll have to sell investments when they're down.

Large investment losses in early retirement are compounded over time, so avoiding them is imperative. However, when you're well into retirement, timing risk isn't a major concern anymore.

Next, look at the key asset allocation decisions you first explored in active retirement (refer to Tip #71 for details).

Rethink Income Annuities

If you decided against purchasing an annuity during the active stage of your retirement, you may want to reconsider your decision now. If your updated retirement income plan indicates that you'll probably live longer than your assets will last, an annuity may provide the lifelong income to meet your needs.

Next, decide whether to purchase an annuity with an income stream that increases yearly to protect against inflation. Because you face fewer years of compounding inflation than you did when you first retired, an annually increasing income isn't as essential as it was then. Look at the current rate of inflation to see whether it's been trending up or down over the last several years. And look at the rate of inflation for home care and long-term care services; these costs increase by a higher rate than the cost of normal goods and services.

Assess the value of annuities in regard to your current financial realities and goals. If you can afford to purchase the amount of annuity income you need, including an inflation benefit, you reduce the impact of the other three elements of retirement uncertainty. You may place a high value on the peace of mind you get from a guaranteed income.

If you can't afford to purchase the level of income you need with inflation protection, evaluate how close you can come to meeting your current needs if you avoid the additional cost of the inflation protection. And if you decide against investing in an income annuity, you need to continue to invest wisely. Refer to Tip #16 for more on annuities.

Examine Your Stock, Bond, and Cash Asset Allocations

As you enter the slow-down stage of retirement, determine whether and how to change your investment portfolio to better suit your circumstances.

When thinking about your asset allocation for the slow-down stage of retirement, keep the following in mind:

- ✓ **Cash and bonds:** Your first concern is still to secure the cash flow you need over the next eight or so years; set this amount aside in cash and bonds.

- ✓ **Stocks:** Depending on your age and life expectancy, you may want to go from seeking inflation-beating investment returns to achieving inflation-matching investment returns. This method allows you to reduce your allocation to stock investments within your portfolio. Reducing your overall stock holdings to 35 or 40 percent of your portfolio is perfectly reasonable.

All the principles of rebalancing that Tip #71 discusses still apply. In fact, you should be even more vigilant and disciplined here because you have less time to make up for mistakes. Replenish the cash with your profits from the stocks as you get them so you're protected when the markets disappoint.

For the most part, the advice about bonds and bond funds from Tip #71 holds. Look for bonds that seek to provide inflation-matching returns (or better); your bond allocation should include 50 to 60 percent of these bonds. Keep a portion of your stocks in all the major categories, but favour the more-conservative categories of Canadian (versus foreign), large company (versus small company), and value (versus growth) stocks.

Allocate Your Assets During the Late Stage of Life

By Kay Conheady, CFP

Hopefully, you can continue living independently during your later years. If, however, you need help taking all your medications on schedule, getting up and going in the morning, fixing your meals, or maintaining your home, consider the cost of long-term care. Whether you receive this care in your own home, an assisted living residence, or a skilled nursing home, your outflow of cash is likely to increase considerably, and you may be more concerned than ever about outliving your assets.

Now is a good time for a financial review. Your nest egg has probably been slowly shrinking as you've been withdrawing an ever-increasing income to keep up with inflation. You may be withdrawing income faster than your nest egg is growing. With good planning and investment management, you've survived ups and downs in the economy; but if the cost of long-term care is now the most pressing uncertainty you face, this tip can help.

Assess Your Assistance Needs

Before focusing on your investments and whether you need to make changes to your allocation strategy, assess your situation:

- ✔ Determine your needs for assistance.
- ✔ Figure out who's available and willing to be involved with your care. Family? Friends? Acquaintances?
- ✔ Determine what kinds of care professionals should provide.
- ✔ Investigate available federal, provincial, and municipal government programs and what kinds of services they provide.
- ✔ Determine whether your current living environment supports your ability to stay there.

✔ Look at what kinds of modifications to your home or technologies would help you to remain in your home.

✔ Look at other living alternatives and compare the cost of staying where you are to the cost of living elsewhere.

Use this information to determine whether your income sources will continue to cover your living expenses (and your spouse's) and whether you can cover long-term care expenses with your income. Then figure out how much more you need from other resources to meet your needs. Other resources may include the following:

✔ Provincial services such as nursing, homemaking, and respite services, as well as services such as Meals on Wheels

✔ Long-term care insurance benefits if you have such a policy and meet the requirements for receiving benefits

✔ Subsidies for long-term care facilities based on income (*Note:* These subsidies generally only cover ward rooms.)

✔ Annuities or life insurance that includes benefits to cover long-term care if you meet the requirements for receiving benefits

✔ The equity you've built up in your home

Tailor Your Asset Allocation Strategy to Your Savings

You need to keep at least three years' worth of upcoming living expenses in cash and replenish it at least every two years. Factor in the cost of long-term care that other resources can't cover. If you're still in your home, factor in any large expenses for home modifications and/or assistive technology devices or systems.

After you calculate how much to allocate to your cash stash, you'll know how much of your nest egg is left over. Explore your asset allocation challenges by analyzing the two common scenarios outlined here.

Scenario 1: Your nest egg is adequate relative to your anticipated needs

If you determine that your nest egg is adequate relative to your anticipated future income needs, you can now

✔ Sell your riskier investment holdings

✔ Buy securities such as Guaranteed Income Certificates (GICs) and bonds (especially inflation-tracking bonds) that have relatively stable values

At later stages of life, the potential reward of investing in risky assets is no longer worth the risk. The higher returns you may enjoy from risky investments won't significantly extend how long your nest egg lasts, but investment losses, large or small, can significantly shorten it.

Scenario 2: Your nest egg is sizable relative to your anticipated needs

If you have plenty of available resources, consider yourself fortunate! Then consider the following:

✔ Continue to invest for growth to build your legacy for heirs and charitable intentions.

✔ Invest assets that are reserved for your remaining needs conservatively. But assets you anticipate passing on to your heirs can be invested up to 100 percent in stocks. A good asset allocation may be 20 to 30 percent stocks, 30 to 40 percent bonds, and 30 to 40 percent cash.

✔ Continue to rebalance regularly and stay vigilant about your investments.

Get Help with Long-Term Care Planning

The following resources can help you plan for aging or long-term care:

✔ **Seniors Canada Online** (www.seniors.gc.ca): This comprehensive government Web site provides tonnes of information to assist you with healthy aging. It has information on assistive devices, home-care programs, transportation when you're disabled, pension planning, and more.

✔ **Long Term Care Planning Network** (www.ltcplanning network.com): This Web site offers products and services related to aging and long-term care for caregivers, health-care providers, and professional advisors.

#74

Preserve Assets to Pass on to Your Heirs

By John Vyge, CFP

If you want to leave assets to your heirs, you have to balance your need for current income with preserving your assets. If you play it too safe, your portfolio won't keep pace with inflation. If you take too much risk, wild fluctuations in the stock market may shrink your nest egg. After you put your assets in the right place, then you can implement wealth preservation strategies to guide your future financial decisions.

Put Your Assets in the Right Place

One way to preserve assets for your heirs is to draw retirement income from fixed-income securities. Having a sufficient base of these types of assets, which aren't subject to the fluctuations of the stock market, allows you to put other assets in more growth-oriented investments. Here are some fixed-income options:

- ✔ **Individual bonds:** Individual bonds provide regular interest payments, but you need to be willing to hold the bonds until they mature. Bond mutual funds also pay interest regularly, but they fluctuate in value, so you have no guarantee of having a specific amount on a specific date. Consult an investment advisor before building a bond portfolio. (Also read Tip #15 on government bonds and Tip #24 on individual bonds.)

- ✔ **Guaranteed Income Certificates (GICs):** A GIC is one of the safest ways to earn interest and avoid loss of principal. However, a GIC often pays an interest rate that's less than inflation. (For more information on GICs, refer to Tip #14.)

- ✔ **Money market accounts:** A bank money market account may pay a slightly lower rate of interest than some GICs, meaning it still may not protect against inflation. Mutual fund companies offer a variety of money market funds, which also pay interest regularly. (For more information on how these accounts and funds work, refer to Tip #14.)

Also consider the value of tax-deferred accounts. Not only do tax-deferred retirement accounts save you from current taxes, but they can also protect you in the event of bankruptcy.

Draw Down Your Assets Wisely

At some point, you're probably going to spend some of that money you've saved and invested over the years. The whole point of putting that money away was to enjoy it during retirement, right?

The appropriate mix of equity and fixed-income investments is important. The assets you'll use for retirement income will be targeted for income and safety of principal. A smaller percentage will be geared towards growth (you may live a long time!).

If you have enough to see you through retirement (including possible emergencies and long-term care), you can allocate the remainder based on your heirs' time horizons. If you'll be leaving money to young grandchildren with years before university or college, you can invest that money more aggressively. If your heirs are adults with financial pressures, put the money in more stable investments.

Plan Your Estate

When you die, your existing debt, final expenses (funeral costs and so on), and lawyer's/probate fees will decrease your estate. You can minimize or avoid some of these costs, depending on the estate planning strategies and documents you use. You should consult a competent estate planning lawyer before acting, but knowing some of your options can help you start the planning process now.

There are no federal or provincial estate taxes or death duties in Canada. But given the uncertainty of estate tax laws after 2010, planning between now and then can be challenging. Basic information includes the following:

✔ **Pass registered and non-registered assets on to your spouse:** When you die, the government basically treats your registered investments (Registered Retirement Savings Plans and Registered Retirement Income Funds) as if you'd cashed them all in and taken all that freed-up cash as income. You can sidestep the tax hit by passing those assets on to your spouse or a dependent child.

Similarly, with the exception of your home (which, as your principle residence, passes tax free to your beneficiary), the taxman acts as if you'd sold all your non-registered assets for fair market value the minute you kicked off (called *deemed disposition*). Your estate has to pay taxes on the resulting net net capital gains. You can avoid this scenario by leaving assets to your spouse, but if you're not married or your spouse is already dead, your estate will certainly be hit with the capital gains tax.

✔ **Annual gifting:** Give cash and assets away to family, friends, or charity during your lifetime. You may save tax and you get the pleasure of being generous. You can give cash away without any tax implications. But when you give an asset such as property or stock to anyone other than your spouse, the tax implications are as if you'd sold that asset for fair market value on the day you transfer ownership. This could trigger a capital gains tax hit. Measuring the tax cost before giving away certain assets is in your best interest.

✔ **Avoid probate:** *Probate* is a process used to validate your will and make sure your wishes are carried out. Your estate pays the costs, which can run as high as 3 percent of your gross estate at death, depending on where you live. An accountant may be able to minimize probate fees by setting up trusts, establishing joint accounts, or giving money away before you die.

✔ **Name your spouse as beneficiary on your Registered Retirement Savings Plan (RRSP) or Registered Retirement Income Fund (RRIF).** That way the assets in those accounts can be transferred to your spouse's RRSP or RRIF tax free when you die. Ditto for a financially dependent child.

✔ **Consider life insurance.** Although life insurance doesn't actually reduce your taxes on death, it covers the tax bill. That's particularly important if you want to pass a cherished family cottage or a family business on to your kids. The growth in value of the asset could result in an enormous tax bill. Life insurance proceeds can help cover the taxes so your heirs can keep the property or business.

✔ **Choose carefully which accounts to dip into.** If you have taxable accounts, balance the preservation-for-heirs goal against how much you'll pay in taxes along the way.

Establishing a *testamentary trust* can help reduce taxes. Why? Because a testamentary trust is treated like a separate individual, so it gets Canada's graduated tax rates. Say, for example, that you had assets that earned about $30,000 per year. If you left those assets directly to an heir, that person would have to claim the earnings as part of his or her annual income, potentially getting taxed in the top marginal tax bracket as high as 48 percent. If that money belonged to a trust instead, the marginal tax rate would be almost half, depending on what province you live in.

Part VII
The Part of Tens

The 5th Wave

By Rich Tennant

@RICHTENNANT

BRAIN TWISTER PUZZLE

"That reminds me – I have to figure out how to save for retirement and send these two to university."

In this part...

Every *For Dummies* book includes a Part of Tens, which consists of top-ten lists of important information the authors think you should have. In this part, we give you ten tips for building a solid financial foundation and ten ways to minimize risk.

Ten Tips for Building a Solid Financial Foundation

*G*etting your financial household in order helps prepare you financially for all the ups and downs you may face in your lifetime. With a solid financial foundation, you can withstand just about every bout of market turmoil or financial crisis that may be heading your way. Here's how to set yourself up for success:

- **Establish adequate cash reserves.** In the event of a downturn in the markets, a family emergency, or loss of income, nothing is as comforting as having enough money in the bank to get you through those rough times.

- **Invest in your ability to earn money.** One of the biggest — if not *the* biggest — assets you have is your ability to earn money. In uncertain times, invest in yourself. Continue to sharpen your axe, whether you're securely employed, between jobs, temporarily retired, or permanently retired. Often, the easiest way to reduce the stress and strain on your investment nest egg is to keep earning money, even for a short period of time.

- **Give yourself credit.** Managing your debt wisely — by minimizing or eliminating debt — reduces personal and financial stress. Building an excellent credit history provides you with options to access money if and when you need it.

- **Insure your income.** If you're not yet retired, make sure you have adequate disability insurance. If you need your paycheque to survive, you need disability insurance, just in case you can't earn that paycheque due to a prolonged illness or injury. If others (such as your spouse or family) depend on your income, you also need adequate life insurance to replace your income if you die prematurely.

- **Provide for health-care expenses.** Make sure you have enough cash for costs that your provincial health-care plan doesn't cover. Consider whether long-term care insurance is right for you.

✔ **Cover your assets.** Periodically review your homeowner's or renter's insurance, automobile insurance, and liability insurance to make sure you're adequately insured.

✔ **Diversify your investment portfolio.** One of the best things you can do to minimize most investment risks is to effectively diversify your portfolio.

✔ **Monitor and rebalance.** After you establish the proper diversification for your investment portfolio, spend a little time on it once or twice a year. Make sure you're monitoring your portfolio's performance relative to its peers on a risk-adjusted basis, and be sure to rebalance your portfolio back to your original target allocation.

✔ **Plan for certainties in life.** Many of the major events that occur in your life shouldn't come as surprises. Maybe the timing is a surprise, but the event itself shouldn't blindside you. Think about these potential events. Is your car on its last leg? Do you have children whom you want to help through college or university? Would you like to be able to retire and maintain your standard of living someday? These events are near certainties. The details or timing may be fuzzy, but these events will most likely occur. Prepare in advance — as much as possible — for these eventualities.

✔ **Get help.** If you're unsure of where to turn for personal help and direction about your personal financial situation, be proactive. Get help sooner rather than later. With time on your side, you have many more options.

Ten Tips to Minimize Risk

*Y*ou face a variety of risks in your financial life. You can and should avoid some of these risks. Others you can transfer to an insurance company. But some risks are a normal part of your investing life. The following list identifies the primary risks and the most common ways you can best handle them:

- ✓ **Understand risk.** Possibly the best thing you can do for yourself is understand investment and financial risks and discover which ones you can transfer through insurance and which ones you can minimize with different investment strategies. Understand history and plan for the future.

- ✓ **Be aware of volatility in the financial markets.** Check your risk profile and select a portfolio allocation that lets you tolerate all market climates. Then diversify your portfolio across a broad mix of investments that aren't all subject to the same risks.

- ✓ **Watch out for inflation.** Invest in equities (stocks, mutual funds, or exchange-traded funds) that tend to do well during inflationary periods, such as consumer staples (toothpaste and toilet paper), energy, real estate, and alcohol and tobacco. Put some of your fixed-income allocation into Canada Real Return Bonds (RRBs).

- ✓ **Set goals.** Determine where you are now and what you need to realize your goals. Periodically review your overall financial picture and make adjustments as necessary.

- ✓ **Have a plan for unexpected expenses.** Financial issues can derail even the best plans. Think through all the potential what-if scenarios in your life and explore how you can best handle these issues. Adequate cash reserves, ample liquidity, a steady income, and good insurance can get you through the majority of life's financial emergencies.

- ✓ **Maintain liquidity and flexibility.** Avoid unnecessary expenses. Avoid all consumer debt, and build up a comfortable emergency reserve. Have a line of credit available for true emergencies only. Maintain a great credit score.

✔ **Control costs.** When you think of investments, keep in mind three primary factors that influence total returns:

- The returns provided by the markets
- Income taxes
- Investment expenses

The latter two factors can make up a significant chunk of your total return. You have little control over what the markets provide; however, you have a lot of influence over the taxation and expenses on your investments. Exercise that control!

✔ **Make sure your retirement money lasts.** As for the risk of outliving your money, you have a few options. You may be able to accumulate gobs of money, so this may not be a concern. For everyone else, strongly consider working and postponing Canada/Quebec Pension Plan (CPP/QPP) benefits until full retirement age, or better yet, age 70. If you're lucky enough to have a defined benefit pension plan, do the same. If you don't have a pension plan, consider taking a portion of your nest egg at retirement and purchasing an immediate annuity to provide you with guaranteed income for the rest of your life.

✔ **Wisely tap into retirement income.** Have a plan for drawing down your assets in retirement (see Part VI). This plan can help you minimize taxes, make sure money is available to fund the distributions, and maximize any remainder for your heirs.

✔ **Hedge your risks.** Investors often achieve hedging by purchasing insurance to protect themselves from risks they can't afford to bear; however, insurance isn't available or appropriate for all risks that you face in your financial life. Hedge most of your financial risk with insurance. In select circumstances, you may want to hedge a portion of your investment portfolio with stock options (refer to Tip #25).

Index

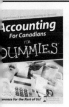

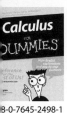

FOOD, HOME, GARDEN, & MUSIC

978-0-470-15491-5

978-0-7645-9904-0

Also available:

✔ 30-Minute Meals For Dummies
978-0-7645-2589-6

✔ Bartending For Dummies
978-0-470-05056-9

✔ Brain Games For Dummies
978-0-470-37378-1

✔ Gluten-Free Cooking For Dummies
978-0-470-17810-2

✔ Home Improvement All-in-One
Desk Reference For Dummies
978-0-7645-5680-7

✔ Violin For Dummies
978-0-470-83838-9

✔ Wine For Dummies
978-0-470-04579-4

GREEN/SUSTAINABLE

978-0-470-84098-6

978-0-470-17569-9

Also available:

✔ Alternative Energy For Dummies
978-0-470-43062-0

✔ Energy Efficient Homes
For Dummies 978-0-470-37602-7

✔ Green Building & Remodeling
For Dummies 978-0-470-17559-0

✔ Green Business Practices
For Dummies 978-0-470-39339-€

✔ Green Cleaning For Dummies
978-0-470-39106-8

✔ Green Your Home All-in-One
For Dummies 978-0-470-40778-ͣ

✔ Sustainable Landscaping
For Dummies 978-0-470-41149-€

HEALTH & SELF-HELP

978-0-471-77383-2

978-0-471-77383-2

Also available:

✔ Breast Cancer For Dummies
978-0-7645-2482-0

✔ Depression For Dummies
978-0-7645-3900-8

✔ Healthy Aging For Dummies
978-0-470-14975-1

✔ Improving Your Memory
For Dummies 978-0-7645-5435-ͳ

✔ Neuro-linguistic Programming
For Dummies 978-0-7645-7028-ͳ

✔ Pregnancy For Canadians
For Dummies 978-0-470-83945-ͣ

✔ Understanding Autism
For Dummies 978-0-7645-2547-€

OBBIES & CRAFTS

3-0-470-29112-2

978-0-470-29112-2

Also available:

- Crochet Patterns For Dummies
  97-0-470-04555-8
- Digital Scrapbooking
  For Dummies 978-0-7645-8419-0
- Home Decorating For Dummies
  978-0-7645-4156-8
- Knitting Patterns For Dummies
  978-0-470-04556-5

- Oil Painting For Dummies
  978-0-470-18230-7
- Origami Kit For Dummies
  978-0-470-75857-1
- Quilting For Dummies
  978-0-7645-9799-2
- Sewing For Dummies
  978-0-7645-6847-3

OME & BUSINESS COMPUTER BASICS

3-0-470-11806-1

978-0-471-75421-3

Also available:

- Blogging For Dummies
  978-0-471-77084-8
- Excel 2007 For Dummies
  978-0-470-03737-9

- Office 2007 All-in-One Desk
  Reference For Dummies
  978-0-471-78279-7
- PCs For Dummies
  978-0-7645-8958-4
- Web Analytics For Dummies
  9780-470-09824-0

TERNET & DIGITAL MEDIA

3-0-470-25074-7

978-0-470-39062-7

Also available:

- eBay For Canadians For Dummies
  978-0-470-15348-2
- MySpace For Dummies
  978-0-470-09529-4
- Pay Per Click Search Engine
  Marketing For Dummies
  978-0-471-75494-7

- Search Engine Marketing
  For Dummies 978-0-471-97998-2
- The Internet For Dummies
  978-0-470-12174-0
- YouTube For Dummies
  978-0-470-14925-6

MACINTOSH

978-0-470-27817-8

978-0-470-05434-5

Also available:

- iMac For Dummies
  978-0-470-13386-6
- iPhone For Dummies
  978-0-470-42342-4
- iPod & iTunes For Dummies
  978-0-470-39062-7
- MacBook For Dummies
  978-0-470-27816-1

- Mac OS X Leopard For Dummies
  978-0-470-05433-8
- Office 2008 For Mac For Dummies
  978-0-470-27032-5
- Switching to a Mac For Dummies
  978-0-470-14076-5
- Upgrading & Fixing Macs & iMacs
  For Dummies 978-0-7645-0644-4

PETS

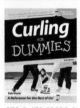

978-0-7645-8418-3

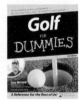

978-0-470-06805-2

Also available:

- Birds For Dummies
  978-0-7645-5139-0
- Boxers For Dummies
  978-0-7645-5285-4
- Cockatiels For Dummies
  978-0-7645-5311-0

- Ferrets For Dummies
  978-0-470-12723-0
- Golden Retrievers For Dummies
  978-0-7645-5267-0
- Horses For Dummies
  978-0-7645-9797-8
- Puppies For Dummies
  978-0-470-03717-1

SPORTS & FITNESS

978-0-470-83828-0

978-0-471-76871-5

Also available:

- Coaching Hockey For Dummies
  978-0-470-83685-9
- Exercise Balls For Dummies
  978-0-7645-5623-4
- Fitness For Dummies
  978-0-7645-7851-9

- Rugby For Dummies
  978-0-470-15327-7
- Ten Minute Tone-Ups
  For Dummies 978-0-7645-7207-4
- Yoga with Weights For Dummies
  978-0-471-74937-0